Praise for *We've Been Too Patient*

"*This book's message honors the diversity of each person's mind and body by moving us outside the limited scope of the biomedical model. This message needs to be spread to counter the stigma, labeling, and pathologizing entrenched in the current mental health system. I share the vision of this book: a mental health system that is not based on forced treatment as its default, where people choose services and supports because they serve their needs as defined by them. This would be a system that does not reduce people to chemical imbalances but sees them holistically with myriad needs and influences.* We've Been Too Patient *moves us all toward this substantially different perspective of mental health.*"

—SALLY ZINMAN, pioneer of the consumer movement and executive director of the California Association of Mental Health Peer Run Organizations

"We've Been Too Patient *is a must-read for all. Through mad rage, mad resistance, and mad pride, this brilliant collection creatively and provocatively challenges the structural oppression, stigma, and sanism in our everyday lives as well as within the very mental health services that are purported to support us. This book is not only silence shattering—it moves adeptly beyond revealing the harm and shame experienced by so many of us to expose the triumphs, creativity, dignity, and self-agency attached to mutual aid and other alternative approaches to healing. In short,* We've Been Too Patient *is a courageous, powerful, and important contribution to radical mental health and to the field of mad studies.*"

—BRENDA A. LeFRANÇOIS, social work professor at the Memorial University of Newfoundland and coauthor of *Mad Matters* and *Psychiatry Disrupted*

"*This powerful anthology shines a spotlight on the mental health system, highlighting serious flaws. The authors, often retraumatized by the care they received for real and perceived mental illnesses, explore their journeys in rich, vivid language. Rather than accepting victim roles, the writers detail 'call-to-arms' epiphanies that allow them to embrace their experience and emerge as activists. This powerful book is a game-changer for anyone serious about looking at the mental-health system from a patient's perspective. An excellent read."*

—NICKI BREUER, owner of Odin Books, a mental health, education, and special needs bookstore

"For too long those living with mental health conditions were marginalized, dismissed, and distrusted by the very communities in which they lived leading to isolation, often in the name of treatment. The power to overcome this forced isolation and faulty identification to instead construct a community built on mutual trust and support has taken enormous faith and courage. You can hear the courage in the voices found throughout this anthology. The courage they inspire is contagious and serves as a guide to building the healing communities that those living with mental health conditions need and deserve."

—JOSEPH ROBINSON, program manager of Each Mind Matters

"Justice is not possible unless we make space for the stories of the margins. What more powerful elucidation can there be than to cast light on the margins of the mind? We've Been Too Patient *shreds stigma and replaces it with dignity, autonomy, and power. This anthology heralds the necessity of our messy radical neurodivergent brains so that we might call forth a world where we are never again forced to be 'too patient.'"*

—SONYA RENEE TAYLOR, activist and author of *The Body is Not an Apology: The Power of Radical Self-Love*

"Nothing beats the advocacy and ideas of someone with lived experience in a subject and this book is proof. The insights and ideas might be radical to some, but anyone who has lived experience with mental illness and/or suicide can see this is actually a long-overdue and very reasonable plea for basic human dignity, compassion, support, and sense of community. This is how we should treat people who are suffering. Whether you are a loved one, someone who suffers, a politician, or a mental health worker, please read it."

—PAUL GILMARTIN, comedian and host of *Mental Illness Happy Hour*

We've Been Too Patient

Voices from Radical Mental Health

STORIES AND RESEARCH CHALLENGING
THE BIOMEDICAL MODEL

EDITED BY
L. D. GREEN AND **KELECHI UBOZOH**
FOREWORD BY **ROBERT WHITAKER**

North Atlantic Books
Berkeley, California

Published by
North Atlantic Books
Berkeley, California

Cover art © gettyimages.com/Vadimas Lisicinas
Cover design by John Yates
Book design by Happenstance Type-O-Rama

Printed in the United States of America

We've Been Too Patient: Voices from Radical Mental Health—Stories and Research Challenging the Biomedical Model is sponsored and published by the Society for the Study of Native Arts and Sciences (dba North Atlantic Books), an educational nonprofit based in Berkeley, California, that collaborates with partners to develop cross-cultural perspectives, nurture holistic views of art, science, the humanities, and healing, and seed personal and global transformation by publishing work on the relationship of body, spirit, and nature.

DISCLAIMER: This book contains personal stories that include institutional and interpersonal trauma, self-harm, and abuse of all kinds. We believe these stories and contexts are important, and they may be triggering. We encourage you to take care of yourself as you take this book in.

North Atlantic Books' publications are available through most bookstores. For further information, visit our website at www.northatlanticbooks.com or call 800-733-3000.

Library of Congress Cataloguing-in-Publication data
is available from the publisher upon request.

1 2 3 4 5 6 7 8 9 KPC 24 23 22 21 20 19

CONTENTS

FOREWORD

ROBERT WHITAKER

Robert Whitaker is a science journalist and the author of several books about the history of psychiatry, including *Mad in America* and *Anatomy of an Epidemic*. He is also the publisher of the webzine *Mad in America*.

. . . .

There is a risk, I think, in writing a foreword to an anthology written by those who have been—as the title of this fine anthology cleverly notes—"too patient." The problem is that you have been invited to add your voice into the mix, even though what this book calls upon a reader to do is to "listen."

Indeed, after having finished the book, I was struck mostly with this one thought: from the first page forward, I simply wanted to empty my mind of my own thoughts, and quietly listen to the writers tell their personal stories and to their thoughts for creating a new narrative of "radical mental health."

With that hesitation in mind, I thought I would simply write a bit more about "listening" to this book, and why I believe, from a societal perspective, that we need to become much better listeners to the voices present in these pages. In the past, we as a society have regularly turned a deaf ear to those deemed "mad," and for the most part, that societal deafness continues today. This is one reason why *We've Been Too Patient* demands that readers, first and foremost, just "listen" to this group of talented writers.

There are many aspects to the act of listening, and my first response with this book was to simply enjoy and often marvel at the use of language in the poems and essays. The writing is direct, clear, and most important of all, authentic. You can easily recognize that the writers are striving, with their choice of words, to be "true" to their own life stories, and how that authenticity then lends a moral authority to their arguments for "radical interventions."

The opening poem by Leah Harris, "dear dr," immediately put me in the mood to just listen. However, you shouldn't just read this poem to yourself. You need to *hear* it, and after my first silent reading, I read it out loud.

Here is the first stanza:

dear dr
on that proud, glorious day
you graduated from medical school
you took an oath as old as Hippocrates
remember?
   "above all, do no harm"
   above all, do no harm
   do no harm
   no harm

We see, in those first four lines, the sight of newly minted doctors, ready to enter a seemingly noble discipline, guided by the moral light of Hippocrates. And then, with the most delicate touch imaginable, Harris drops in the word "remember." That one word propels us forward in time and tells of doctors who, years later, have lost their way. Then the echo of "no harm" begins to reverberate, a lament that will linger in the reader's mind.

The next nine stanzas tell of the author's passage through that "medical" world of psychiatry, a story of suffering, coldness, and scientific biobabble, all of which tell of harm done. And then comes the moment when the poem turns: we hear of how the author has emerged stronger from that passage, the locked wards of the asylum giving way to an inner world of spiritual freedom, where her voice can begin "charting a course of humanity and dignity / with scribbles and shouts of my own."

After I read the poem aloud, a second and then a third time, all I could think was "wow." There are other fine poems in this anthology, and I have to confess that reading them made me wonder why I ever stopped reading poetry on a regular basis.

The first half of *We've Been Too Patient* is composed of poems and essays that tell of "personal stories of lived experience." There are several authors who forgo telling of the tribulations of being a psychiatric patient, and instead jump straight to telling about the paths they took to reach a better place in their lives. A common theme is how important friendships are to mental well-being, and how the peer movement helps engender such relationships. Healing spiritual journeys are recounted here too.

Several writers do tell of a larger span of their lives, and readers will recognize that their stories often fall into a pattern: childhood loss or trauma, then entry into a world of diagnosis, psychiatric medications, and hospitalization, and finally, from that darkness, a long struggle to regain autonomy over their own selves. While individual writers may tell of a helpful therapist, or of medications that help them today, most tell of a larger "system of care," starting with diagnosis, that increased their suffering.

When you listen to these personal stories, you are reminded anew that whenever a person trusts you with the larger narrative of his or her life, they are giving you a gift. It is, ultimately, the gift of intimacy.

The story that Chris Anastasia tells in "Untitled" fits the general pattern described above: childhood loss led to diagnosis, multiple drugs, and hospitalization, and then came a long struggle, as an adult, to find "ways to support my mental well-being." What makes Anastasia's story particularly memorable is that it intersects with the very psychiatrist, Joseph Biederman, who did perhaps more than anyone to create a mental health system that can do such great harm.

Beginning in the 1990s, Biederman—with pharmaceutical money flowing into his coffers—played the pied piper for recruiting children and adolescents into psychiatry, telling of how so many of them had chronic brain illnesses, which needed to be treated, on a forever basis, with powerful drugs. Anastasia was treated by Biederman from age twelve to sixteen, and during those four years, Anastasia writes that Biederman "had me on varying combinations of sixteen different medications, including mood stabilizers, antianxiety medications, tranquilizers, antidepressants, an antiepileptic medication that he believed could treat bipolar, antipsychotics, and stimulants to counteract the fatigue I experienced from the other medications."

This reads like a diary of assault with a prescription pad. It was also during this time that, at age twelve, Anastasia was hospitalized on a psychiatric ward for the first time, where they were strip-searched and left to cry out, "Mom, please don't let them take me." The ward door slammed shut, their mother disappeared, and the wailing of their twelve-year-old self can still be heard in these pages today.

Anastasia is careful to write that as an adult, psychiatric medications have been helpful. Yet, at the same time, they raise this haunting question, which I wish all of American society could hear. "I don't know what my life would have been like if I hadn't been medicated as a child. One thing I can be sure of is that my brain wasn't allowed to develop as it should have."

Anastasia's closing words will remind readers that, when someone tells you their life story, the gift of that telling imposes a responsibility too.

> Up until very recently, fear of judgment kept me from sharing my history with others. I wanted to maintain a façade of normalcy and was afraid I would be regarded as too damaged to relate to if I were to divulge my past. I worried that the people I told might tell others, and that my story would precede me. I have found, however, that stories of survival—survival of all kinds—are not uncommon, particularly in the queer community. There is strength in our narratives, and I have come to a place where I am willing to tell those who are willing to listen.

Which brings us to the essential question: are we, as a society, willing to listen? Unfortunately, there is plenty of reason to doubt that we will. The past tells of a societal deafness toward those we call "mad" or "mentally ill," while the conventional wisdom today specifically tells us *not* to listen to the mad (unless, of course, they agree with the conventional narrative).

The promoters of that silencing even have a word to explain why we should turn a deaf ear: *anosognosia*.

I remember when I first encountered this word. It was in 1998, when I was reporting a series for the *Boston Globe* related to abuses of psychiatric patients in research studies, which included the testing of antipsychotics. The academic psychiatrists I interviewed told me how these drugs fixed a dopamine imbalance in the brain, like insulin for diabetes, which I understood to be true. However, interviewing David Oaks from MindFreedom left me mulling over a different possibility, which was that there might be good reason that some people didn't like antipsychotics. When I questioned the psychiatrists about that, they all had a one-word answer: "anosognosia." There were some patients who "lacked insight" into their illness, and thus didn't understand that antipsychotics were good for them.

While I knew little about this world of psychiatry then, I immediately understood this: it was a statement made by the powerful that justified their control over the powerless, and it was a statement of far-reaching impact. It provides a rationale for forced treatment, and, even more profound, informs the society that the mad person is an unreliable witness to their own life, and thus unworthy of being listened to.

This is the very concept that has led psychiatry to "do harm," over and over again. Psychiatrists know what is "best" for their mad patients, and if their patients have a different idea of what is "best" for them, that is too bad. This is the medical stance that led to spinning chairs, tranquilizer chairs, and drowning therapies in early American psychiatry; the embrace of convulsive therapies and lobotomies as miracle brain surgeries in the first half of the twentieth century; and forced injections of haloperidol in the latter half of the twentieth century.

With the "mad" silenced in this way, you have to dig deep into the library shelves to find any written accounts from patients locked up in nineteenth-century asylums. It is much the same for the first half of the twentieth century, although, with the proper library search, you can eventually find several powerful accounts of life behind the locked doors of a psychiatric hospital. Not surprisingly, those patient accounts regularly tell of a society that is deaf to their plight. In his 1947 book *If a Man Be Mad*, Harold Maine lamented that there was simply nothing a patient could do to "prod the nation into an awareness of the way it had been duped with the folklore about modern institutional psychiatry."

In the 1970s, the rise of the psychiatric survivor movement punched a dent in this societal deafness. Ex-patients organized political groups with such names as the Insane Liberation Front and the Network Against Psychiatric Assault. These groups held demonstrations, organized human rights conferences, and, starting in 1975, took their arguments against forced treatment to state courts. Judi Chamberlin's 1978 book *On Our*

Own became a rallying cry for ex-patients to develop their own "alternative" forms of care to help each other.

The moment that this voice of resistance was heard most loudly came in 1975, when *One Flew over the Cuckoo's Nest* appeared on the nation's screens. This was a film that turned conventional wisdom upside down: reason could be found in the speech and thoughts of the mad, while madness was most evident in those who ran the asylums.

But that high-water moment was more than forty years ago, and so Anastasia's essay brings us again to this essential question. Are we, as a society, willing to listen?

Today, I think the answer is both yes and no. The voice of those with "lived experience" can be broadly grouped into two types, depending on whether they understand their own lives within the context of the conventional medical paradigm, or in resistance to that paradigm, and it is only the first group that is well heard by society. The authors of this anthology fall into the second group, which has a much more difficult time finding a public megaphone.

In the 1970s, the psychiatric survivor movement presented a fairly uniform message to the public. Forced treatment was a violation of their civil rights, and a violation of their basic constitutional right to be the governors of their own lives. But this was a narrative told mostly by ex-hospital patients.

Then, in 1980, the American Psychiatric Association published the third edition of its *Diagnostic and Statistical Manual (DSM)*, which greatly expanded the criteria for diagnosing someone as "mentally ill." This invited a much larger group into the "patient" camp, and this naturally has led to an explosion of writings—memoirs, personal stories, and such—about this experience.

The *DSM* narrative tells of distinct brain illnesses within the individual, which can be more or less successfully treated with psychiatric medications, and those with "lived experience" who locate their lives within that narrative have told their stories in books, on television shows, and so forth. As could be expected, the pharmaceutical industry—and psychiatry as an institution—has helped promote that voice. A celebrity tells of having bipolar disorder, as Mariah Carey recently did, and she is publicly praised for her bravery and for fighting stigma.

This is the "lived experience" voice that is most loudly heard by the public today. I do not want to speak poorly of that voice here. When you encounter anyone telling of their life, and the difficulties they may have, the only right thing to do is to listen and honor their personal narrative. They are serving as witnesses to their own lives, and their own self-understanding.

At the same time, it is that conventional narrative that allows for psychiatry, and our legal institutions, to promote the idea that those who don't see themselves as ill lack insight into their own illness, and thus their voices should be ignored. The conventional narrative undercuts—and serves to silence—the "radical narrative" that resists psychiatry's diagnostic conceptions, and its "illness-based" treatments.

Unfortunately, this "lived experience" voice is not so well heard by the public, which is why listening to the voices of the authors in this anthology is so important. They are putting forth a vision, rooted in lived experience, that challenges society to rethink our current conceptions of "mental illness," and create new understandings—and new "radical interventions"—for helping one another as we struggle with our minds and our emotions.

In the second half of the book, the authors lay out their ideas—and arguments—for radical interventions, and, frankly, it is a rather damning indictment of our current paradigm of care that their thoughts and beliefs would be seen as "radical." Their agendas for "radical mental health" are all rooted in timeless—and what should be quite ordinary—ways of helping each other.

Any remaking of our current paradigm of care would begin with throwing out the *DSM*, with its ludicrous setting of diagnostic boundaries between the "normal" and the "abnormal." The "normality" that haunts the pages of that manual is not to be found in any world depicted by novelists, playwrights, or the authors of the Bible. It is a make-believe "normalcy," and the writers of this anthology, with their poetry, narratives, and essays, thankfully invite readers into the very literary world absent from the *DSM*. Their writings tell of the "normality" of suffering, and how such suffering and mental distress regularly arise from one's interactions with an environment that, starting in childhood, can be frightening, painful, and horribly unfair.

These two different narratives represent a fundamental dividing point for a society. The illness conception, with the suffering located inside the individual, regularly leads to harm done, while the radical voice for change articulated here, which tells of suffering and misery that can arise from social injustice and other life experiences, naturally leads to efforts to create more helpful environments.

If there is anything that the history of psychiatry teaches us, it is that a conception of "mental illness" that prompts society to think of people so diagnosed as abnormal—and thus as the "other"—will inevitably lead to abusive therapies and societal assaults on the civil liberties of those it calls "mad." In contrast, if there is a conception of "madness" or "mental suffering" that calls upon our common humanity, then that naturally leads to "treatments" that provide some of the environmental supports that we all need to be well: friendship, meaning in life, shelter, good food, and so forth.

It is that second conception of "madness" or of "mental illness" that is the foundation for the "radical interventions" that are presented in the second half of *We've Been Too Patient*. The irony is that if this conception were to take hold, and we came to see each other as "alike," then the interventions described here—while described as "radical" by these authors—would instead be seen as belonging to the "of course" category. Of course this is what we, as a society, should do.

There is a description of one intervention, the DE-CRUIT program, written by Alisha Ali and Stephan Wolfert, that filled me with utter delight. Wolfert developed it "after discovering firsthand the healing power of Shakespeare's plays" in work with veterans. Each veteran learns to recite a Shakespearean monologue and then performs it before the group. It's easy to see why this would be healing: if there is any writer who has explored the wild corners of the human mind, and yet normalized such extremes as a regular part of the human experience, it is Shakespeare.

Such was my experience of "listening" to the writers of this anthology. There are poems that took my breath away, personal stories that I felt privileged to read, and arguments for "radical interventions" that I can only hope rapidly take hold.

ACKNOWLEDGMENTS

Liz's Acknowledgments (L. D. Green):

Thank you to all our contributors.

Thank you also to:

Erin Wiegand, dear friend and former acquisitions editor at North Atlantic Books, for liking my articles on The Body Is Not an Apology and approaching me about putting a book together, and coaching me and Kelechi through the process; Sonya Renee Taylor for giving me a platform to write about radical mental health on TBINAA; Ma'ia Williams for being a kind and incisive editor at TBINAA; my dear partner Ramon(a) Rio for reading drafts and for her endless love and support; Salaams, Stella Sheldon, Deb Cuny, Julia Hazer, and the rest of my mutual aid friendship community for being awesome and keeping me striving and thriving; old dear friends Meredith Summs and Ainsley Story who will always be stars that make me face east; my colleagues at Los Medanos College; Meg Schoerke, my friend and critique partner for valuable feedback on drafts; and my mother, Susan Donahue, and my stepfather, Peter Donahue, for their love and for their excitement for me about this project. Thank you to my sister Tana for being my first mutual aid friend.

Thanks to The Icarus Project for existing and for being there when I needed it, introducing me to great ideas and great people (especially thanks to Jacks McNamara), and for continuing to do amazing work. Thanks to my co-editor Kelechi for being a rock star collaborator and friend. I loved making this book with you. Thanks to Gina Goldblatt for all the amazing work you do in the world, and for introducing me to Kelechi!

Thanks, finally, to everyone who has shown up for me in support of my well-being. You give me faith, you keep me going. And thank you to those who have let me support you.

We've Been Too Patient

Kelechi's Acknowledgments

Thank you to my mother, Janet Bivens, my rock and my gem, a virtuous woman who fills my life with love, laughter, and magic. To Aunt Beth, for being a second mother and helping me grow up. To my father, Ferdinand, and brothers Uche, Chimezie, and Nnaemeka Ubozoh—with whom I finally shared my whole life and who opened their arms wider to embrace me. To the Kendrick, Lewis, and Bivens families for a lifetime of love and encouragement.

Thank you to my supernatural friends Miguel Jimenez and Erin Huestis, who move across all realms with their support and love; to Lisa Torchia, who keeps me laughing during the darkest days and quietly models courage; to Gina Goldblatt for celebrating my story and amplifying my voice through her work at Liminal; to Lucie Lie-Nielsen for helping me reclaim my voice; to Causha and Chanel Spellman-Timmons for showing me that love and friendship take grace and grit; to Tawny Estrella for being a guiding light; to Roberta Chambers for affirming my dreams; to Lisa Klein for including me in *The S Word*; and to my love James Hill who stands by my side and makes me feel powerful and seen.

Thank you Sally Zinman for your groundbreaking leadership and unwavering commitment to the consumer movement. Thank you to all the contributors for sharing your soulful stories and your life-altering work so we can all learn, heal, and grow.

And lastly, thank you Liz for the partnership, for the joyous work, and for helping to create something beautiful. My dear friend, you demonstrate this movement.

EDITORS' INTRODUCTION

Kelechi Ubozoh

From my head to my steel-toed combat boots, I believe that just like people, systems can get better, healthier, stronger, and smarter. Over the past twenty years, the role of survivors/consumers/ex-patients and folks with lived experience in the mental health service system has grown. However, the reality of stigma and injustice for our community is far too real. I've experienced this firsthand. I am someone who has been fired for disclosing a mental health diagnosis at work and experienced discrimination in seeking help and receiving help in hospitals.

I was told I was "broken," and that I would never get better. I was also told that my experience wasn't real, and I needed to stop being so dramatic and pray. It didn't take long for me to realize that that my and other's mental health self-healing journeys are not realized or accepted by everyone. I wanted large-scale change, so I moved west to work in mental health advocacy. As mental health advocates, we work to ensure that there is "nothing about us without us." What happens when our voice is missing from the system? Well, very bad things. In the name of treatment, we've experienced injustice, neglect, and abuse. Labeled with being too dangerous, too sick, too unpredictable, and unable to understand what we need.

This anthology is about putting power back into the hands of people seeking mental health services, specifically about the types of interventions that we want, that we need, and that work. Stories are powerful, and not because of a "Hallmark feel-good feeling." Stories dispel myths and show us that we are not alone. We may experience things differently, but we all deserve respect and to have our stories heard and, more importantly, listened to. Want a cliché quote about it? "We are the ones we've been waiting for." We have been too patient with the system, but we are ready to act now on our own behalf.

I used to think recovery meant not ever being in a dark place again, getting so depressed you can't leave your bed, or never hearing a suicidal thought again. I was wrong. Recovery, for me, is about the choices you make when you are in those spaces. For me, healing was developing boundaries, trauma-informed therapy, psychoeducation, adopting a cat, starting yoga, removing toxic people from my life, quitting yoga, cooking lessons with my mom, poetry, and karaoke singing. Thankfully, I had built a community of mental health advocates who reminded me to take care of myself. I had done enough work to create a safety net to catch myself.

As Liz says about herself, I have big emotions too, so I have a big life. Now, I plan for it. Today, I am an advocate, a mental health consumer with mad pride, and a suicide attempt survivor shattering the silence, because if my Black community doesn't start talking about it we'll lose more people to the tenth-leading cause of death. I will never stop working on ending the stigma of mental health and suicide through story, and I am so *honored* to be in this book of so many survivors, system-changers, and researchers, who are in this fight with me.

L. D. Green

As I write my part of the introduction to the book Kelechi, I, all our contributors, and our publisher have brought into being, I must admit I am filled with both excitement and trepidation. I urgently want to claim my seat at the table of what contributor Jonah Bossewitch calls "the new wave of mad resistance" in his article, and by doing that, I am compelled to disclose that I, too, am … a "mental health consumer"? A "psychiatric survivor"? A lifelong "patient"? A mental health advocate with lived experience? That last one sounds best, safest. But I must claim the others, too.

As a "consumer," I am frustrated with "services rendered" that have been, well … insufficient at best. As a "psychiatric survivor," I am healing from the traumas inflicted on me by the mental health industrial complex

(MHIC). As a lifelong "patient," I have many stories to tell about psychiatry's and even therapy's limitations. (Although a few of my therapists have been really rad, in both senses of the word.) Hence the title: we've been too patient, too long suffering, too "compliant," "concordant," whatever they want to call it now. This is a movement that demands awareness of the oppression of the MHIC while allowing for a nuanced understanding of radical healing for those who need it.

To say I am now a mental health advocate, and not just a survivor/patient/consumer, feels right. I have worked with The Icarus Project[1] in the past, and my artivism through my poetry and other writing first published on The Body Is Not an Apology (one article is included in this book) was my beginning as an advocate with lived experience, and this book represents a new dawning of what I can contribute to this movement. But I must admit there is another reason I would like to cloak myself with the title "lived experience." It feels neutral. It could suggest that my suffering, due to childhood trauma as well as psychiatric trauma, is housed within the realm of less stigmatizing troubles like depression and anxiety. True, the bulk of my everyday distress can be labeled as such. But I feel compelled to disclose more, to speak truth to power about what I have suffered, and yes, honor the *strengths* of my "condition."

My reluctance to assert my mad pride stems from the ableist capitalist power structure, which is the very thing this book resists; namely, I fear the repercussions of stigma that could cause me to lose my job—a job I have worked very hard to land. This is a reasonable fear. My work with Kelechi, and her brave modeling of being "out" in a stigmatizing world, brings forth another desire that eclipses my reluctance. The other contributors to this book are also helping me take this stand because the slogan Nothing about Us without Us is vital and is the pioneering contribution of this book. Every story or essay in this anthology comes from someone with "lived experience,"[2] and denying all the complexities of mine in the hopes of protecting myself from the structure we are resisting would be counter to the ambitions of this project. So, let me just say that I have been psychiatrically hospitalized. I have been diagnosed with "bipolar disorder"—and while I choose to take medication as one tool to mitigate the intensity that characterizes my life, I have many other tools: mutual aid, therapy, creativity, spirituality. Those are the tools that save me. Personally, I am suspicious of any narrative that says medication is *the* method to solving something so complex as mental and emotional distress. This book actively resists the mainstream pseudoscience of the biomedical model in favor of other alternative frameworks, such as the recovery model, trauma-informed care, the mad pride movement, the consumer movement, the neurodiversity framework, and more.[3] As you will see, mental health care looks different for each person.

I also believe that my "disorder" is really a complex response to early childhood traumas, compounded by psychiatric traumas and other violence I have experienced later in life, much of which can be viewed through a lens of structural oppression. But the biggest tool for me is radical acceptance that I will have hard days. As Kelechi said to me once, "Life doesn't get better, but we do." Life still shows up, dishes out more rough experiences. So, I build up my buttress of support and use more tools. And I do my best to not shame myself for the days when I simply cannot function in society and need to sleep binge with my cats. I have also learned to anticipate these days, so when they happen I am less distressed by my distress. Depression and anxiety (responses to trauma and stress) riddle together and can immobilize me. That's okay. My range of feeling is wide and deep. I am lucky for that. I live a big life filled with love, friendship, community, art, a great job, and I also have big emotions—I have a "dangerous gift," as they say in Icarus, and I tend to this flame so it doesn't erupt or die out. This flame lights the passion I have at my job, and my ability to be a good partner and friend, and it fuels my creativity.

With this book, I give myself the permission to be out and proud as a survivor/advocate/neuroatypical artivist. Just as I have continually come out in various contexts as queer since adolescence, I have had various moments of disclosure throughout my life as a "mad" person, too. But this is a book with my name on it. Pretty public. So, let me say it here: because of trauma (and perhaps some predisposition to intense mood states that trauma activates) I am neuroatypical. Because I am neuroatypical, I have dangerous gifts. Because I have dangerous gifts, I have mad pride—a pride that calls on me to heal the ragged edges while I call on my differences to be a force for change. And while the Americans with Disabilities Act (ADA) should protect me from losing my job, I am sadly aware of the perniciousness of stigma, so I am reasonable enough to make this choice thoughtfully and with no small amount of courage. My spirituality guided me, years ago, to make more conscious steps toward this calling: to speak my truth about what I have struggled with, to join the mad movement, and in this telling and in this gathering, light a new fire that is not just within me but grows ever outward into other people's minds and hearts.

L. D. Green and Kelechi Ubozoh

Our vision and passion for this book has been a process that mirrors its product. We are both wounded healers and mental health advocates with lived experience. When we first started working together on this project, we had a whirlwind of ideas about what in particular we wanted to contribute to the mental health dialogue. We knew for certain that we wanted to have the stories from people with lived experience at the forefront. From our twenty contributors, only one does not have lived experience with mental health issues. We explored a lot of different modalities— would we use art? Would we use poetry? Would this all be research based? A combination? We settled on a combination of research-based analysis and narrative.

People heal themselves through stories. Stories help combat stigma and also challenge the biomedical model because they offer an alternative in the recovery model. For people without lived experience with mental health, hearing from survivors humanizes the teller. An epiphany for us was that these stories are not just useful for the reader or audience, they are empowering for the writer as well. In that regard, we as editors engaged in a process of mutual aid with our contributors that helped all involved. Because both mutual aid and narratives are radical mental health interventions, our process reflects our product.

Any book takes intellectual labor. This process took emotional labor, too. What does that mean? It means sitting with someone and listening to their story of trauma and triumph as they craft their written work, it means shaping the nuances of their recovery through their narrative, it means building a community of diverse experiences, backgrounds, and views. It means we cultivated a space where all of these diverse voices could thrive.

This first part of the book is titled "Narrative as a Radical Healing Strategy: Personal Stories of Lived Experience with Mental Health." Our writers in the first half reflect on serious abuses in the mental health industrial complex, such as overly medicating minors, police brutality, and electroconvulsive therapy, as well as a range of traumas and struggles that lead to intense altered states and suicidal thoughts and actions. But these stories are not without hope. Many of them speak to the healing powers of spirituality, friendship, physical movement, and story itself.

We decided ultimately that while stories speak volumes on their own, we also wanted to hear from writers who could articulate the context for this chorus of voices. We must be heard, yes, but what are our demands and concerns? Part Two, "Radical Interventions: Challenging the Biomedical Model and Stigma with the Recovery Model," begins to consider these questions, and more.

Through expository essays, part two illuminates central questions about what this radical mental health movement is really all about and offers what amount to common-sense solutions (as Whitaker describes in the foreword); people should care about each other and see each other as equal and human, which will lead to humane, creative, and compassionate interventions into distress. This "common sense," however, ultimately has the power to radically reshape society beyond just the scope of mental health care reform if we don't stigmatize differences, if we offer each other mutual aid and listen to the "dangerous gifts" of the neuroatypical. We must build our society outward along such principles and visions. The "radical" here is not just about our orientation to the treatment of those who struggle with mental health concerns; the way in which we conceive of these concerns, and the way we practice healing, are the acts with implications for intersectional, radical social transformation.

In part two, Sascha Altman DuBrul advocates for transformative mutual aid practices in the peer-support mental health movement. Alisha Ali and

Stephan Wolfert's essay details a richly creative trauma-informed care practice for veterans. Psychologist and well-known mental health advocate Patrick Corrigan bravely "comes out proud" as someone with lived experience himself and discusses the complex choices behind disclosure in various settings, particularly professional ones, due to the reality of stigma. Researcher, writer, and activist Jonah Bossewitch threads together seemingly disparate movements to make a case for where the "mad" movement has come from and where it's going.

We hope you find yourself in these pages just as we found ourselves in this process.

NOTES

1. See Sascha Altman DuBrul, Jacks McNamara, Jonah Bossewitch, L. D. Green, Imogen Prism, Jeffrey Goines, and Anita Roman's work for mention and description of The Icarus Project, a part of "mad pride" and "mad resistance." The organization was founded in 2002 by Altman DuBrul and McNamara as a mutual aid support network for folks labeled as mentally ill. The new group reframed this experience as having "dangerous gifts." The collective co-authored a zine with the Freedom Center, *The Harm Reduction Guide to Coming Off Psychiatric Drugs,* which has been translated into many different languages. The Icarus Project continues to lead workshops and webinars. Leadership has changed—Agustina Vidal, Kifu Faruq, and Byul Yoon now direct the organization. This is from their current website: "The Icarus Project is a support network and education project by and for people who experience the world in ways that are often diagnosed as mental illness. We advance social justice by fostering mutual aid practices that reconnect healing and collective liberation. We transform ourselves through transforming the world around us" (www.theicarusproject.net).

2. One is co-authored by an ally: "Treating Trauma through the Imagination: Therapeutic Effects of Simulation and Mimetic Induction."

3. See the glossary at the end of this book for more definitions.

PART ONE

Narrative as a Radical Healing Strategy: Personal Stories of Lived Experience with Mental Health

dear dr

Leah Harris is a mother, storyteller, and intersectional activist. She has spoken and written widely on her experiences as a trauma survivor and a suicide attempt survivor, as well as on her paths to resilience. Leah is the founder of Shifa Consulting, a social enterprise promoting holistic and creative arts approaches to healing trauma. Her 2016 solo storytelling show, *Aliens, Nazis, and Angels,* was named among the Best of the Capital Fringe Festival. She serves on The Icarus Project Advisory Board and the National Suicide Prevention Lifeline's Consumer/Survivor Subcommittee. She is an advisor to *The S Word,* a documentary about suicide.

. . . .

dear dr
on that proud, glorious day
you graduated from medical school
you took an oath as old as Hippocrates
remember?
    "above all, do no harm"
    above all, do no harm
    do no harm
    no harm

ah but the trouble is
you thought you were doing Good
by warehousing us in that
sterile, oppressive, un-hospitable place
you called the hospital
you practiced the toughest form of tough love there is—

so tough
i could not see no love
nowhere

you placed the blame
squarely on our brains
squarely on our serotonin flow
our synapses
labeling us with whatever diagnosis
on whatever page of your book
you found appropriate
at the time—

you thought you could turn us around
make us productive future citizens
make us fit into this
  authoritarian
  sexist
  racist
  ageist
  militaristic
society your generation
the greatest generation
built

you always insisted that we were the problem
and that you were the solution
but your treatments, your cures
your directives issued from on high
  did not heal our brains
  did not open our hearts—

they merely transformed these organs
into impassive lumps of bitter rage

if anything, dear dr
you taught me how to act
you taught me all the world's a stage
you pushed me to award-winning performances
 the award being
  life away from your indifferent eyes
  your pronouncements of health or ill
  your indecipherable scribbles
  on the prescription pad—
  the infernal fifteen minutes
  you gave me each week
in a word, dear dr, the award was
freedom
or at least a glimmer

perhaps I give you too much credit, oh dr dear
assuming
that you saw me as something more than
 billable hours
 business as usual
 another bed, filled
 until the money ran out
 this time

dear dr
you'll never know
in your ivory tower on the second floor
of the locked teen ward
how many years i've spent
sweating and struggling
to undo all the harm you did
the harm you did
with the best of intentions
paving my road to hell

i declare war on all you scribbled
in my chart
building a new chart
charting a course of humanity and dignity
with scribbles and shouts of my own
and all the while Hippocrates's bones
are twitching in their grave
dear dr

To Call Myself Beloved

LEAH HARRIS

> *To call myself beloved, to feel myself*
> *beloved on the earth.*

> —RAYMOND CARVER, "LAST FRAGMENT,"
> FROM *ALL OF US: THE COLLECTED POEMS*

The bell rang to signal the beginning of a forty-five-minute sit. I listened as its sound rose high and clear through the meditation hall with its vast domed ceiling, until my ears could no longer perceive its tone. I adjusted my posture. Reached the crown of my head toward the sky, lifting and straightening my spine. Felt the weight of my body seated upon its cushion, the density of my hands resting on my thighs. Settled into the familiar rhythm of my breath as it rose and fell through my lungs. This human body, breathing.

In July of 2004 I was twenty-eight, sitting my first intensive silent meditation retreat. I had flown all the way from my home in Washington, DC, to this hippy-dippy place called Spirit Rock in Marin County, California, for twelve hours of sitting and walking meditation per day. For seven days.

In-breath. Pause. Out-breath. Pause.

When my mind wandered, as minds do, it meandered over to my lie.

I had lied on the application to get into this retreat. I was not proud of it. That dreaded part where it asks about previous or current mental health conditions. It did not ask about a history of suicidality that I can recall. If it had, I surely would have answered "none" to that as well. I knew that if I had been honest, they would have turned my application down. I did not want to explain or expose myself in this way, on an online form, where they could not see my face, where they could not see in my eyes: *Yes, I tried to kill myself. Yes, I have five different psychiatric diagnoses. But despite what this form says, I can handle this.*

I once heard a teacher say that the entirety of the Buddha's teachings can be distilled down to two subjects: suffering and the end of suffering. I knew about suffering. I knew it intimately. What I wanted was to begin to understand a way out of suffering that would not necessitate death at my own hand.

———

Just six months before, if you had told me that I was going to go meditate for a week at some crunchy retreat center in California run by aging hippies, I would have laughed in your face. I hated anything I deemed as "New Age bullshit," which definitely included meditation, yoga, and anything involving "vibrations." All a navel-gazing waste of time, in my opinion.

It was an especially painful dark night of the soul that brought me to the Buddha's feet.

I was beginning my life as an activist, organizing and speaking out for compassionate alternatives to a mental health system that is all too often punitive to people in pain, especially if that pain is suicidal pain. At the time, I was traveling around the country and connecting with all of these other survivor activists. I went from being someone who had my story narrated in medical records, in the language of damage and disorder, to reclaiming my narrative and telling my story on my own terms. In front of people! What was once my mess had become my message. There was a very exhilarating high to it all.

In late 2003 I was going to be speaking on a panel at a conference in Washington, DC. Jennifer, one of my fellow panelists and an acquaintance from activist work, arrived from out of town to stay with me for the weekend.[1] When I opened the door, I could immediately tell that something wasn't right. Her face was drawn. There were huge circles under her eyes. She looked like she had lost a lot of weight.

She spoke in a low, quiet monotone and wouldn't meet my eye. She would disappear for long periods of time into my bathroom and then emerge with downcast eyes. Finally, I knocked on the door. She opened it a little, then all the way. *I've been cutting myself*, she confessed, showing me her arms. *I want to die*, she continued in a barely audible voice, telling me about a few of the ways she was thinking about ending her life.

I began to sweat. I was fourteen again and in my room, door locked, razor pilfered from my grandfather's medicine cabinet. My grandmother, screaming at me to open the door. I couldn't. The police, banging, banging on the door. The young cop's disgusted eyes when I finally opened it. *Why would you do that to yourself?*

I didn't call 911 on Jennifer. Couldn't, wouldn't bring the cops to the door. Behind her back, I called one of my fellow panelists and told him what was going on. He got ahold of her family. Picked her up, and made sure she got safely onto a plane back home.

When he arrived at my apartment to remove her, she finally looked me in the eye. A mixture of surprise and hatred, swirled with accusation. If the look could talk, it would say, *You're a hypocrite.*

That's what I was saying to myself. You're a champion for the human rights of suicidal people, but someone who is suicidal right in your own home? You shut down. Kick her out. You're a complete fraud.

Today, I know that my nervous system was overloaded with memories of unresolved trauma. Suicide is traumatic, and the responses of others can add more trauma still. Intellectually, I know I froze in a situation I wasn't prepared to handle at the time. But deep inside, I loathed myself for how I responded. I crawled into a psychic hole of self-blame and recrimination. The world beyond my bed felt like an uninhabitable place.

In the midst of this rapidly spiraling shame-fueled depressive state, I was scheduled to give a talk at a conference in Charlottesville, Virginia, a few hours' drive away. The talk was supposed to be about my lived experience as an attempt survivor. I considered canceling. But I couldn't bring myself to do it.

Before getting on the road, I pored through the audiobooks section at Politics and Prose, seeking something to distract. My eyes darted over novels and biographies, and then landed on a title that would have definitely fallen under my "New Age bullshit" category: *Creating True Peace* by this Vietnamese Zen Buddhist dude named Thich Nhat Hanh. But my hand shot out and selected it.

As I drove, I was mesmerized by the perspective of this extraordinary monk and activist. He talked about mindfulness meditation as a way for us to learn how to choose how we respond, rather than be ruled by our unconscious reactions. He talked about how people hurt one another out of their own unconscious pain. Something about his message lodged a crack in the wall of judgment I had built between myself and my own heart.

The incident with Jennifer was the mirror that showed me my shadow. How I had been expending tremendous amounts of energy trying to fix the world "out there," while neglecting my own pain. Living this way caused me to shut down in the face of another's suffering. To cause harm.

I knew I needed to try this mindfulness thing.

———

Listening to a fifteen-minute guided meditation on a CD, sitting cross-legged on a pillow in my living room, I discovered for the first time that the breath is an anchor. A place to return to. A home inside of me that I never knew existed.

When I opened my eyes after that first fifteen-minute sit, the world was somehow *different*.

Please. I am not saying I was struck enlightened. Far from it. But through mindfulness practice, I discovered something within that a decade of traditional talk therapy had never unearthed. The Observer. Also known as "witness consciousness." The part of my consciousness that can *notice* what is happening in this body, heart, and mind, and meet it all with nonjudgmental curiosity. Kindness, clear seeing, and compassion: that's the Observer.

For much of my life, I had wanted to stop myself from breathing. But the first time I sat in meditation, I learned how to follow my breath. To love it, even.

———

May you be safe and protected from harm.
May you be happy and peaceful.
May you be healthy and strong.
May you live with ease.

On that silent retreat at Spirit Rock, I was introduced to the phrases of *metta,* or lovingkindness. The Buddha originally taught these phrases to a group of forest monks as an antidote to fear. Instead of focusing on the breath, you repeat these phrases over and over in your mind. Prayers of well-wishing. Starting with yourself and extending out to all beings, everywhere.

The meditation teacher was speaking from the front of the hall. The metta phrases may bring up the opposite emotions. We may begin to think about all the ways in which we and others are not happy or healthy, or don't feel safe, or peaceful, or at ease.

I was grateful for that reminder. Traumatic experiences had imprinted a sense of hypervigilance on my nervous system. Right now did *not* feel safe. The suffocating sense of being trapped in a body, in a life not of your choosing. That feeling of wanting to claw your way out of your own skin. The fertile ground of suicidal imaginings. Edwin Shneidman, the founder of modern suicidology, called it the *psychache.*

May I be happy. May I be peaceful. May I be—

Who was I kidding?

I stood up and silently padded out of the meditation hall. My feet needed to move. They moved and they moved until I found myself standing on a vast hill covered in bleached tan tufts of grass, overlooking a small valley. The sun gleamed in a cerulean sky. The air smelled of warm, dried grass.

I laid myself down on the earth, my eyes toward the heavens, arms and legs splayed out like a star. *Savasana.* Corpse pose, they call it in yoga. The hardest pose. I never understood why yoga teachers said that. Until one day, I did. Letting go is the hardest thing to do.

I felt the presence of my suicidal girl, floating above me like a ghost, demanding that I meet her baleful gaze. We overlapped, she and I, a human Venn diagram through space and time. The suicidal girl whose body was the only thing under her control. Until she crossed a line, and it wasn't anymore. *Danger to herself.* That suicidal girl who was handled with rough male orderlies' hands, thrown onto stretchers, deprived of human eye contact, deprived of liberty, left alone in hallways and rooms both locked and unlocked for hours with her traumas old and new. Left with a fist of shame lodged halfway between her throat and her heart. Convinced of her original, irreparable damage.

The body remembers. It waits, patiently, until we feel strong enough to meet the parts we have abandoned. The ones we want most to forget.

The Observer stepped in, as vast as the sky, witnessing our reunion. For the first time, I was able to feel compassion for the girl who hurt herself, who swallowed the pills, who inflicted the scars that were only now finally beginning to fade. I no longer hated her. No longer wanted her gone.

My heart opened wide enough to allow her to climb in, to take her rightful place there, no longer confined to a graveyard in the recesses of my unconscious. No longer a frozen ghost.

The dam between my heart and me broke. I howled on the hilltop with grief and rage for my suicidal girl inside. For Jennifer. For all the girls who feel they must drop their bodies, because life is too much to contain. For all the girls whose voices have evaporated into the dust because they saw no choice but to leave. For all the girls who survive, with a host of visible and invisible scars.

I will stay for them, I decided.

A strange calm rushed in. For the first time, I felt myself as beloved upon the earth. Belonging to it. Not separate from it. Whole in my brokenness.

———

Nowadays, people in suicidal distress contact me fairly often, because of the very public ways in which I tell my own story as an attempt survivor. While I will never be able to change how I responded to Jennifer, I have since learned and practice the fundamentals of peer support and resource referral. How to be an ally to someone who is suicidal. How to listen without needing to fix people or talk them out of their feelings. I have since learned the art of staying grounded in the face of another's distress. How to have boundaries around what I am and am not able to give. How to express my needs and to be authentic in relationship with others. How to let myself receive. It's an ongoing process and it's messy. I'm far from perfect at any of it.

Mindfulness meditation did not "cure" me of suicidal thoughts and urges. From time to time, my mind still wants to convince me that death is a good idea. That my preteen son would be better off without such a damaged mother.

Meditation has taught me to see the suicidal thoughts as an early warning system. I must not take the thoughts literally, believe them, or obey them. What the suicidal urge is showing me is that something about how I have been living needs to die. My brain points me to all the ways in which I abandon myself, drive myself unforgivingly in the name of whatever pursuit I falsely believe is more important than caring for my sensitive soul. I am forced to acknowledge my vulnerability. The places where I need love, care, and understanding.

The suicidal thought is now my cue to stop. To tend. To seek solace.

When my suicidal warning system sounds, sometimes all I need is to connect to another human being who receives me without judgment, without fear.

Other times, I need to find the nearest patch of grass and lie down, letting the earth cradle my entire body. I practice the art of letting go. *Savasana*. Corpse pose. The hardest pose. Letting all doing slip away. Letting life live through me. I allow tears of grief and rage to stream down my cheeks and onto the grass, where they become one with the ground.

I stare up at the bowl of the sky until I remember the truth. My deepest-held truth, echoing throughout the chambers of my beating heart. *I want to stay. I want to stay. I want to stay.*

NOTE

1. For privacy purposes, her name has been changed.

Can't We Just Pray It Away?

Faith Communities and Their Role in Mental Health Support

JENEÉ DARDEN

Jeneé Darden is an award-winning journalist, public speaker, mental health advocate, and proud Oakland, California, native. Her debut book, *When a Purple Rose Blooms*, is a collection of poetry and essays about her experience with love, sex, and mental health as a Black woman. Jeneé hosts the website and podcast Cocoa Fly. She is pitching a book on Black sexuality. Visit CocoaFly.com to read her research series *Under the Covers: The Popularity and Debate over Black Erotic Literature*.

. . . .

"Depression is a result of spiritual starvation. Overcome depression and emotional hardships by immersing yourself in God's Word."

New York Times best-selling author and megachurch pastor John Hagee tweeted this misinformed message to his 312,000 followers in 2018. His tweet triggered teenage memories from Sunday mornings when I heard similar messages in church. While I sat in the pews confused as to why I couldn't just be happier, my pastor preached that people are depressed because they don't have a strong relationship with God.

That's like saying someone has cancer because they don't pray hard enough. Depression is a health issue. People of all faiths encounter health issues, whether they're physical or mental. Being a Christian doesn't exclude you from depression. Even the Reverend Martin Luther King Jr. struggled with depression during his lifetime.[1]

Reading that tweet made me feel bad for people who are struggling with depression and are in a mental space where they're not feeling good about themselves. I know the feeling. Those of us with depression can be hard on ourselves. Pastor Hagee gave them one more thing to add to their "Why I'm Worthless" list—not being spiritual enough.

Pastor Hagee's tweet didn't surprise me because many faith leaders have shared this sentiment for a long time. There are some churches that still believe a person with a mental illness is possessed by an evil spirit. However, what did surprise me about Pastor Hagee's tweet were the responses.

> I'm a pastor. My job is to immerse myself in the word of God. I also have depression. The two are not related.
>
> —*Steven W. Barber, @RevSWBarber*

> Nope. It's an illness that needs treatment. Much like a physical one. God loves people with depression just like everyone else. They are not starved of his presence.
>
> —*Mind and Soul, @mindandsoulUK*

> The same is true of fractures. You see people coming back from skiing holidays with their legs in plaster, and you know it's a problem with their faith journey.
>
> —*Tim Jinkerson, @timjinx*

You gotta love Twitter sometimes. I was amazed that most of the responses criticized the pastor. Where were these people when I was in church back in the day?! This pleasant surprise speaks to how far we have come when it comes to mental health and faith communities.

Spirituality and Mental Health Work Together

While I disagree with Pastor Hagee and my former pastor that depression is caused by "spiritual starvation" or not being Christian enough, I do know that my spirituality plays a part in my mental wellness. When I feel depression kicking in, one of the first things I do is pray. I pray for

God to give me the strength to keep going. I play gospel music to fill me with hope. Mindfulness meditation and repeating mantras help me with my anxiety. Those practices calm and center me when I feel myself on the verge of an anxiety attack. I do all of this in combination with going to therapy and applying non-spiritual tactics to fight the depression.

Many people with mental health challenges use spirituality as a tool to help them manage their wellness. According to a 2010 survey by the California Mental Health and Spirituality Initiative, 79 percent of people with mental health challenges and family members agreed spirituality is important to their mental health.

Former newspaper editor Dick Peterson lives with bipolar. He does peer-support work with homeless people in the Chicago area. Peterson also attended divinity school. During his serious bouts with bipolar, he lost his job and his marriage fell apart. But he told me in an interview that spirituality got him through then, and today. "It's brought me closer to God," said Peterson. "There was always this calm feeling in the back of my mind through ordained ministry."

Years ago, I worked for a mental health nonprofit in Oakland, California. Like many people who work in nonprofits, I juggled a few positions. One of them was facilitating a speakers' bureau with consumers. The empowering people in the group were diagnosed with a range of challenges, including depression, bipolar disorder, schizophrenia, and dissociative identity disorder. Just about all of the twenty people in the group referenced their spirituality when we had check-ins. They praised their God for the good, and asked us to pray for them during rough times. Sometimes their check-ins turned into mini-sermons. Whether it was Judaism, Islam, Christianity, art, or nature, they often spoke about finding strength in their Higher Power. And this came up when they gave.

Faith without Works

For some people, their place of worship is their first stop when in emotional distress. I'm African American, and that's definitely the case in our community.

"[They say], I can pray about it. And the Lord is going to provide," said Dr. Patricia Jones, a psychotherapist in Oakland, California. "Well believe me, I agree. But, the ministers are not licensed or trained in counseling and therapy. Which means the church members need to start getting trained."

The training is happening in more churches and other faith communities. In my other role at a mental health nonprofit, I attended and later organized interfaith meetings where people gathered to talk about their spirituality and mental health. People discussed ways of enlightening faith communities about mental health and eliminating stigma. People around the country are bringing these conversations to their temples, synagogues, churches, etc.

In Oakland, I attend a Buddhist temple called the East Bay Meditation Center. It hosts daylong, donation-based retreats on the weekends. Some retreats focus on using mindfulness to help ease depression, anxiety, and trauma. Although I'm not Buddhist, it has been a tremendous help for me. The leaders aren't shaming people for having these conditions. Instead, they're encouraging the use of spiritual tools to help with our afflictions.

Mental health advocates in the Bay Area's Alameda County have partnered with churches to host trainings called Mental Health Friendly Communities. There, participants learn about mental health stigma, and how to bring more awareness to their congregations.

In 2011, counselor Kameelah Rashad founded the Muslim Wellness Foundation in Philadelphia. According to its website, the organization's mission is to "reduce stigma and promote healing in the American Muslim community through dialogue, education, and training."

Organizations such as the National Alliance on Mental Illness, the Substance Abuse and Mental Health Services Administration, and the American Psychological Association have published research and more information on the impact of spirituality on mental health. Of course more needs to be done to share this information. But at least we're having the conversation. I hope more people of faith become more open to this information.

Civil rights activist Fannie Lou Hamer said, "You can pray until you faint. But unless you get up and try to do something, God is not going to put it in your lap." I imagine her words were inspired by the Bible verse James 2:26, "For just as a body without a spirit is dead, faith without works is dead." That's how I look at mental health. Managing my depression takes both work and faith. Just like anyone else facing a health challenge. My faith fuels me to take care of myself. My faith fuels me to get out of hopeless feelings when I'm in a deep depression. My faith fuels me to tell my story so that others suffering won't carry the shame I did. No matter how much I pray or read scripture, depression still comes back. But I have the spiritual tools to fight it. And no, it's not always easy. I try to keep my spiritual tank on full, so when I encounter people with theories like Pastor Hagee's, I leave them with their stigma tank on E.

NOTE

1. Nassir Ghaemi, "Martin Luther King: Depressed and Creatively Maladjusted," *Psychology Today,* January 16, 2012, www.psychologytoday.com/us/blog/mood -swings/201201/martin-luther-king-depressed-and-creatively-maladjusted.

Untitled

CHRIS ANASTASIA

Chris Anastasia is a San Francisco–based educator and activist with an MA in human sexuality studies. When not writing or teaching, Chris can be found playing the oud, baking, or dancing tango.

. . . .

"Daddy died."

My mother struggled to hold back tears as she spoke these words to me on the morning of March 28, 1988. I remember this morning more vividly than any other memory I have from my early childhood: I was sitting on my parents' bed preparing myself for the school day when Mom opened the door and told me the news. I did not understand why she was crying, or what "died" meant. Days later my brother and I were sent home early from his funeral with some family friends because we kept attempting to rouse my father from his casket. "Why won't Daddy wake up?" my brother asked.

I've heard my mother recount my life story many times, and she always begins in the same place—when I was four my father went to work in the morning and never came home. He was very depressed, had been abusing narcotics, and had threatened suicide on multiple occasions. He never left a note, and my mother still insists it was not a suicide. "He'd been taking a new antidepressant and was feeling better; he didn't kill himself." I tell her that these periods of enhanced mood after lengthy bouts of profound, debilitating depression are the exact circumstances in which many suicides occur.

I was always a very quiet, introverted child, easily frightened and incredibly anxious. I remember having obsessive-compulsive disorder (OCD) symptoms at a very young age: a vague and overpowering fear would grip me to the point that I was afraid to go out in public. Later, I learned that these episodes were called "panic attacks," and they became more frequent as I grew older. When I was around nine, I became so anxious that I would literally regurgitate after I ate. I would have panic attacks and have to leave class. The bullying I'd always experienced because of my gender non-normativity intensified, and I stopped going to school. When I was six, my mother met the man who would eventually become my stepfather, and he was physically and emotionally abusive toward my two siblings and me. Eventually I began self-injuring.

My mother took me to see a psychiatrist who put me on an antidepressant medication, during which time I attempted suicide at age eleven. Soon after, my mother learned of Dr. Joseph Biederman, who was the chief of child psychiatry at Massachusetts General Hospital. She took me to see him for the first time when I was twelve. She recounted my troubles, beginning with my father's death, and he made a hasty diagnosis of bipolar disorder—a diagnosis he used for the basis of his "treatment" of me over the next six years. He told my mother that she should come to terms with the fact that children like me "rarely lived to see eighteen."

I strongly distrusted Biederman—he was cold and blamed me for my problems; on the one hand I was being told that I was very sick, that there was something terribly wrong with my brain, but at the same time I was being held responsible for the fact that I couldn't function like other children my age.

Looking back, it was becoming clear to all that I might not grow up to be an economically productive member of society as my white, upper-middle-class background demanded; I needed to be "fixed." The problem, according to the adults in my life, was not my unhappiness but my inability to attend school. It was around this time that I was sent to a "therapeutic" school where they mixed kids with emotional difficulties with other kids who were violent. I witnessed classmates' psychotic episodes, watched as staff members physically restrained them, heard them screaming in agony on a nearly daily basis, and watched their constant comings and goings as they were taken from school and placed in psychiatric wards. It was here, at age thirteen, that I met the man with whom I had my first sexual experience; he was nineteen, and I later found out he had also raped a classmate's twelve-year-old cousin a couple of years prior. Every day, I would cry hysterically and plead with my mother to not make me go to this school, but her answer was always the same: if I didn't go to school, I would end up in the hospital or in a residential program.

I have Biederman's clinical notes from when I was twelve until I was sixteen. Within those four years alone he had me on varying combinations of sixteen different medications, including mood stabilizers, antianxiety medications, tranquilizers, antidepressants, an antiepileptic medication that he believed could treat bipolar, antipsychotics, and stimulants to counteract the fatigue I experienced from the other medications. When I was twelve, I experienced lithium toxicity at a dose of 1,050 mg per day, so he switched me to Neurontin, a drug that has since been found to halt the formation of new synapses in the brain. He prescribed Luvox, Klonopin, Tofranil, Paxil, Risperdal, Concerta, Elavil, Anafranil, Adderall, and Celexa. He had me on Serzone, a drug that was never approved for pediatric use and was eventually taken off the market for causing liver failure in a number of patients. The manufacturer's recommended highest dose for adults was 600 mg per day, yet Biederman had me on 750 mg per day when I was thirteen and weighed 110 pounds.

It was when I was twelve that I was hospitalized in a psychiatric ward for the first time. I remember being strip-searched, and I remember crying to my mother at the door, "Please don't let them take me." She left looking forlorn and unsure, but soon the heavy door to the ward locked behind her, and I wailed. "If you don't stop crying," warned the nurse, "you'll have to go in the quiet room." I could not stop crying. She escorted me by the arm down the narrow, dimly lit hallway, at the end of which was an even more dimly lit room. It was too small to lie down in, and completely barren except the bench that was built into the wall. "I will come and get you when you stop crying," the nurse said as she locked the door behind me. I don't remember how long I cried for, or exactly how many times I was locked in solitary confinement in this tiny, barren room during my hospitalization. I still suffer from post-traumatic stress disorder from this experience, which manifests as hypervigilance and a constant, urgent sense of needing to flee wherever I am. That which was supposed to "help" me in fact only served to debilitate me; the label of "mentally ill" was used to justify a paradox in which my accounts of depression and anxiety were believed, yet my accounts of what was contributing to my suffering were not. Although my sense of reality was never compromised, I was deemed incapable of knowing what was best for me and what was traumatic and ineffective.

I was made to see many child psychotherapists and social workers. When I was nineteen, I went to a neurology clinic where doctors administered transcranial magnetic shocks to my brain. None of this ever helped alleviate my depression or anxiety.

In 2008, Biederman was charged with conflict of interest when it came to light that he had been taking millions of dollars—the vast majority of which he failed to disclose—from pharmaceutical companies with promises of favorable research results. It wasn't until my midtwenties that I came to the realization that the way I'd been treated was wrong, and it wasn't until Biederman was indicted and a *Frontline* documentary was made about him that my mother apologized for what I'd gone through. Since Biederman, I've seen four different psychiatrists, all of whom agree that I do not have and never had bipolar, and that the doses of medications he had me on were enormous, especially for a child. He attempted to change the diagnostic criteria for childhood bipolar (which, according to the *DSM-5*, no longer exists), likely so that he could diagnose more children and turn to the drug companies for funding to research this epidemic he created.

When I reached adulthood, I began to navigate ways to support my mental well-being that allow me to more easily live in a society that was not designed for people with nervous systems that are considered "atypical." It took a great many years to accept that there is nothing inherently wrong with me, or with people deemed mentally ill. People are sometimes surprised to learn that despite my history, I am not categorically anti-psychiatry. I am adamantly opposed to prescribers having business relationships with drug companies, and I am opposed to the use of psychotropic medications for young children whose brains are not yet fully developed. Finding a medication regimen that addresses my actual symptoms—as opposed to the misdiagnosis and subsequent medical abuse I was subjected to by Biederman—has been a key component of the fact that now, in my midthirties, I feel like I am finally living. However, it is impossible to say whether I have an organic chemical imbalance that predated my "treatment," or if my brain has become so accustomed to the presence of psychotropics that I now find it difficult to function without them (empirical research in this area has found that long-term use of psychotropics does indeed alter one's ability to produce certain neurotransmitters). My history isn't one about a happy, healthy child who was indiscriminately subjected to psychiatric treatment; it is one about a child who could not function according to the standards their society had set and was met with severe and irreversible measures to make them conform. I'm still someone who struggles with anxiety and OCD, a condition grossly distorted by the media, which is in reality characterized by intense fear as opposed to arbitrary compulsive behaviors. I consider myself incredibly lucky to have access to the resources I need and at the same time I feel guilt for the fact that I was allowed to survive largely because of my economic privilege. Often I think about my classmates at the therapeutic school, and the kids I was hospitalized with, and wonder how many of them are no longer with us because of a woefully unjust health care system.

I don't know what my life would have been like if I hadn't been medicated as a child. One thing I can be sure of is that my brain wasn't allowed to develop as it should have; the reason psychiatrists are allowed to medicate young children is that it is impossible to prove damage in a brain that wasn't fully developed prior to treatment. The thought that I will never know that most vital part of me, and that I can't get back what I never was allowed to have, is never far from my mind. If anything has ever made me feel like life is not worth living it is the knowledge that my body and brain were profoundly and irreversibly violated, and that not only will there never be any accountability, but that the burden of proof is on me, the adult who was once a child who was, in a very real way, punished for my hardships. "What did this do to me?" is not a question that anyone should have to answer.

Up until very recently, fear of judgment kept me from sharing my history with others. I wanted to maintain a façade of normalcy and was afraid I would be regarded as too damaged to relate to if I were to divulge my past. I worried that the people I told might tell others, and that my story would precede me. I have found, however, that stories of survival—survival of all kinds—are not uncommon, particularly in the queer community. There is strength in our narratives, and I have come to a place where I am willing to tell those who are willing to listen.

Unfrozen

LYNDSEY ELLIS

Lyndsey Ellis is a cultural worker, fiction writer, and essayist who blends community activism with the literary arts. She has led trauma-informed trainings and creative writing workshops for survivors of domestic violence, transitional age youth, and individuals with mental health challenges. A VONA/Voices and Squaw Valley Community of Writers alumna, Ellis was a recipient of the San Francisco Foundation's Joseph Henry Jackson Literary Award in 2016 for her fiction, which explores intergenerational struggle and resiliency in the Midwest. Her work appears in *Joyland*, *Entropy*, *The Offing*, *Stockholm Review of Literature*, *Shondaland*, and elsewhere. For more information, visit www.lyndseyellis.com.

. . . .

I once read about the experiences of patients with anesthetic awareness. They describe themselves as lying on the operating table, in a state of paralysis, with a medical team performing surgery on them. They don't endure physical pain because the anesthesia hasn't completely worn off, but there's an uncomfortable and persistent pressure, besides the horrifying feeling of being immobile while still under the knife, a predicament no one else is aware of at the time.

I've never experienced anesthetic awareness, and my heart goes out to those who have. I could be wrong, but I'd imagine that, figuratively speaking, it's much like childhood trauma, which, if not addressed, can leave you emotionally numb for a long time, whether others recognize it or not.

When I was seven, I began seeing a child therapist for depression after my parents' divorce. It forced me to recall a climactic night—one that involved the witnessing of physical abuse in the hallway of the home I was raised in. An only child, I remember feeling stuck between what to do, who to protect, and which parent to cling to. Everything in me froze and I fell inside myself, even as I ran after my father—to do or say what, I still don't know—and left my wounded mother lying on the floor in a state of shock.

I wasn't big enough to fight back and win, so I did nothing after I followed him to the garage door. I watched the first person to hold me as a newborn, the man who unbraided my hair while I habitually ate Fig Newtons and watched *Moonwalker* or played records while I bounced on the trampoline after school, the one whose colossal arms I'd fly into every evening when he picked me up from day care, drive off into the night never to return to the place that he and my mother had once built into a happy home together.

My parents' ugly feud following that night, soon compounded with school bullying, turned me from an energetic, outgoing girl into a sullen, inert child who basically went into survival mode by shutting down. I retreated and didn't talk much. I had nightmares and cried very easily. I was often a ball of nerves, anger, shame, and guilt that found solace only in reading books.

Despite this rough period, my mother and a love of books, which inevitably grew into an overwhelming passion for writing, helped me reset my future by focusing on my strengths. The close community that existed for me within my extended family, my childhood church home, and my mother's "adopted" students from the performing arts school she taught at, helped me gradually recover from the past trauma and awkwardness that came with preadolescence. My teenage and college years were almost typical—a blur of textbooks, hormones, and fashion trends—but there was this underlying anxiety that lay dormant, a dull pressure on a wound that ran jagged across what's typically regarded as the best years of one's life.

Continuing to balance recovery with external factors, like the hustle of everyday work life and the current socioeconomic climate, remains a process, even in my thirties. Still, I'm at a place where I feel more at peace with myself and my parents. I'm finally able to see both of them not as infallible authority figures I constantly feel obliged to choose sides with, but as people with their own hurts and hopes who are doing the best they can with the choices they've made.

I'm learning to walk unfrozen on this journey, welcoming new opportunities that enable me the space to feel my emotions more freely without completely letting them rule me. I've accepted the mental and emotional challenges that have colored my past and use them as unique lessons and a testament to the resilience inside all of us. Although I haven't pursued traditional forms of therapy in adulthood, I'm actively involved with combining my spirituality, my community service as an activist/cultural worker, and my writing in the literary arts field as pathways to sustaining wellness and allowing these outlets to speak to others, if only in small ways.

How to Tame a Flying Dragon

ANITA ROMAN

Anita Roman was born in communist Romania and raised in capitalist New York City. By day she is a family nurse-practitioner at a community health center in Oakland, California. By night she is a traveling, trapeze-flying writer of stories. Her work has appeared in *The Sun, Riverbabble, So To Speak,* and the San Francisco–based anthology *Your Golden Sun Still Shines.*

. . . .

Once upon a time there was a young woman who wanted to learn how to tame a flying dragon. The dragon had been a part of her and her Romanian family for many, many years, perhaps centuries. Once every decade, this black-winged beast would rise from its cave in the molten lava core of the earth and snake to the surface to snatch one of her family. The dragon would arrive silently, unexpectedly, and pluck them up from the roots of their lives, taking them on a wild ride through the heavens and the underworld, through radiant skies, flaming microcosmos, exploding planets, and down into the darkest underbelly of the quietest places beyond life.

In 1983, when I was three years old, the black-winged dragon came swooping down for my twenty-nine-year-old mother. A few months after arriving in the United States, while balancing the harsh demands of her new immigrant life, working a minimum-wage job, learning English, and parenting a small child on her own, my mom was hospitalized for suicidal depression. We were living in a third-floor walk-up apartment in Astoria, Queens. It was late spring, the air heavy and the sidewalks slick with rain. I knew something was wrong because my mom didn't pick me up from preschool one day. Instead, her friend Cati came to get me. Kneeling down to my height, Cati whispered softly in Romanian, "Your mama is really sick, but she's going to be okay. You're going to go and stay with your family in California until she's better and can take care of you again." I had no idea what these words meant, but I felt scared. I remember how my mom's voice sounded on the phone that day from the mental hospital, thin, tired, and far away: "I'll always love you, baby."

I was sent across the country to live in San Diego with Romanian relatives I'd never met. Doina, Soni, and their twelve-year-old son, Vlad, were kind and welcoming, but strangers nonetheless. That summer I learned to swim with inflatable orange plastic wings in the pool of their apartment complex and took my first trip to Disneyland. My mother spent those months locked away, sedated with Thorazine and medicated with lithium. When she finally came home, it felt as though her spirit had been irrevocably crushed. No one ever spoke of that time again, and the word "depression" was never uttered in our home or family.

Maybe we were averting our eyes, hiding from the inevitable, but no one saw the dragon when it finally came for me, picked me up onto its scaly back, and pounded its glistening jet-black wings to begin my wild descent into the underworld.

In truth there had been foreshadowing of the black-winged beast's arrival in my life for quite some time.

As a teenager, I hovered between periods of calm happiness, juxtaposed with hyperactivity and insomnia, segueing into weeks of intense depression and despair. Maybe no one saw the dragon coming for me because when I was well, I was so well, and when I wasn't, I was good at hiding it. The ups and downs of my mood changes were easy to miss and easily confused with normal teenage stuff. I white-knuckled it through the rough times and tried my best not to let anything stop me from achievement in school, work, theater, and sports. In May of my seventeenth year, a few weeks shy of graduating high school, I had my first nervous breakdown. I didn't sleep for eight days, moved out of my mom's house, and stopped going to classes. I come from a dramatic Romanian family with mental illness so entrenched that everyone believes life's soaring highs and crushing lows are precisely what make it worth living. Perhaps I simply blended in with the madness around me.

It was 2006 and I was twenty-five years old, following my dream of living in India, but also struggling with a painful breakup from my first love and boyfriend of nine years. I landed a volunteer post in Mumbai, teaching writing and English to children who lived on P D'Mello road—a small slum community of interlaced aluminum shacks with dirt floors, tucked away behind the crumbling colonial glory of the Victoria Terminus train station. Unexpectedly, three months into the trip, the bright saffron, violet, crimson, and sapphire hues of the India I had come to love began to dissolve into sleet gray. Sounds muted, and soon the singing at Mahalakshmi Temple, the hiss of trains at VT station, the *chaiwala*'s song, and the joyful noise of children's laughter got quieter and quieter, until all I could hear was the heavy beating of the dragon's wings beneath me.

The dragon's wings beat faster and faster, and my thoughts were no longer my own. My mind would involuntarily shift from grocery lists and lesson plans to dreams of death and a thousand permutations of suicide. I hadn't seen it coming, but now I was barely holding on. Where at first I had excelled in teaching and my work with children, I now limped along at half-mast, still showing up without fail for work with my students every day, but consumed and exhausted by a deep depression and an inexplicable longing for death. I knew something was very wrong, but I muscled through the rest of the India trip, trying to see if working hard, eating a vegetarian diet, yoga, meditation, and daily journaling could make me better.

I set up phone sessions with a family therapist who had seen me as a teenager in New York, and used phone cards and pay phones to call her at our weekly appointed time. The sessions helped a little, and I decided to continue onward, backpacking though Europe and Thailand on long-distance buses and trains, eventually landing in South Africa. I kept thinking at each turn and every new destination that if I just tried hard enough, I could "snap out of it." The truth was that no amount of speed or distance would allow me to outrun the dragon. One of the most adventurous and beautiful chapters of my life was marred by a deep, dark, numbing depression, punctuated by brief days and weeks of sleepless nights, joy, creativity, and brimming passion.

By the time I arrived in San Francisco later that year my mind was tattered, frayed, and worn thin. I settled into a communal house of radical women roommates, took a part-time job running an after-school program in Oakland, sought care at a free mental health clinic on Twenty-Third and Mission Streets, and decided with certainty to "get my life together." I hadn't been able to turn the tide of my moods despite months of my best efforts, and I became willing to try medication. The clinic assigned me a well-meaning but burned-out psychiatrist who, with very little information about me or my symptoms, prescribed Wellbutrin, a standard medication for depression. Desperate to feel better, I dutifully imbibed the medication, not knowing that for a person with a mood disorder, this medicine could cause serious harm. With the new medicine, I got worse. Although I continued my work at the after-school program overseeing 161 kids and 21 teachers in a daily frenzy of snack time, story time, homework help, coaching kindergarteners on how to tie their shoes, and playing four square on the playground, the thoughts of wanting to end my life got more and more intense. Within two weeks of starting the medicine, the dragon ride took its most vicious turn yet, pulling me further and further into the silent black underworld, to that place beyond life.

Counter to its intended effect, the Wellbutrin made me feel really nervous and on edge. The suicidal thoughts that had been present throughout the previous year were now more powerful than ever, and I found myself crying inconsolably for hours on end, something that had never happened before. The medication had been a last resort, and now, instead of getting better, I was getting worse. With hindsight, I wish that I had been able to recognize that the medication was making me sicker, intensifying my despair and completely unhinging my grasp on reality.

I hit bottom, hard. On January 29, 2007, still living in my communal San Francisco apartment with the door of my tiny room locked, I tried to kill myself. In a trancelike state, I swallowed pills, lay down, and went to sleep, hoping that my life would end. I still don't understand how, but fourteen hours later I awoke in my own bed, in a panicked, drug-induced fog. I was frightened, ashamed, and completely in awe that I had lived through the night. Now desperate to stay alive, I called my mother in

New York, who called the San Francisco Police Department. My mother's call activated a 5150, an involuntary hold where a person who is a danger to themselves or others is forcibly admitted to a hospital. Within minutes, two uniformed cops arrived at my Folsom Street apartment. They banged on the front door, pushed past my worried, confused roommates, and walked me into the back of the police car. We drove straight for Saint Francis Memorial Hospital.

The next hours fade to blackness in my memory. I woke up connected to a labyrinth of IV tubes, wires, and a beeping heart monitor, with my exhausted and worried best friend and ex-boyfriend, Halsey, at my side. I thought I'd gotten lucky and survived my suicide attempt. Instead, I spent the next several days in the intensive care unit teetering between life and death, with liver enzymes one thousand times the upper limit from the overdose. My family and closest friends arrived one by one, pacing the carpeted hallways of the hospital, waiting. The ICU doctor said that I'd swallowed "enough medication to kill a horse." Two days into the hospital stay, a slim, white-coated liver specialist arrived at my bedside to speak with my mother and me. After some quiet minutes of him rifling through the paper chart at my bedside, brow furrowed, he explained to us that my liver enzymes were going up and not down. The situation was dire, and he laid out the options: (1) in the next forty-eight hours I could die of liver failure; (2) if I made it through the next forty-eight hours but my liver was still in peril, I would be transported by helicopter to another hospital across the bay in hopes of getting an emergent liver transplant; or (3) if I was extremely fortunate, my age and strength would allow me to survive without a transplant and, in time, my injured liver cells could regenerate completely.

I responded automatically from my young, stubborn, twenty-six-year-old self and told the doctor, "I don't need a different liver." I told him I thought I could make it on my own. While my mom was still arguing with me about my stubbornness, I fell into a deep sleep where I saw the "white light" that people talk about and met with my dead grandparents, who told me it wasn't my time, and I believed them. The next day my liver enzymes started trending down. I took a turn for the better, and we all breathed relief.

There is no apology that can repair the suffering I caused to those I love in that week, and no end to the shame that I will always feel about the day I tried to end my life. In that moment, in that hospital bed at Saint Francis, I glimpsed the very real specter of my own death and decided that even though I didn't know how, I would find a way to live and to thrive.

I was released home with the understanding that I could not be left alone overnight for at least a month. For weeks, a benevolent team of friends and family took turns "supervising" me overnight to make sure I didn't try again to kill myself. After my hospitalization, I stopped working for several months and attended an adult "day treatment program" with other recently hospitalized adults. It was like preschool for people with mental health issues, for those well enough to live at home but not yet ready to return to regular life. We had group therapy every morning at 9:00 a.m., art therapy in the afternoons, weekly visits with a psychiatrist, meditation, and snack time with milk and graham crackers. In the day program I befriended a kind, bespectacled, seventy-five-year-old Korean War veteran named Doug, with a shock of white hair and mischievous brown eyes. Doug taught me I should make my bed every morning like they did in the military. He felt bed making was one small victory you could start the day with, and so he clocked his daily bed making down to the second, always trying to shave a few seconds off yesterday's time. Doug cautioned me against a life spent worrying too much for others: "You've got to look out for number one, first," pointing to his own heart. Doug and I stayed friends after the program, even sailed the Golden Gate together one day with a disabled veterans sailing group. One day Doug stopped answering my calls, and I still don't know to this day if he made it.

I wish I could say that I was healed after being hospitalized, that the medications the psychiatrist at Saint Francis gave me worked, but they didn't. Dr. Blaustein cycled me through many different meds—Lamictal, Effexor, Abilify, and lithium—but nothing could stave off the suicidal thoughts that skipped in and out of my mind, day after day, month after month, even though I no longer had any serious wish to die. When each of the medicines failed, Dr. Blaustein had little to offer besides a new prescription. Being in his office made me feel broken and deficient.

I eventually found a skilled and empathic psychiatrist named Dr. Quick, who seemed capable of relating to me as a fellow human and not just a "patient." Dr. Quick was funny and quirky; he listened patiently to my life story and had me start tracking my moods every day to see what the patterns and triggers were. After so many medication failures, he wanted to try an experimental treatment with an antipsychotic called Seroquel that was "off label" for people with severe depression and rapid cycling moods like mine. At first, the medication made me so sleepy I could barely function and I felt hungry all the time, but soon it seemed to start working a little, taking the edge off my depression, allowing me to sleep deeply at night. Over time the sleepiness and hunger diminished, and the medication seemed to create a floor that limited how low my moods would drop. Even so, I knew that medication was only a small part of the answer, and I worked hard to find other avenues of healing.

I interviewed several therapists until I found someone with experience who had a sliding-scale fee and who I thought could really help me. Anne Stallard was strong and wise and calm, a masterful psychotherapist who worked with me twice a week until I got better and continued to see me a few times each month for the next seven years. She taught me the skills I needed to tolerate suicidal thoughts when they came, to offer compassion and kindness even to the part of me that wanted to die. We worked backward through my life to try to unravel the threads of neglect, trauma, and sexual abuse that had brought me to this point. I understood through our therapy that depression and suicidal ideation weren't moral failings, but rather an understandable reaction to my family's intergenerational trauma and the difficulties of my early life. Anne helped me step out of the shadow of the black dragon and create a different kind of life for myself. My family and friends rallied around me, answered my phone calls at all hours and in the darkest moments, conveying to me, over and over again, their supreme faith that I would find a way through this.

A few months after my time in the hospital a friend brought me a bound paper volume of a zine by a group of people called The Icarus Project, created by people who had survived mental illness. I pored over the densely packed, handwritten and illustrated pages and savored stories of people who were working to find alternatives to medication and therapy, who'd found healing through creativity and community. I was comforted to find others for whom the medication and hospital-focused mental health system had come up short and was excited to know there was still hope.

I'd heard about Al-Anon as a safe place to talk about family issues. After my suicide attempt, I felt ready to face some of the harder truths about my growing up and learn from other people who'd survived dysfunctional families and were willing to talk about it. Walking into my first Al-Anon meeting, I was surprised by how kind and welcoming people were. It was a relief to realize how many people's families were plagued by addiction and mental health challenges. Being able to share what seemed like the worst possible things about myself and my upbringing with others who had experienced similar struggles helped me not feel so alone anymore.

I had been a secret writer since the age of eight. As part of my healing I signed up for my first creative writing class and found a wonderful alchemy in the act of writing stories and poems. The experience of sharing my stories with others who found strength and beauty in my words was profound, and my writing continues to be a deep source of healing and connection.

The spring after my suicide attempt I also bought a bicycle and started riding, tentatively at first, up and down the hills of San Francisco. With my two friends Emmanuelle and Roseanne, I joined an all women's triathlon training group and committed to a structured routine of bike-run-swim every week. None of us had ever completed a triathlon, but we held each other accountable for the 8:00 a.m. practices every Saturday and Tuesday-Thursday 6:00 p.m. track and swim workouts. The endorphin rush of exercise helped me to feel just a little bit better. In June of 2007, I completed my first triathlon. Simply to arrive at that finish line, having lived through so many months of wanting to die, felt like a victory. Over the years I've held fast to exercise as one small but reliable lifeboat in the stormy seas of my intense moods.

I knew I needed to find work that could sustain me, financially, mentally, and emotionally. In the week I spent as a patient in the hospital, I saw and felt the difference that a nurse could make between a good day and a bad day. Almost all of the nurses who cared for me in the intensive care unit at Saint Francis were exceedingly kind and loving toward me and my family. Their humor and warmth helped my family and friends tolerate the scariest moments of having someone you love almost die. They were encouraging about each day's small triumphs. (Eating solid food! Getting the IV tubes taken out of my arm! Being able to get up and pee!) As I got better, I was able to talk to my nurses about their experiences doing this work. Many nurses shared feeling deeply fulfilled by their careers, and they encouraged me to seriously consider becoming a nurse. One of my favorite nurses, a young woman named Georgie, gave me a pair of her blue nurse scrubs to wear when I complained about the hospital gowns with the awful opening down the back that left your butt exposed. Changing into her scrubs, I suddenly looked like a nurse and not a patient. Georgie smiled wide, with a twinkle in her brown eyes: "You look good in those scrubs. You should keep them—you may need them one day." The good nurses I met inspired me to change my career path from teaching to becoming a nurse-practitioner.

In the year after my suicide attempt I applied to and was accepted to nursing school at UCSF. When I started school, I was still struggling with suicidal thoughts, but slowly something shifted in me as I took care of patients. I cleaned gunshot wounds. I helped to reattach the fingers of a man who'd had a chainsaw accident. I played checkers with veterans from Afghanistan who were now patients in the VA's locked psychiatric ward. I cared for terminally ill kids who would likely spend the rest of their short lives within the falsely cheerful pastel painted rooms of Stanford hospital. Between hanging IV antibiotics and feeding tubes, we played with monster trucks and a dollhouse. I was witness to the births of six miraculous, squalling, newborns.

As the months went by, I began to change from a person who couldn't count on herself and was consumed by her own sadness to someone who could be a rock of caring, support and service to patients. By graduation day in June, it felt like I had passed through a portal, that despite my profound broken-ness, I had become a healer. Bit by bit, I came to know that I loved this work and that it was a key part of my recovery. Being a nurse-practitioner and working as a hospital nurse require me to get up every day and be there, fully and completely, awake to the experiences of others, connected to those I care for and to my own capacity for empathy.

In the decade since my suicide attempt, I have slowly, haltingly continued to heal. Two steps forward, one step back, I have found medication that wears away the jagged edges and a therapist and psychiatrist who understand me. Now, a delicate balance of sleep, work, creativity, community, the mutual aid of Al-Anon, and exercise helps me to tame the flying dragon of my mood disorder. I do not have to go back to the underworld. On this journey, I have learned immense compassion for all the wounded people in this world and the dragons we ride.

How My Friends Showed Up: Mutual Aid

KELECHI UBOZOH

I've been here before. When the sadness is so thick it can choke me, and I have terrifying thoughts swirling in my mind trying to seduce me with an escape plan from my pain, it can be horrifying, especially because I am a suicide attempt survivor. Lately, I've reflected on my recovery, and how I get through really difficult times like this past year. I've learned a lot about loss with the ending of my engagement and uncertainty of my future. Recently, I was harassed by someone who violently attacked me years ago. This triggered some familiar shadowy thoughts.

But this time was different. This time I asked for help. When it was too scary to be alone in my head, I reached out. I'm lucky: I have a fantastic support system. I called my mom, my therapist, and my friends to let them know what was going on. My mom immediately booked a ticket to California. During filming of *The S Word,* I admitted to the director of the film, Lisa Klein, that I wasn't in a good place. We stayed up till 1 a.m. talking, and she listened and held space for me as I cried. My friends and family offered love and support, and we worked on a plan of what was going to get me through this difficult time.

This is how I showed up. I was honest and accountable. I told my loved ones what was going on and that I needed their help, time, and support. I didn't lie and pretend that everything was okay when it wasn't. I stopped trying to "power through" or "be strong." I remembered that everything I put before my mental health, like relationships and jobs, I've lost. So this time, I put my mental health first. I took some time off work and decided to focus for an entire month on my mental health treatment.

This is how my friends showed up. When someone is physically sick, people know exactly what to do. They bring casseroles, they send flowers and cards, they make phone calls, and they think about what someone who is in pain needs. I don't think it should be any different for folks who are feeling suicidal. But I get it, it's scary. What the heck do you do? What do you say? How do you show up for someone who is going through darkness you might not understand? I don't know the answer for everyone, but this is how my friends showed up.

When I was so depressed I couldn't get out of bed, my friends brought me groceries. My friends took me to poetry readings and hiking in the redwoods, brought me to dance classes and karaoke, invited me to dinner, and sent me inspirational texts featuring unicorns and/or vampires. One friend made sure we had a weekly walking date to check in on me and give me some physical activity. A friend in New York sent me an adult coloring book and crayons. Another friend brought me to an art exhibit called *The Black Woman Is God*, where I got to see beautiful creations from Black women all over the world. Some friends called, other friends sent letters or emails.

One of my closest and oldest friends did something pretty phenomenal. She wanted to make sure that I didn't feel alone during my month of recovery and that I had a daily reminder that I am loved. So for each of my thirty days of mental health recovery, she left me presents, all numbered, to open. Every morning I'd wake up and unwrap something lovely. She sent lavender, which is under my pillow for sleeping, sage for cleansing, chocolate—because, well, chocolate is healing and delicious, and letters of our fondest memories and inside jokes, and reminders that I could get through this.

None of these acts of kindness required a background in therapy—just plain old thoughtfulness and care, which any human is capable of doing. Nothing was too small to make a difference. What I needed was connection and an interruption to the isolation and negative thoughts in my head.

In the past, I pretended everything was okay while I secretly broke down. But this time was different. If we can create a world where the stigma of suicide is decreased so people speak out when they are in pain, maybe we can prevent anyone else from dying. **And fighting this stigma and silence, well, that's how we can all show up.**

We've Been Too Patient*

How Mutual Aid Can Improve Therapy and Transform Society

L. D. GREEN

The Pitfalls of the Therapeutic Relationship

I had my first therapist at the age of six after my parents' divorce. My mom says she did it as a kind of preventive measure. Yeah, we got to play with toys, but we had different agendas. My therapist wasn't a playmate. She was the observer, and I was the observed. Like the male gaze, this is the therapizing gaze.

I've written a lot about psychiatric power, and anyone who has had both psychiatrists and therapists can tell you therapeutic relationships can be healing and beneficial. In my experience, most psychiatrists are traumatizing pill pushers. There are the rare few who are compassionate and offer trauma-informed care, but this is a far cry from the industry norm that damages more than it heals.

But even the therapeutic relationship can be flawed. Any relationship based on professionalization, where there is a helper and the helped, where one person is perceived as having a problem, and the other is perceived as being capable of fixing that problem...well, this can lead to more problems.

---

* An earlier draft of this essay was published in 2016 by The Body Is Not an Apology as "We've Been Too Patient: Mutual Aid Practices for the Twenty-First Century." Republished with gratitude. www.thebodyisnotanapology.com.

Don't get me wrong. I greatly appreciate several of the therapists I've had, including my current one. They've all helped me tremendously. It's kind of like capitalism though. It's not that I don't like working (although we could all stand for some more leisure time), it's that I don't like the system that alienates and exploits.

Similarly, I love the healing work that happens in therapy. But the money does taint it—does render the therapist more powerful, some-how—and we can't pretend that it doesn't.

Not all methods of healing have to be burdened by power relationships or capitalism. The practice of therapy has much to learn from networks of healing outside its office walls.

Peer Support and Mutual Aid

In peer support or mutual aid, both parties look at their stuff. It seems like a no-brainer that this would promote deeper, more radical growth. We all know the best intimate relationships of our lives, be it with dear friends, romantic partners, or family, can make or break us—and at best can lead to profound spiritual growth. bell hooks defines love as the conscious decision to aid in the spiritual development of ourselves with another human being.[1]

When we are in a relationship of mutual respect and equality, when the connection is between two peers struggling along the same road together, *working* to love one another, we can become powerful and beautiful beyond measure. When mental health care recognizes mutuality, "patients" are transformed into people, and health is restored beyond expectation. And more than this. As people come into wellness and self-love, society is transformed.

As Shery Mead, founder of Intentional Peer Support, says, "As peer support in mental health proliferates, we must be mindful of our inten-tion: social change. It is not about developing more effective services, but rather about creating dialogues that have influence on all of our under-standings, conversations, and relationships."[2]

My experiences of peer support have come in both The Icarus Project and in the 12-step community. Both have been critical for my mental health and well-being. Icarus interrupted the self-stigma shame cycle by giving me mad pride and creating a network of joyously neurodiverse support that got real about how rough things can get for the neuroatypical in this world. The 12-step program has helped regulate me, given me tools for handling life's inevitable challenges, and created a community focused on wellness and spiritual principles that ground and heal.

I am blessed to have friends from many spheres. I have friends from these mutual aid circles, from activist circles, and from artivist and writing circles, and just the friends I have been blessed to pick up through life in one way or another. When I was in mental health crisis about eight years ago, friends from all of these realms (and some family) showed up in an abundant outpouring of love and tangible support: helping with laundry, shopping, visiting me so I wasn't isolated, preparing meals, setting up a care calendar online and coordinating volunteers to the project of helping me, and on and on. I am forever grateful. This experience has cemented my ardent belief in the power of community to heal and transform. This was service to me based in love with no expectation of any kind of payment. That kind of radical act didn't just help me. That generosity was a coming together that renewed my life so that I could continue to be of service to others through my writing and teaching. These kind acts seem simple, but are profound and prefigurative; they reflect the kind of world we should live in—they anticipate a future world I hope one day exists.[3] This is how we really recover. Thank you. You know who you are.

Let me be clear: we do need dedicated therapists. This world inflicts suffering and trauma on many, if not most of us, and there are tools that clinical training provides that can bring clients closer to wholeness and peace. I have, blessedly, received this kind of help. I would not be the person I am today without it. But the best experiences I've had involved seeing my therapist as a human being with limitations and a life beyond their office. Knowing that a real person with a specific identity actually cares is the real transformative power of those relationships. In that sense, the best therapists break through the invisible wall in mindful, boundaried ways, and are informed by mutual aid. This is how we interrupt the gaze.

Mutual aid transforms society. Clinics don't. And yet we need skillful healers. We don't need a false dichotomy. In and outside of offices, therapists with clinical training and "patients" themselves can learn from one another about their experiences with healing themselves and others.

Pause.

I can't finish this article for weeks because I started a new job that is consuming me. It pays me better, so I can be a better consumer. It is asking me to labor, and with this labor means I have fewer spoons (less bandwidth) to be of service to my friends, to be in the mutual aid society.

Because mutual aid is labor. Emotional labor. And I do get uplifted by it. I do believe in being of service. But work obligations take me away from this work, this heart work, and my art work. I try to carve out time, but mutual aid has now become incidental, a hobby, not the place where my soul sparks. It is an afterthought.

Emotional labor is gendered. It's stereotypically feminine work. It is devalued. It is expected that femmes or people assigned female at birth (AFABs) do this work for free.

The mutual aid society is anti-capitalist, it is anti-patriarchal. It encourages all genders to participate. It is gender nonbinary. We can use these principles of self-reflection and support to deprogram all of our oppressive impulses. It could be, but is often not, anti-racist.

And now I enter the world of professionalization. I am a full-time community college professor. No longer a marginalized adjunct. With this, I am more supported to be of service to my students—offering academic coaching, instruction, and often the "soft" support of what the industry calls "managing the affective domain."

And I manage it to the best of my ability, but sometimes I slip. Because I, like professional therapists, am imbued with too much power in the relationship. Yesterday, I witnessed, and was unconsciously complicit with, bullying in my classroom. I am not as accustomed to the younger age group. These students are seventeen and eighteen. I have taught college for eight years, but have never encountered bullying in such a bold and insidious way. I was proud of how I handled the bully; I pulled her aside and emphasized that she is a good person and needs to get it together—I didn't shame, I praised, and it called on her best impulses, and she turned her behavior around. I was not as sensitive with the victim, largely because I can relate to her and I have plenty of self-hate. I am afraid I may have hurt her, and I don't know how to repair the damage.

I am not her peer. I am older. I have degrees that validate my authority. I can try to relate, but there will always be a boundary—a boundary that does allow her to be mad at me.

Which may be exactly what she needs.

The biggest advantage I can see to the professional relationship is having a safe space to project anger, fear, and other socially unsanctioned emotions onto the professional helper. They are being paid to hold what can often be too painful to hold on your own. But what if we were smart enough to see that need, and made agreements to hold each other's projections? To create boundaried, ritualed space and time to let each other do what we need to do? Co-counseling does this. BDSM communities and relationships sometimes do this. Peer support does this.

Sponsors in the 12-step community put up with a lot of this, knowing that it's part of being of service.

This is not permission to act out and treat people like crap. This is acknowledging that we all have a need to exorcise our demons, that we have to put them somewhere, lest we take out our pain on loved ones in a way that is not boundaried, not conscious, and thus abusive.

Therapy Is Often Inaccessible and Unaffordable

Another argument for a larger social investment in mutual aid practices is that there are plenty of people who can't afford therapy due to a multitude of intersecting factors that speak to how broken mental health care is in this country. Yes, we should strive to make therapy accessible to all. But that, especially in the age of Trump, is a difficult proposition, and meanwhile, people need help.[4]

I cannot underscore the importance of this point enough. I have plenty of relative privilege. I am a white, middle-class person with health insurance and can access a good, experienced therapist now. But I couldn't always.

I also have bipolar disorder, so within the biomedical model I am supposed to get long-term care. At nineteen, I was told by a psychiatrist I would have to be in therapy for the rest of my life. This is a pretty toxic and dubious message to give someone whose brain hasn't even finished developing. Within the recovery model, I know that I have a lot of trauma to recover from, so I agreed I needed therapeutic support over the long haul. But because I have such doubts about the biomedical model, and because psychiatry has traumatized me, I do still question the "prescription" for lifelong therapy that many like me are saddled with. Isn't it possible that I will grow and heal and "graduate" from my need for it (vis-à-vis the recovery model)? This is also part of why mutual aid appeals to me; for someone with my diagnosis, therapy can sound like a lifelong mandatory sentence. The complex nuance here is that recently, a rad therapist validated my experience that being given that message at nineteen is wounding and reprehensible.

In my twenties without insurance, this message left me desperate for any care I could afford, whether it was good, adequate, or damaging. At that time, the only mental health care I could access was graduate student interns on a sliding scale. Forming long-term attachment with them was not possible because they often moved on to other jobs after they graduated, so I cycled through less-experienced and short-term interns rather quickly. Some of them still helped, but I felt sorely how access to the real help I needed was out of reach.

I had an intern therapist who hugged me at the end of every session. It felt obligatory, but I was so stuck in the posture of denying my own agency from a lifetime of giving mental health professionals too much power that I did not have the inner resources to drop her and find someone better. I am not opposed to therapeutic touch if it is truly consensual and purposeful. She also handled me poorly in crisis and dropped me suddenly, without a closure session, when she relocated for a new job.

Again, I am a white, middle-class person. Consider this struggle for working-class people, and for people of color who are also struggling to find someone who is culturally responsive.

In a recent article from the *Village Voice,* journalist Jennifer Pozner writes about her search for therapeutic care in her twenties when she had few financial resources:

> I could barely afford rent and food. As I researched my options, nothing was affordable except for students in training, or group therapy, which—though often extremely useful—I determined wouldn't be helpful for my specific challenges.
>
> Activating my local network, I finally found one supposedly feminist therapist who I was told offered sliding-scale payment options. I called and asked the therapist if she was taking clients. She said she was. I told her I was living one bare step above poverty and did not have any savings or health insurance, but that I was suffering from a deep depression and I had finally accepted that I needed help. I asked what her rates were at the lowest end of the scale. I can't remember if she said $75 or $100 per hour; I do remember the burning feeling of internalized shame rising up in my throat as I regretfully explained that I couldn't afford that rate. Did she have any other options, or could she suggest other therapists with a lower scale? She replied, in a derisive tone I will never forget: "If you are unwilling to pay that little for therapy, you are not dedicated to improving your mental health."
>
> I hung up the phone and sobbed. I felt even more defeated, demoralized, and depressed than I had been before I reached out, and I quit the search for therapy right at that moment. It wasn't just that I felt shamed; it was that my research had led me to a brick wall. It seemed as if there was no point in trying to seek additional resources.[5]

I have heard friends tell me similar stories. The therapist in Pozner's article is, unfortunately, not a cruel anomaly. This message is brutal, damaging, and beyond offensive. If you can't afford therapy, this says nothing about you other than your economic situation, and the last thing that should happen is for someone you are reaching out to for support shame you for your bank account and doubt your "dedication" to your mental health within a deeply flawed system.

Not only is affordable, quality therapy inaccessible to many, being put into the therapizing gaze without a practice influenced by mutual aid can be dehumanizing.

And therapists don't do your laundry for you when you just can't manage it. That is a tangible benefit to forming communities of mutual aid that isn't just practical; the friend who did this for me gave me a feeling of deep care and regard that healed; my inner child felt cared for and loved. That physical labor became an emotional labor. When I said, "Thank you," he said, "Happily." And meant it. That is a gift. Years later and on my feet, I helped get his partner a job at my college. They first met because this partner set up a care calendar for me at the time. I was their first mutual (aid) friend.

Part of being radical involves being the best human you can be in a world not designed for love, in a world that trains us to be competitive, individualistic, selfish, hierarchical, and discriminatory. Every act against that norm is a radical act.

When Therapy Works: How to Relate
Inside and Outside of the Clinic

I am lucky enough to have had a therapist for several great years (until, sadly, they had to relocate) who had a radical perspective. When I was sick with the flu, they gave me soup they had made in their restaurant. This is an act of tangible care that opened up the clinic into the kitchen and made my therapist into a person capable of both asking the right questions and choosing the right spices. But more than that, the choice to treat me as a full human and bring another dimension of *their* humanity into the room with us opened up a window into friendly behavior, which is a relationship of equals. But probably the deepest gesture of mutual aid they gave me was disclosing they were a member of the same 12-step community that I was—not that they were an "expert" in the field, but that they were a member of this mutual aid society. I knew they had suffered in the same way. I knew I wouldn't be judged or evaluated as "the problem" when they shared in the problem. Also, they had some of the same tools and spoke the same language but were further along on the path and had therapeutic training to boot; unlike some previous therapists, they kept great boundaries, which are fundamental for therapeutic work. Also of significance is that they are genderqueer, like me. We related on this level as queer humans of similar genders, too, which also healed me profoundly. I saw them once at Pride.

When I told this same therapist once that I was mad at them—because I had self-hate I was projecting outward—I told them gently, I told them with awareness. They said, "Okay," and I was relieved. Then I said, "Thank you for going over time." What I was really saying was, "Thank you for letting me be mad at you, and still being here." That is a gift, too.

But it's a gift we have to pay for. Literally.

There's something weird about paying someone to be okay with you being mad at them. It heightens the sense that maybe this has shades of abuse. And only some can afford that luxury.

What if no money were exchanged? What if honoring taboo emotions and serving others' wellness were just part of being in community with people? What if safe expression of anger were accepted as a gift of mutual aid? What if absorbing the anger of the person in need released a need for the person listening? And what if we did something with that anger besides hold it with the chains of capital?

What if we related?

And what if, in addition to creating a society that honors mutual aid, skilled emotional healers were accessible to all, and these healers didn't behave with the arrogant sanctimony of a priest class?

I just got off a mutual aid phone call with a 12-step program friend. I saw in her patterns my patterns. Seeing her survival strategies helped me see mine. I said, "You know that's just a story, right?" And I remembered my stories, and in that moment, was able to let them go.

NOTES

1. bell hooks, *All about Love: New Visions* (New York: William Morrow, 2018).

2. "What Is IPS?" Intentional Peer Support, www.intentionalpeersupport.org /what-is-ips.

3. "Prefigurative politics are the modes of organization and social relationships that strive to reflect the future society being sought by the group. According to Carl Boggs, who coined the term, the desire is to embody 'within the ongoing political practice of a movement [...] those forms of social relations, decision-making, culture, and human experience that are the ultimate goal.'" Wikipedia, s.v. "Prefigurative politics," https://en.wikipedia.org/wiki /Prefigurative_politics.

4. Trump slashed the budget for the National Institute of Mental Health by 30 percent in 2019.

5. Jennifer L. Pozner, "Who Are We Telling Depressed People to 'Reach Out' to, Anyway?," *Village Voice*, June 12, 2018, www.villagevoice.com/2018/06/12 /who-are-we-telling-depressed-people-to-reach-out-to-anyway.

Who Do You Think You Are?

SHIZUE SEIGEL

Shizue Seigel is a Japanese American writer and visual artist. She is a largely self-taught writer whose five books include the multicultural anthologies *Endangered Species, Enduring Values* and *Standing Strong! Fillmore and Japantown.* Her poetry and prose have been published in numerous anthologies and literary journals, and her artwork has been exhibited locally, nationally, and internationally. She has been awarded San Francisco Arts Commission Individual Artist Commission grants; workshops at VONA/Voices of Our Nation, Atlantic Center for the Arts, and A Room of Her Own; and residencies in Wyoming, Georgia, and the state of Washington.

. . . .

"Who do you think you are? You don't know what you are talking about!" My father's indignation sputtered into life whenever I voiced an opinion as we watched the news together. In San Francisco in the early 1960s, Dad was a staunch Republican who thought Martin Luther King Jr. was a dangerous radical.

I thought, but dared not say out loud, Who am I, Dad? I'm a straight-A student! My teachers think I'm brilliant. Why can't you ever be proud of me? And how can you disparage Blacks, Koreans, and Jews, and then turn around and complain about how Japanese Americans were treated during World War II?

But in the face of conflict, I kept silent. My American-born father was a good man, but *oyakoko,* filial piety, was a major star in my father's moral firmament, along with American patriotic duty, even to the country that had put him and his family behind barbed wire. Dad did not tolerate talking back. In his eyes, seventeen-year-olds didn't know anything. We were immature. Our judgment was not to be trusted. Japanese American children were expected to respect and obey their parents at all times and in all matters, large and small.

In 1963, my father had a very clear idea of who *he* was. In 1942, he'd been incarcerated in the aftermath of Pearl Harbor, along with 120,000 other Japanese Americans. After his release, he'd devoted his career to vindicating his family's honor and proving his loyalty by serving in US military intelligence.

He was a charter member of the "model minority," and he expected no less from me. Dad had been incarcerated just weeks before he was supposed to graduate from the University of California, Berkeley. According to him, Cal was the best school in the world, then and now, and that was where I was going. No discussion.

Though he was American born and raised, his strict immigrant father had taught him well. Children should honor and obey their parents without question. Parents gave you life, so they owned you. Women should keep their mouths shut and the house clean. They should walk ten steps behind. And they should never, ever bring shame on the family.

My parents rarely used the Japanese words, but traditional values suffused their expectations of themselves and of me: *gaman*, patience and perseverance; and *giri* and *on*, duty and obligation. I should be *chanto*, diligent, earnest, reliable, perfect, proper, neat, and punctual—at all times. If I didn't like something, *shikata ga nai*, I should to let it go. Only perfection sufficed. It was expected, so why should it draw praise?

I should never be *bakatare*, stupid; *itazura*, naughty; *kitanai*, dirty; or *kichigai*, crazy. But try as I might, I could never be quiet and neat enough. I walked like a boy, squirmed in my chair, and put my feet on the coffee table. At seventeen, I felt like an abject failure even at sitting like a lady. Decades later, I realized that I had to kill the person my parents raised me to be in order to find out who I really was.

At the time, I was a heaving mess of self-conscious, resentful misery, and the life my parents had laid out for me looked like a lifelong desert of dutiful boredom. I was not interested in the elaborate Buddhist church wedding to a nice Japanese American engineer, the house in the suburbs with a two-car garage, the immaculate house, the perfect children, midlife crisis, cancer, and dementia. Why not cut to the chase and end it all now?

———

I wasn't planning to humiliate my parents when I took an overdose of sleeping pills in 1963. In Mom's eyes, I was being a typical teenager—thinking only of myself. In actuality, my parents were probably distraught that their only child had almost died, but from my bitter teenaged perspective, I could see only their embarrassment and humiliation for my having damaged the family reputation.

My timing could not have been worse. It was Mom's turn to have her family over for Thanksgiving. Too bad I couldn't have held out until an even year, when it would have been Auntie Sumi's turn to host the family dinner. But no! A week before Thanksgiving in 1963, I had to be in a coma at Letterman Hospital, and Mom had to call the whole family and disinvite them to a family celebration.

My actions announced to the world that she and Dad were inadequate parents who had raised a defective child. It brought shame, *haji*, on the family. Japanese American girls didn't commit suicide in those days—not that anyone knew of. Decades later, seventy- and eighty-year-old ladies in the writing class I taught in Japantown assured me that Japanese and Chinese American girls did all sorts of things back then *and* now. But nobody talked about it. In the '50s and early '60s, girls who were pregnant or suicidal got "appendicitis" or went to live with relatives in another town.

I was equally inconsiderate of my best friend, Catherine. She had stolen twenty sedatives from her mom. Every Monday morning as we walked to school, we transferred the romance of suicide, and custody of a little plastic vial of bright red sleeping pills. Simply possessing them was a badge of sophistication, like smoking or going to see depressing French movies at the Surf Theater. When I swallowed all the pills, it didn't occur to me that Catherine might get in trouble. Our parents never let us see each other again, so I never got a chance to ask her.

My dad never liked Catherine. He didn't trust white people in general, and he thought Catherine in particular was a bad influence. I wasn't sure who was influencing whom. In any case, we were best friends largely because we were both social nonentities who happened to walk the same route home from school.

I'd realized I was sick of school not long after senior year began. My parents had sent me to take college courses at a six-week summer session at beachy-keen UC Santa Barbara. After a summer of freedom, it was hard to get back to foggy San Francisco and the straight-A treadmill.

What was it about my Santa Barbara summer that ruined me for senior year? Was it the relaxed and sleepy campus? The mellow beach climate? Or the friends I made there—Roxanne and Emily, who exuded a complex bouquet of ennui, cynicism, fear, and rebellion fostered by moneyed parents, fancy prep schools, and the prospect of prestigious small colleges. I didn't know anything about their world, except that they hated and feared it and wanted to escape. They were, like Catherine, "a bad influence."

My whole identity since kindergarten had been based on excelling in school, so when I started to procrastinate on assignments or forget them entirely, I was frightened.

The day Miss Martin announced a surprise classroom essay, my gut twisted. I had forgotten what we were supposed to read for homework. I'd glanced at the first line: "No man is an Iland, intire of itself," then closed the book. Did John Donne continue in the same Old English vein or veer off in another direction? I had no idea. Gripping my pen tightly, sweating the blue lines off my notebook paper, I faked a dissent. In my experience, every man, woman, and child *was* an island, locked in inescapable isolation, no matter how hard we tried to connect.

At home, my parents rarely talked. My dad came home from work tired and grumpy. He popped open a Coke and glumly funneled his nervous energy into scanning the newspaper while flipping TV channels, chain-smoking, and folding origami animals out of neatly torn squares of Christmas wrap.

My mother compulsively cooked and cleaned and vacuumed. She complained about every single hair I left on the white tile bathroom floor and every drop of water I missed sponging off the kitchen counter.

My mother lived in a small, safe world. She had few friends, so she relied on me for company. While washing dishes or going grocery shopping, she kept up a constant litany of negativity. She could not drive without criticizing other drivers; she could not go out without worrying what other people thought of her.

———

It did not occur to me—at least not consciously—that I might need liberation, too. I didn't know *anyone* who was happy. My classmates were terminally shy nerds. We kept our noses buried in books so we wouldn't have to meet each other's eyes. We talked to each other only by raising our hands for classroom discussion.

In the early '60s, there was only one gifted class per grade level, so I had gone through junior high and high school with the same thirty kids. We were the cream of the crop, our teachers said, the best thirty out of a thousand seniors. And I was in the top four or five, the 99.99th percentile, according to my SATs.

Being a "brain" was like living behind an invisible force field. It made it a little less terrible that your slip showed or your shoelace was untied. The lettermen and cheerleaders, class officers, debate team members, aspiring thespians, and potential dropouts that thronged the hallways between classes left you alone. Nobody picked on you, but nobody talked to you either. And nobody expected you to be popular or have a date on Saturday nights.

I needed that protection. I was morbidly shy. I had no idea what I wanted to do with my life. I lived in a haze of borrowed lives, reading my way through the public library. I found no solace in Anna Karenina's Moscow, Blanche DuBois's New Orleans, or even Holden Caulfield's New York, but at least I had the satisfaction of knowing that I *knew* that life was fucked, while most people were in denial.

I was perched on a lonely, meaningless pinnacle in a tiny little world. I was tired of it. But I didn't have a clue about how to get down.

My self-consciousness ratcheted up after a stranger approached me in the hall with an intensity that made me look over my shoulder to see who she was looking at. But the stars in her eyes were meant for me.

"Are you Linda Matsumoto?!" she asked with a fawning intensity that filled me with dread. "Oh, God, I can't believe I'm talking to you! I see your essays and artwork up in the hall all the time."

"Teachers put up a lot of people's work. It doesn't mean anything."

"They never put mine up. I loved your essay 'Every Man Is an Island.' It was so …"

"I'm gonna be late for class," I interrupted, and fled.

The attention made my skin crawl.

As October passed into November, I still could not make myself pay attention in school. The teachers had become talking heads; I could no longer hear the words issuing from their mouths. My classmates were ants with horn-rimmed glasses crawling up a perpetual ladder. Judging from the adults I knew, growing up meant decades of misery and boredom, with nothing to look forward to but mortgages, insurance payments, and washing machine repairs.

I could not face another half century of this. I didn't believe in an afterlife. Why not cut to the chase and end it now?

I didn't know how many were a lethal dose, but I naively hoped that the sedatives in Catherine's pill bottle were sufficient. And they almost were. Unfortunately, they made sounds of my breathing loud and labored enough to penetrate my closed bedroom door, rise up the stairs through another bedroom door, and wake my mother. I was rushed to the hospital at 2 a.m. Three days later, I awoke from a coma with deep cutdowns in my ankle and my arm where they had inserted transfusions.

I was at Letterman Hospital, whose sunny glass-windowed corridors were lined with wheelchairs filled with young men in blue bathrobes. They'd been injured in some place called Viet Nam.

My parents were upset. "How could you do this?" my mother moaned. "We've given you everything." My father said nothing. I could tell he was disgusted.

"I don't know," I said. What was I supposed to say? *I hate you and your miserable boring lives? I can't face a lifetime of this?*

At night I was locked in a room with a metal door. Every few days, I was taken to a green-walled office to talk to a psychiatrist. The psychiatrist wore the rank insignia of a major, or "oak leaves" on his shoulders. I lay on a couch and had nothing to say to him, so I suspect he spent the hour doing paperwork. Once he invited my parents, suggesting that we each examine our roles in the situation. Dad stormed out, declaring, "This has nothing to do with me!" At the time I thought he blamed it all on me. Much later, after he divorced Mom and married someone more confident and sociable, I realized he blamed her, too.

I was in and out of Letterman for the better part of eighteen months. The two rounds of shock treatments did nothing to lift my depression, but increased my sense of paranoia and powerlessness.

The sole benefit of hospitalization was getting away from my environment. I hung around the hospital dayroom with a bunch of psych techs, homesick small-town recruits just a year or two older than I, who adopted me as their little mascot. Since it was their job to assist with patient recreation, they took me bowling and taught me to play pool.

When I was released to go home the first time, I didn't last long. My self-consciousness was overwhelming. I could hardly bring myself to go out of the house. I didn't want to run into anyone I knew. I felt as though the letter *S* for suicide was blazed across my forehead, telegraphing my shame. My back felt exposed, as if I'd be shot down by machine guns as I crossed the street.

After two stays at Letterman, I went to a continuation high school where I didn't have to see anyone I knew. I got through senior year at an accelerated pace. In the fall of 1965, I enrolled at UC Berkeley, my dad's alma mater. Things were looking up, my parents thought.

I lasted three weeks at Cal. I hated my roommate, a bland suburbanite who spent much of her free time cleaning her white tennis shoes. My genetics and philosophy classes were held in auditoriums so big that the professors were pinheads in the far distance. My two favorite subjects, art and English, were major disappointments. I was taking art to improve my representational painting skills, not to spend an entire semester imitating cubist violins or Pollock drip paintings. As for English, Mr. Fish waxed rhapsodic about British essayists, one in particular. *Who the hell is Matthew Arnold?* I thought. *He was probably all that was left when you had to pick a subject for your graduate thesis.*

I could have gotten involved with the free speech movement or the third world movement. But from what I could see, there was too much anger and testosterone. The males competed for power, while the women cooked and supplied "free love."

I considered jumping off the Campanile, but I was afraid of pain. I decided to haul a small, empty suitcase to the Golden Gate Bridge to use as a step stool to get over the high railing. When I got safely out of sight around the backside of the south tower, I looked down at the water and saw that a concrete fender surrounded the bridge footing. I couldn't bear the possibility of hitting it, so I dragged myself and the suitcase back home. I was a failure at everything, even suicide.

My parents sent me to a psychiatric day care program that focused on creative expression. Every day was filled with arts and crafts. I enjoyed making copper wire bracelets and mosaic tile trivets. When we read plays aloud, I loved inhabiting different characters and giving rein to their emotions. We took field trips to a sculptor's studio on a Sausalito houseboat, and a nationally known metalworker's forge. It was a revelation that people could actually make a living from their art. Therapy was group sessions. Instead of having nothing to say to a silent psychiatrist, I listened to other people's problems and felt a little less weird. I began to think I wasn't so crazy to want a different life from my parents, but the artistic, romantic life I yearned for still seemed absurdly out of reach.

I had a few sessions with a younger psychiatrist who said the one useful thing I ever heard from a shrink. When I complained that I was paralyzed by self-consciousness, he said with a twinkle, "What makes you think any-body's paying any attention to you?"

The idea was like a thunderbolt. He didn't try to talk me out of feeling worthless. He simply pushed it to its logical conclusion. At home I was the only child, pinned under my parents' scrutiny, the focus of all their hopes and fears. In the gifted class, we were the highlight of the teachers' day. It was humiliating, yet wonderfully liberating, to think that to the rest of the world I was invisible.

My parents gave up on me. They sent me to secretarial school. It was the last educational help I ever got from my father. I got a job as a typist clerk. In less than a year, I married a man I didn't love to get out of my parents' house. The year was 1966, and the apartment we rented happened to be in the Haight-Ashbury.

By the following year, the Summer of Love showed me I was not an oddball; I was part of a full-fledged movement. I was not so different from thousands of first-year baby boomers. We were born in 1946, just after the war ended in a flash of atomic catastrophe. In 1963, when I felt the first stirrings of rebellion, my generation was poised for another change. But I was a little ahead of my time. By 1965, Catherine and I might have been trading marijuana, not sleeping pills.

If my parents had not been Asian American, my struggle to find myself might have been less extreme. I might have been able to talk back to my parents, slam doors, goof off from school. I might have enrolled in a small private college instead of an industrial behemoth. I might have found role models who looked like me. I might have found psychologists who understood the Asian American experience.

But for all the acid-dropping, Aquarian fellowship of the times, I didn't see any other Asian American hippies. The few Asian Americans I did run across were either quiet and conservative or didactically political. In both groups I sensed a deep undercurrent of insecurity that I didn't want to reinforce mine. I steered clear. I didn't want to be white or male, but I wanted to feel truly equal to them.

I searched for ways to build my self-confidence, consciously seeking to replace my parents' negative voices with positive ones. Ironically, much of what I found was flavored by Eastern thought. I went to India to study at an ashram. My shelves filled with Buddhist folk poetry, Tibetan teachings, and self-help books. I learned to connect with the Infinite through a singing meditation called *bhajan*. I learned to still my mind and breathe my consciousness into light. I learned that it was imperative to follow my bliss. When I focused on being here now, fear of the future and guilt from the past dropped away.

By the early 1980s, through a series of accidents, I became an advertising art director—what the ad biz called a "creative." *This is who I am!* I realized. I excelled at putting elements together in new and different ways and suffusing them with emotional resonance. It was the antithesis of received wisdom, the tried and true path of my parents. I learned that my inner voice was neither cracked nor contrarian, but simply a bit ahead of its time. My bosses paid me to think ahead of the curve—if I thought like everyone else, why would they need *me?*

This revelation didn't lessen life's upheavals; advertising was an unstable, inherently consumerist profession. I was too patient with bad situations for another twenty years. A nagging need for approval drove me to work too hard. I fell into crash-and-burn cycles, alternating eighty-hour weeks with months of fatigue. I had to train myself to rest by telling myself, "Fun is a vitamin. You need to take some every day!" The disciplinarian tone was not entirely facetious. Depressions arose when I felt trapped between someone else's expectations and my own desires. They stopped recurring as I gathered confidence to take intuitive leaps of faith instead of waiting to be pushed off cliffs. Experience taught me that when one door closed, another opened. I learned that every winter would be followed by a thaw.

By the early 1990s, I was applying my creative skills to social change in the African American and Asian American communities. By 2006, I was invited to archive my work at the California Ethnic and Multicultural Archives at UC Santa Barbara, the very institution that triggered my first step off the beaten path. I suspect this honor points less to my modest accomplishments than to the continuing invisibility of Asian Americans. I was lucky to fit at least one model minority stereotype. I was "smart." I wonder how many other Asian Americans in distress quietly slip through the cracks.

Back in the 1960s, my suicide attempt forced me out into the open and set me on a long and individual path of recovery and discovery. For many years, my own shame blinkered me into thinking that I was the only family disgrace, but over the years, I've realized that in many ways I was simply a pioneer. As one of the first Asian Americans I knew of to marry and divorce a white man, to have mixed-race children, to choose unstable employment, and to be downsized and outsourced, I encountered criticism and judgment at every stage from my parents and other conservative Asian Americans.

I felt like an Artic trawler heaving its way through pack ice. Yet each of these circumstances is commonplace today, both in the Asian American and mainstream communities. Contrary to popular myth, the model minority is not so perfect after all. When I look carefully at my contemporaries and their children, I can see alcoholism, depression, domestic abuse, cutting, eating disorders, drug abuse, bankruptcy, chronic illness, underemployment, workaholism, codependency, and all the other ills of our larger society.

But even today, many Asian Americans fear visibility as much as or more than they complain about being overlooked. Asian Americans remain unseen and unnoticed even in my hometown, where we constitute 30 percent of the population. Fifty years after my mental health crisis, healthy and realistic Asian American role models are still hard to find. Fully fleshed Asian American characters are almost nonexistent in films and literature. And professional literature on Asian American mental health is scant.

Many Asian Americans find it difficult to share their deepest emotional challenges even with close friends or family. The suicide rate for Asian American women aged fifteen to twenty-four is twice that of all races, yet they seek professional help at half the rate of others. Studies show that Asian Americans fear the stigma of mental illness. They believe that seeking professional help will disgrace the family. They try to resolve problems on their own. They blame themselves for not avoiding bad thoughts or for not having more will power. They don't believe existing resources are culturally competent to counsel them on their particular issues. Where, for example, do family ties bleed into codependency and discipline become repression?

Asian Americans often somatize dis-ease and develop migraines, ulcers, fatigue, and other symptoms. Depression is so common that when I went to my medical doctor for fatigue, she tried to prescribe Prozac. "All my Japanese American friends are taking it," she said. "*I'm* taking it."

I refused the Prozac. "I am not sick because I'm depressed," I insisted. "I know what depression feels like, and this isn't it. I'm exhausted. I haven't bounced back from the flu after two months. I'm sick of being sick, but I am *not* depressed." A blood test finally revealed that my fatigue was caused by an easily treated vitamin D deficiency.

Advertising taught me to love the give-and-take of discourse—arguing with my copywriter, selling an idea to a client. I truly felt equal to most white men, and yet sometimes I replayed the smallest criticism over and over. The voices that persisted and prickled were the very ones I knew were dead wrong. The projectiles of bullies and mean girls, the envious and insecure got under my skin like poisoned darts that seeped a steady self-doubt. Why did I give them credence? I realized I was replaying an old discussion: *Dad, my teacher says I don't have to listen to them; they're just jealous.* And my father's voice: *Stop giving yourself alibis. You don't know what you're talking about! Who do you think you are?*

As difficult as my parents were, I kept ties with them throughout their lives. I was never who they wanted me to be, so their criticism, fear, and negativity never stopped. Nevertheless, I never doubted that they loved me. I worked hard to release my fear and anger and to respect them for their many good qualities. They did the best they could, given their challenges. Now that they're gone, I can say wholeheartedly, "Who do I think I am? I'm Japanese American enough to be hardworking, responsible, and appreciative, but I'm also a unique and creative person, and I trust my own thinking."

ECT: Day One

ALICE MIGNON

Alice Mignon lives in the San Francisco Bay Area. When not undergoing invasive psychiatric procedures, she works and writes and plays with her dog.

. . . .

I'm dropped off for my appointment at the main entrance to Herrick Hospital, which looks like it has been holding its breath since the 1980s. I still can't believe this is happening. I've opted to undergo electroconvulsive therapy (ECT) to deal with my persistent medication-resistant suicidal depression. Opted. Voluntarily. I had to convince the doctors why I was a good candidate. Thirty years ago, I'd voted to ban this procedure based on movie depictions of its cruelty. Last week, I found myself sitting at the end of a quiet hall fervently pleading my case to two different doctors.

I check in for my appointment at admissions ("Really, I check in for an outpatient appointment at admissions?" "Yes, really.") and then go to the hospital lobby to wait as instructed. There are others in the lobby, including at least one other ECT patient I am pretty sure. Her hairstyle is confused and there's a brittle quality to her presence. Sure enough, an ECT nurse comes to get her. Five minutes pass. A 150-year-old doctor approaches me and confirms I'm there for my first ECT appointment. He says since I'm having ECT, there's a requirement that I speak with a non-ECT doctor for a neutral assessment of my fitness for the procedure. I blink. I don't even know what this means. Why hadn't anyone warned me of this? I have to have this medical conversation in the lobby? Has the entire hospital decided it's not-give-a-shit day?

I stiffen in my 1984 faux leather chair. He smiles widely and says, "If the president had depression, he would get ECT." So, this is my last-minute "neutral" physician consultation. I wonder what twist of retirement-planning fate has him still roaming the scuffed hospital halls. Maybe he retired and his wife was like, "Jesus, Frank, get out of the house, I'm going to kill myself if I have to listen to you breathe through your mouth all day." He asks me if anyone is forcing me to do this. I say no. He then asks me what the day, date, and season are. I answer correctly and wonder if he would have been able to do the same if I hadn't just told him. Satisfied I have met this very low threshold, he tells me a nurse will be up soon to get me, and he ambles off.

Ten minutes later, a nurse comes to the lobby to get me, and we take the elevator down to the basement. The ECT "department" is right at the foot of the elevator. There is no reception desk or waiting room, and I realize this is why they oddly and awkwardly had me wait in the lobby. In keeping with the hospital's mission to keep it real, the dingy beige walls haven't been painted in decades. There are a couple of mismatched chairs from the Eisenhower era.

As you enter the department, if you walk straight about ten feet, you'd be in the area where the procedure is done. Instead we go to the left where there's a small nurses' station and six beds lined up on the other wall. One is empty.

The nurse goes to grab me a gown and pauses. "Do you want to wear your own pants?" I'm confused but instinct takes over. "Yes." She takes me to a bathroom, which pretty clearly seems to have been a storage closet previously, where I can change. In fact, it feels like the entire ECT department was a storage unit at one time. When they decided to change its function, they probably decided to just keep those chairs where they were. As I head into the restroom she asks one more time, "Are you sure you want to wear your pants?" "Why …" but then I figure it out. People probably pee involuntarily sometimes from the shock. That or the seizure. What the hell am I doing here?

I emerge from the bathroom wearing their gown and my pants. The same nurse directs me to the remaining empty bed where six of us are waiting, an assembly line of sorts. I try not to look at the other patients as I walk past them. My peripheral vision can't help but note that they're all women in their fifties or older. I guess we get to a point in life when we realize the mainstays in the depression battle have failed us despite our best efforts. Therapy? Check. SSRI? Check. Tricyclics? Check. MAOI? Check (only for the hale and hearty). Miscellaneous categories of antidepressants? Check. Not working so far? Check. Oh, maybe you have bipolar II! Mood stabilizers? Check. Anticonvulsants? Check. Exercise? Check. Not straining at it so much, just going with the flow? Check. Raise a family? Check. Career? Check. Check check check. Never being fished out of the dark waters, we end up trapped in the drain in the basement of Herrick Hospital.

Several nurses are tending to me at any given time and continuously apologize for how long it's taking, but the first time there are a lot of questionnaires to fill out. They're putting an IV line in and hooking me up to a heart monitor. The delay is fine with me. Take your time. I'm tightly wound and terrified by now. How is this not going to be like *Frances?* Or *One Flew over the Cuckoo's Nest?* Sure, I'll be under general anesthesia and they weren't, but that doesn't undo the procedure's violence.

After about an hour, it's my turn. They wheel me in my bed back to the procedure area. Terrified, I wonder if the women who pee in their pants do so before rather than during the procedure. The anesthesiologist says something; the ECT doctor says something else. Their mouths move. My mouth moves. I listen to the heart monitor beeping but can't quite follow the conversation until the anesthesiologist speaks again. "The medicine is going to start going in your arm now, so ..."

If the doctor does what he told me he would, he holds the two electrodes against my right temple in a unilateral position. That's all I'm sure of. How does he instruct the machine to deliver the current? How does my body physically respond to the cue it should convulse despite the muscle relaxants I'm given? If my brain could talk, what would it say? Would it look at me with hooded eyes steeped in betrayal?

I wake up sobbing back in the recovery area. I don't wake up, feel sad, and then start crying. I'm already crying when I wake up. The oxygen mask is interfering with my ability to breathe; I need to take big gulps of air to sob this hard. I mildly wonder what I'm sobbing about, but I have no idea, and it doesn't interest me that much anyway. More interesting are the mechanics of sobbing. My face is wet. I can't catch my breath. When my fingers touch my face, my fingers are wet. Something is wrong. I have no idea what. Something is wrong, but I don't want to know what.

One month of treatment passes. I remember nothing of that time. Now, I have to pore over emails from the time I know it happened to reconstruct that month of my life. Needless to say, ECT was not a panacea.

For Psychiatric Survivors, Friends Make the Best Medicine[*]

IMOGEN PRISM

Imogen unfortunately recognizes the difficult reality of stigma and so writes with a pen name. If you would like to get in touch with her, email the editors of this book at beentoopatient11@gmail.com, and we can make that happen.

. . . .

Psychiatric Survivor: The Trauma of Involuntary Hospitalization

I have been locked up in psychiatric facilities four times in my life. The first hospitalization was at sixteen, and I had never had any kind of episode before. The next three somewhat had to do with my ambivalence toward medication, but much also came from incompetent psychiatrists. I've been in a cop car for this. The code for mental health legal violation in California is 5150, which can be made into a verb. I've been fifty-one fiftied. Supposedly, this can be done when a person is deemed being "of danger to self or others." And yet, oddly, I have never been homicidal, and while I have had suicidal ideation, I've been far from the brink of attempting or even seriously considering suicide. So, what gives? Why

---

[*] First published in 2016 by The Body Is Not an Apology as two pieces: "Psychiatric Survivor: The Trauma of Involuntary Hospitalization" and "Why Friends Make the Best Medicine: Self-Love for the Neuroatypical." Republished with gratitude.

lock me away? Why separate me from society like a contagious pathogen? How can we really effectively label someone as "a danger to themselves or others?" That definition is so slippery.

An Altered State of Consciousness Commonly Known as Psychosis

I have had some pretty intense delusions. Some typical fare, some not so typical. The National Security Agency (NSA) being everywhere, some ideas about being connected with God and/or the Antichrist and seeing the Truth about everything. Some *Truman Show* type of conspiracy theory that my imaginative brain elaborates into a dizzying web of symbols.

My psychosis is, as you may be gathering, not a lot of fun. Actually, it can be excruciatingly painful. It's dysphoric mania, not euphoric mania, according to the textbooks.

The little spider that we all have in our minds, the one that spins stories about ourselves and other people, the thing that gossips, gets creative, makes sense of reality—when I am manic, that spider spins out of control, and I can't tell what's cobweb and what's window anymore. I can't see people clearly, I can't see myself clearly.

I know that I am doing harm to myself when I am in this state. But when I am held against my will in a facility with many other people whose internal storytelling spiders are also in overdrive, hospitalization turns into a big fucking Halloween frat house mess.

I once heard Michael Cornwall (who has been practicing radical, compassionate therapy for folks in altered states of consciousness for years) say that what we label as psychosis is a distortion of latent feelings that are longing to be expressed.

I survived four involuntary hospitalizations. Western medicine's attempt to manage the trauma in my body when it was at its most acute expression was a massive fail for many reasons. They try to clog up the emotional urges with chemicals that have devastating short-term and long-term side effects.

Hospitals have an outdated Middle Ages model of separating the "sick" from the "well" that originated with leper colonies. If that's not enough to make you feel oppressed, there are all those big mirrors everywhere. They were tracking our every move, putting it all in our charts, and they wonder why we think we're being spied on. The panopticon is real.[1]

What I really feel like I need when I'm in those states is a place to rest and someone to listen to me until I run out of the story and land with necessarily rugged emotion. And then people to hold me with care as I release those feelings, not an orderly to hold me down to a bed and inject me with drugs in the hip. There is rarely individual therapy in those places. Group therapy is a joke. And as for rest, while I was sleeping, someone opened my door every hour and shined a flashlight on my bed and my roommate's bed to make sure we weren't hurting ourselves. Or fucking. Hospitals are hotbeds of weird flirtation and sexual compulsion and frustration. If that sounds fun, trust me, it's not.

So you may be asking yourself—what's the solution? And the truth is, I am not sure.

Running Out of Solutions

I have made an uneasy peace with taking medication, and have mercifully found a kind, competent psychiatrist who is trained as a psychotherapist—a rare find. I work hard to stay out of the hospital. I have no plans to return, but I also recognize that I have a chronic condition. I am vigilant about my self-care, but life circumstances could push me over the edge again. I don't know.

And that's terrifying because I know that currently there is no place on the planet that would help me heal from a manic flare-up in a measured, helpful way. I know that there is no place that wouldn't do me more harm than good.

Those places just don't exist yet.

It's more than the history lesson I've given you, though; it's more than the fact that I know intellectually that these institutions are built on a foundation of separating the "good" from the "bad" in society, the same principle that fuels our broken prison industrial complex.

I don't want to say all of the nurses, doctors, orderlies, social workers, and group therapists are missing the mark. But so many are. When I was locked up, so many of them looked at me as the Other. So many of them treated me with condescension, rudeness, syrupy false kindness, or any other tactic that regards me as subhuman. I was terrified, I was disempowered. I was literally not allowed to leave the premises until they decided my metaphors were not so hysterical. I never threatened to kill myself or anyone else, but my rants were deeply unsettling to me and everyone around me, and my language and behavior stopped making sense.

Why is that a crime? What is the alternative?

Healing and Accountability

First of all, I want to question the entire notion of crime and punishment. It's important to acknowledge that this is not an academic point. So many of our country's prisoners have severe mental health struggles, and their experience being "treated" with psychiatry while imprisoned makes my experience look like a cakewalk.

This means that mental health reform is also about prison reform. They are inseparable. The restorative justice movement seeks healing and accountability rather than separation from society and punishment. How can this inform mental health reform? Instead of a 5150, instead of a system that separates the "sick" from the "well" and insists on "compliance" with medication and other treatments, couldn't we have restful places with healthy food, herbalists, acupuncturists, art therapists that help those in an altered state come to terms with the symbols rattling around in their brain? This approach would take more time. People would not be able to return to work as quickly. But they might be able to heal the root of their problems by expressing the deep, primal emotion shaking them into psychosis or major depression. Many of them might not even need medication. They might not keep going in and out of hospitals and prisons.

Respite centers or halfway houses are better than lockup, but not by enough. R. D. Laing and others experimented with radical sanctuaries like Kingsley Hall in the 1970s. It's hard to say if those were a success. Designing, building, and funding alternative sanctuaries for folks in mental health crisis that allow for real healing is a vital part of the work we need to do. Mental health advocates with lived experience need a dialogue with providers of all kinds—from open-minded, humble psychiatrists to herbalists, therapists, social workers, and more—to boldly imagine what is actually needed for people in mental health crisis. And then we need to work on building these centers. The spiritual emergence of a mental health crisis can be an ideal time to undergo transformative healing work in the hands of a gifted practitioner, and that is just worlds away from what happens in hospitals, in my experience.

Most think that going mad is shameful. Of course it is painful, and I for one do not want to suffer under the weight of delusions ever again. But it could happen—I am not so arrogant to think I have escaped that possibility. So for a potential future self, and as an advocate for others, I have to ask: what if we honored the wild and tender green shoots that burst from the cracks in the sidewalk? What if we said—here is growth, let's water ourselves, let's tend to ourselves and move to a garden? Let's see how strong and healthy we can get with the right kind of care.

From a cross-cultural perspective, too, there are many places in the world that don't treat psychosis as an illness, but rather as an expression of a problem, or even as an expression of a gift—that the person experiencing this altered state has insight into the world. I mean, I was pretty sure the NSA was up to no good before Edward Snowden's big day. Sure, I went too far with it and hurt myself, but there was a grain of truth there that a respectful guide might honor, not ridicule or punish for betraying sacred rationality. Ethan Watters published a book called *Crazy Like Us: The Globalization of the American Psyche,* which details how psychiatry and psychopharmacology have collaborated to basically make the rest of the world as miserable as America, even in places where mental health has historically been treated much more holistically, or where those undergoing altered states of consciousness were actually revered.

The symbol for Western medicine is the Rod of Asclepius—you know, that snake winding itself around a stick. Snakes are poisonous, and the Greeks knew this. *Pharmakon* means drug, medicine, poison. I have to get my blood drawn twice a year to make sure the drug/medicine I've been on for twenty years isn't poisoning my liver.

As a child abuse survivor, I hold a great deal of ambivalence in my body—love for my perpetrators as well as justifiable anger. They are both there. Medicine, poison. As a psychiatric abuse survivor, I have gratitude that I can function as well as I can in society and in my various communities of work, creativity, and friendship. I also have justifiable anger at all the ways the psychiatric system has disempowered me, sent the overt and covert message that I cannot be trusted with my own life. That I cannot be trusted to make decisions, and that I am irreparably broken. On my best days, I am proud that I am as well and as successful as I am despite all my traumas. On my worst days, psychiatry's messages land; I believe that I am broken.

I know healing is a life-long journey, and so the practice of self-care has paid off with a more stable life, and for that I am grateful. But a system that tells me I need them forever, my condition is chronic and I will probably have to endure traumatic hospitalization again if I am not hypervigilant—this makes the little spider in my mind anxious, and makes it weave faster. And you already know how that goes.

So, what do I do? I cultivate community. I cultivate spirituality and mindfulness. I go to therapy. I am creative. I do loads of self-care. When will it ever be enough to drown out the voices that whisper I shouldn't be where I am? That any success I've had is an accident of fate, that at my core, I can't be trusted to take care of myself, that at my core, I am dangerous to myself and others?

It's just another story. Another web. I wipe away the mess. I see my reflection in the glass. I smile, open the window. I tell myself a different story.

Why Friends Make the Best Medicine

About a month ago, a friend and I who share many things, including a bipolar diagnosis, were sharing our stories the way folks do in 2019—over text. She asked something about when I first experienced a manic episode. For me, it started at sixteen, so I started to type: "It's a lifelong struggle." But autocorrect wouldn't let me. It made me say:

"It's a lifelong star."

You're damn right. I am a star. Thank you, autocorrect!

But I am not the only star in the sky. This good friend and I have "access intimacy"—intimacy based, at least in part, on a common health struggle/star. And I have been lucky enough to share this with other "Icaristas" too.

Co-founded in 2002 by Jacks McNamara and Sascha Altman DuBrul, The Icarus Project is "a support network and education project by and for people who experience the world in ways that are often diagnosed as mental illness. We advance social justice by fostering mutual aid practices that reconnect healing and collective liberation. We transform ourselves through transforming the world around us."

In 2009 I joined the Bay Area Icarus Project. We had weekly peer-support meetings (where we laughed a lot). We brought speakers and organized events around the many interrelating topics of mad pride, neuro-diversity, mental health advocacy, and so on. We worked together as a collective for several years, and as volunteer groups often do, we faded. A year later, another group of folks took up the mantle and started having meetings.

The Icarus Project continues to be a growing, dazzling, international constellation of stars. But this is an intergenerational human rights movement. Let us never forget "drapetomania." The so-called mental illness that caused slaves to run away and be free. Psychiatrists have historically colluded with systems of power. Homosexuality was considered a mental illness, actually codified in the *DSM,* until 1973. It took activists to reform the system throughout history. It's gonna take a movement to revolutionize the way we think about and treat mental health as a whole. "Crazy" is not a binary phenomenon. It's not either/or—you don't either have the scarlet C or you don't. There is no crazy Jell-O mold formed around your brain in utero. Unless it's the star-shaped one. But maybe we're all stars.

A couple years ago, I went to a phenomenal event here in Oakland. It was the book release for *Outside Mental Health: Voices and Visions of Madness* by Will Hall, activist, therapist, and producer of *Madness Radio*. All my old Icarista friends were there! It was a reunion of sorts. It was at a collective house. There were talks about mental health, readings from the book, and an incredible musician, Bonfire Madigan Shive, a founding member of Icarus. Since I'm a little neuroatypical star, by the end of the night, I was a little overstimulated. As I was waxing perhaps a bit too poetic about sparks, flames, and movement building, one of my friends said: "Your pupils are really dilated honey, you should go home and sleep." And she was right. This is why, as an Icarus zine says, "Friends Make the Best Medicine."

But for me, they're not all I need. Some may describe corporations as giant octopi reaching their tentacles into people's bodies, but for me it is actually true—Eli Lilly is in my bloodstream. I have to make some kind of uneasy peace with this just to accept what allows me to function. But does that mean I am diseased? Does that mean I am genetically different? I don't believe I was born chemically imbalanced. I may have been born with that potential, but trauma didn't just trigger it: it locked, loaded, and fired the gun. I am a child abuse survivor. That shit reaches into my bones. Of course it's gonna shake my brain, too.

I'm still not sure if my diagnosis has any use or only serves to stigmatize. At the same time, I know the realm of my emotional and mental experience is different from most people's. I accepted the meds mostly because doctors with a lot of power told me to take them. At sixteen, forced to take them in the hip, with a needle, held by orderlies and bound to a bed. But I continued to swallow them because I was so terrified about the shadows of my childhood that I wanted to be sedated, wanted to make sure I kept forgetting, and at least meds didn't give me a raging hangover. I also hoped that someday my critique of the biomedical model of "mental illness" would translate into the practice of me being med-free.

It's true that some saddled with a diagnosis of a "major mental illness" can, through meditation, nutrition, acupuncture, exercise, and routine, overcome their dependency on psychoactive drugs and truly recover, mind, body, and soul. For those who have succeeded in drastically reducing or eliminating their need for medication, I have profound respect and admiration. For me, meds do the job. They do it quicker and dirtier, and with potentially devastating long-term results, but they do the job. The blade forged in my mind's fire cuts me, but it also unbinds me. Medication dulls this blade, and that really is its double edge. I have reluctantly accepted, after all my struggles (supernovas and black holes), that simply put, the meds keep me alive and functioning.

I don't do everything the med-free self-care warriors do, but I do a lot, because I know medication is only one piece of my wellness. It's a tool, an instrument, and a pretty blunt one at that. So I try to eat well. I go to therapy. I get plenty of sleep, I get bodywork done. I actively cultivate a rich support network of friends. I pray. I meditate. And fun stuff! In case you're wondering, I work. Quite a bit, and at a demanding job. This is all part of my wellness, too. I have to be creative and social and productive and spiritual. It's what keeps me humming. Also, I limit my alcohol intake and don't do any more drugs than the three pink ones and one little white one I take every night.

The Icarus Project has a pro-choice policy when it comes to medication. Along with MindFreedom, they've co-authored a powerful zine, the *Harm Reduction Guide to Coming Off Psychiatric Drugs*. Its central principle is that for those who deal with altered states of consciousness (otherwise known as mania, depression, or psychosis), the harm can come from both these states themselves and the drugs used to temper them. The question always becomes, what will do me the least harm, since both the trauma-rattled bent of my brain and the drugs can be damaging. Robert Whitaker, author of *Anatomy of an Epidemic: Magic Bullets, Psychiatric Drugs, and the Astonishing Rise of Mental Illness in America*, presents many disturbing trends, including the fact that the number of working-age adults on disability due to mental illness has nearly quadrupled since 1987 with the introduction of Prozac.

I might resign myself to the intricate ambivalence of requiring medication, but I cannot escape the way society marks me as damaged, regardless of what I do to treat my mood challenges. Without the mentally "imbalanced," there would be no movement in the ocean of humanity. Martin Luther King Jr. said: "Human salvation lies in the hands of the creatively maladjusted." Psychiatry's defenders say they are trying to rid the world of suffering. But I can't measure my powerful feelings in milligrams or genetic codes. Pills and friends and other healing practices keep them at bay, but they stay alive in my body, dormant, perhaps, but waiting for their next expression. Whether that eruption is creative or destructive is up to me and each person blessed and cursed with mental "dis-orders." It should not be up to the so-called experts to shape the fire in my mind, to keep it spilling past its borders, to keep it from sparking others and igniting the landscape in dangerous and useful ways. It's up to me to learn to balance my elements to prevent fire or flood.

I have a poem about my experiences being hospitalized and the pain of dysphoric mania. I performed this poem at an Icarus event called Mad Love, and something switched inside me: the poem's delivery had been despairing before. But at Mad Love when I described the way my thoughts soared into madness, I felt like a superhero! Yeah, maybe genes play a role. Or maybe it's all environmental. Or both. But just like "We're here, we're queer, get used to it"—mad pride echoes a similar idea. In fact, it's the same damn chant. To be marked as mad in this society is a kind of queerness. To be off, marginal, away from the norm. So who gives a shit where we come from or how we got this way? We've got mad gifts. "Dangerous gifts." We've got mad beauty. And mad self-love.

NOTE

1. British architect Jeremy Bentham invented a system of surveillance for prisons in the eighteenth century that French philosopher Michel Foucault then adapted into a concept of "panopticism" to explain the systems of surveillance in jails, hospitals, schools, and everyday life. From Michel Foucault, *Discipline and Punish: The Birth of the Prison* (Pantheon Books, 1977).

From Burning Man to Bellevue[*]
A Hero's Journey

Jeffrey Goines is not ashamed of his dangerous gifts and mad sensitivities, but he is keenly aware of the stigma and discrimination that continue to oppress people who disclose their conditions. Out of consideration for his family and his future self, he has published this piece under a pen name, providing a modicum of privacy and protecting them from casual internet searches. If you would like to contact Jeffrey, please write to the editors at beentoopatient11@gmail.com, and we can put you in touch.

. . . .

I will keep them from harm and injustice.... In purity and holiness I will guard my life and my art.

—THE HIPPOCRATIC OATH

"Apple hasn't had a genius working for them since 2011!" I growled.

The scene at Apple's flagship store on Fifty-Ninth Street and Fifth Avenue continued to escalate. It was just past 1 a.m. on a Friday night in mid-October, and I was a few drinks into the evening. To work off some of my nervous energy, I had decided this was a great time to bring

[*] First published in *Blunderbuss Magazine,* www.blunderbussmag.com, in 2014. Republished with gratitude.

my malfunctioning MacBook Air in for repair and to replace my recently deceased iPod.

The scene was fraught, and I was more than mildly tipsy. For the past few weeks my mind had phase-shifted into an altered state. Not nearly as extreme as I had experienced in years past, but one that could be described as an emotional crisis of sorts. Was I going through a nervous breakdown, a meltdown, a manic episode, or a midlife crisis? Sometimes labels make all the difference.

"If you don't get out of here, we're calling the cops," the blue-shirted Apple genius threatened. I hadn't threatened anyone or damaged any property, so I defiantly taunted, "Go ahead. Call them."

Over the past few years I have teased the Apple geniuses on more than one occasion. I've asked them how I could download the app that maps US drone attacks, one that the App Store had censored, and I've showed off my Android's FM tuner which, unlike the Apple model, uses the century-old technology of radio to avoid devouring your data plan. I considered these interventions my solo take on performance art or direct action, although admittedly they can be a bit dickish. But given that Apple's corporate policies have been systematically eroding human and civil rights, sometimes I can't help myself. While my banter with the retail staff may have been smug and inappropriate, it never crossed the line into criminal behavior.

When the police arrived I was composed and fully cooperative. I thought they would likely turn me out on the street. In cases like this, more benevolent officers have even been known to drive people home. At worst, I might face some kind of misdemeanor ticket, for mischief or disturbing the peace. I was genuinely surprised by their next move.

Instead of following any semblance of constitutional due process, the NYPD ignored my Miranda rights and proceeded to hand me off to the FDNY, who subsequently took me for a thousand-dollar ambulance ride to Bellevue's emergency room. The firemen handcuffed me behind my back in a painful stress position, banged my head a few times on the wall of the ambulance, and even mischievously tried to plant psychotic ideas in my head by claiming that their walkie-talkies didn't work and that there are no Wi-Fi or radio waves anywhere in the city.

When we arrived at the emergency room I was still handcuffed, and we waited around in discomfort for over an hour to see the attending psychiatrist. When he arrived he looked like he was sleepwalking, and my fireman escort goaded me into yelling at him to wake him up.

It was a horrifying situation—I was surrounded, restrained, and bracing myself for the inevitable. I didn't hear the order, but I knew what was coming. They stuck me with a hypodermic needle attached to a syringe filled with Haldol. Haldol is a miserable first-generation neuroleptic (a.k.a. antipsychotic), whose short-term side effects include hallucinations, sedation, drooling, compulsive pacing, diarrhea, and muscle aches. I had pleaded with the doctor and nurses to take the medication orally, since that would have cushioned the anvil-like impact of the drug on my mind and body. I knew about the federal statute mandating that patients who are willing to take medication orally can't be forcibly injected, but the law didn't protect me that night. I was left on a stretcher writhing in restraints as the delusional psychosis of the antipsychotic set in. How many patients are assaulted daily in utter disregard of the doctrine to employ the "least restrictive method of constraint?"

I barely remember awaking inside the locked ward, but I do remember what I felt as my eyes opened. Disbelief. I couldn't believe I was back again. It had been over nine years since my last hospitalization, and while I had traversed some tumultuous states of consciousness in the meantime, I had walked between the raindrops and managed my periodic emotional crises as an outpatient.

When I was a freshman in college I was diagnosed as bipolar. Sometimes I think a more accurate description for my condition is post-traumatic childhood stress disorder, and to varying degrees, we all suffer from that. Although there was a history of madness in my family, the condition of one of my close relatives was always described as a thyroid disorder—not as something with a *DSM* label. I later learned that they had been institutionalized for a year after they finished high school, and that they underwent electroconvulsive therapy for three years during my childhood. Additionally, my uncle committed suicide before I ever had a chance to meet him. He was a medic in the Korean War—Lord knows what he witnessed and endured—and jumped out a veterans' hospital window.

That freshman year was intense for me. I didn't really like my friends, and I had my heart broken by an unrequited love. Much of the fall semester, I fantasized about hanging myself with my bicycle chain. I persevered, clinging to a quote that a friend shared with me—"Sometimes it takes a lot of courage to stay alive." By the following spring, I bounced back. In fact, I bounced back like a glitter-filled Super Ball. As has happened many times since, my psychological immune system transformed my intense psychic and emotional pain into (sometimes inappropriate) giddiness, euphoria, and energy. Once I figure out how to bottle this, I'll be a billionaire. Or we'll all be locked up psych wards.

I spent that spring running around barefoot like Socrates, putting out cigarettes in my palm, going to punk shows, and expressing righteous indignation at unsuspecting (and sometimes undeserving) targets. It ended when I was brutally hospitalized, spending weeks subjected to physical and psychological violence. After two court trials and a transfer to another facility, I managed to elope during a group outing and was finally free. In a plotline lifted from the pages of a comic book, I'm an escaped mental patient who has gone on to investigate corruption in psychiatry and the pharmaceutical industry.

The system caught up with me many times over the years, and I have been institutionalized more times than I prefer to count. These experiences have been uniformly violent and traumatizing. I've never attempted suicide, and have been hospitalized only for what they call "manic" episodes. Though I have suffered from melancholy, I have developed coping mechanisms that guide me through those periods with as little drama as possible. Over the years I have developed various strategies to help manage my dangerous gifts, starting with taking care of the basics (nutrition and sleep), cultivating a peer-support network, and developing a "mad map." I have also developed the confidence to believe that "this too shall pass," and have faith that the bad will wane and the good will wax.

———

In the summer of the 2013—the months preceding my fateful trip to the Apple Store—I was yearning for a vision. I had been in an emotional desert for a while, with no oasis in sight. I had known about Burning Man for over a decade, and had always been curious but never quite sure how to pull off the logistics of spending a week in the desert on the other side of the country. Burning Man is not for the faint of body or mind. The conditions are incredibly hostile, with temperatures sometimes exceeding 110°F by day and dropping to almost freezing at night. There are blinding dust storms, and the acidic playa dust can wreak havoc on your skin. But, the experience promised to be unique—visually, socially, and experientially. I entered with eyes wide open, aware that the sleep deprivation and the sustained stimulation might be triggering. My sister played Cassandra, warning me against making the trip, and I promised her I would avoid experimenting with hallucinogenic drugs and be mindful of my emotions.

My time at Burning Man felt, appropriately, like a controlled burn. I distinctly remember feeling that I was *simulating* my psychic extremes, rather than actually experiencing them. I was simultaneously a detached observer of my emotions, while at the same time being fully present. The experience was incredible, and almost indescribable. I've compared Burning Man to a cross between *District 9, Tron,* and Dr. Seuss, but that was just my perspective. With upward of seventy thousand people in attendance, the event was a vibrant metropolis. Its attendees call that stretch of desert Black Rock City, and like any big city, its citizens each experience it differently.

It all felt like an altered state to me. Many of the costume props I had brought along were souvenirs I acquired during my episodes over the years. Impulsive shopping sprees are one of the odd characteristics of my extreme states, and I suddenly realized that all of my eccentric crap felt completely at home at Burning Man. The resonance helped me connect with those extreme states of mind and gain a bit more insight into their roots and causes. I wondered: Could I return back into the cave of my everyday life and preserve these insights once I was re-shackled, stuck staring at the dancing shadows?

On my third night, I finally ventured out into the Deep Playa, a sparse expanse of Black Rock City away from the camps, parties, and most of the people, dotted with errant sculptures and other art installations. I climbed inside a sacred geometric structure called "the transportal" that was designed to tune the passengers inside to each other's frequency. It worked. I made quick friends with former strangers, and we explored a terrain that resembled nothing so much as the far side of the moon. We came across an upside-down couch that we were convinced had teleported there from the previous year. I took one of its cushions and returned to the portal, only to find a friend of mine inside it. We hadn't seen each other all day, but he had just been complaining that his ass hurt. Somewhere along this journey of synchronicity, I had been gifted an old-fashioned skeleton key. In the context of the night, it was a master key, my key to the portal and beyond. The line between inner and outer was blurred at Burning Man, and manifesting and wish fulfillment were regular occurrences. The world was saturated with meaning, and everything was interconnected—a semantic synesthesia where every perception was infused with meaning. It was the external manifestation of some of my most intense inner journeys.

The emotional challenge of returning to the default reality post–Burning Man is a well-known phenomenon. Burners sometimes call it "reentry." In the aftermath of such utopian beauty, it's common to struggle to understand why the world must function as it does. Why don't people greet each other with hugs? Why is it so hard to meet new people? Why is sharing property so difficult? A week is just about enough time to immerse yourself in a foreign culture and begin to internalize it. From what I hear, many attendees have survived the playa, but burned up on reentry. Before for my trip I found telephone books' worth of guidance for burners on how to prepare for their trip, but next to nothing on how to prepare for the return.

I took a few days off work after Burning Man to help decompress. I booked a short stay at a hotel in Westchester that, I discovered, also served as a Pfizer training facility, like something out of *Love and Other Drugs*. Through conversations I learned that Pfizer and Monsanto used to be the same company. Somehow the magic of the playa had followed me home. There were no coincidences. Only beautiful narratives, where often I was the hero.

After the Burning Man vision quest, I realized how discontent I had become with my life, especially at work, and I flailed about desperately to effect a change. The Snowden leaks that summer only served to compound my passions and convictions, fueling my overactive imagination and leading to a sensational theory that the NSA was building a time machine. I basically threw a psychic temper tantrum as I desperately tried to process the rush of insights, emotions, and revelations.

My tantrum landed me in a locked ward, a brutal experience that I wouldn't wish on anyone. While Bellevue delivered surprising moments of empathy (e.g., while dancing to Michael Jackson's "Thriller" on a Nintendo Wii during video game therapy), overall the experience was violent, traumatizing, and humiliating. I witnessed systemic racism, abuse of veterans, and simple, old-fashioned cruelty. One gentleman who kept getting reprimanded for yelling needed a lozenge, not an antipsychotic. Most of the nurses refused to respect the gender pronoun preferences of a transgender patient and insisted on calling her "him." A Pakistani woman who spoke very little English was detained against her will and forced to miss her flight home with no explanation (or translation). Many of the people working at Bellevue were in the right ward but on the wrong side of the nurse's desk. My psychiatrist was downright combative, intrusive, and aggressive, exhibiting many of the symptoms that had gotten me incarcerated. Had I followed the behaviors she modeled, I would have been shot with a syringe full of Haldol and thrown in seclusion. It was enough to drive a sane man crazy. The nastiness and hostility of the staff was evident to all of my friends who visited the ward. I was blessed and privileged to have a steady stream of visitors, and I honestly don't know how I would have survived without them.

———

When I earned my master's degree, I donned the goofy ceremonial robes and walked with my classmates at the university-wide commencement. I distinctly remember my astonishment when I heard the medical graduates recite the Hippocratic Oath, right there on the quad for all of us to witness. I remember thinking to myself that other professionals should be required to recite oaths too, as lawyers, teachers, journalists, and others all have the power to do great harm. But, I suppose that medicine still occupies a unique place, as the power to heal is synonymous with the power to kill.

The psychiatric-pharmaceutical complex is currently violating the Hippocratic Oath. I realize that this is a heavy accusation to make, but the field has gone beyond simple or even gross negligence and has crossed the line into willful harm. Consider that pharmaceutical companies aren't bound by a coherent code of ethics—their charters don't contain anything like Google's "Don't be evil," and their employees aren't required to take the Hippocratic Oath upon hire. Their sole responsibility is to maximize shareholder value (and increasingly, that includes breaking the law as the calculated cost of running a profitable business). I'm under no delusion that adopting language like this would instantly reverse decades of malfeasance, but a formal reminder that that employees have responsibilities more important than profit seeking might help generate a few more whistleblowers in the pharmaceutical industry.

As for the systematic erosion of our civil and human rights, I'm disgusted, but not surprised. Oppressive governments of all ideological stripes have a long history of locking up dissidents with opposing views, and the production of mental illness has historically functioned as a disciplinary mechanism for hierarchical societies. Due process? One psychiatrist, with a wink to a second, can take away someone's freedom indefinitely. You may be initially locked up for being a threat to yourself or to others, but once inside, you won't be released until you can perform "normal." Thoughts become crimes, punishable by forced restraints, chemicals, and seclusion. And, even today, they are sometimes punishable by involuntary forced electroshock.

And the statistics all scream that it's getting worse, but in slow motion so not too many people notice. I keep meeting people who were pulled into the psychiatric system at younger and younger ages—twelve, eight, and even as toddlers. Law enforcement and others in positions of authority are increasingly fearful and risk averse. Their skittish paranoia has claimed collateral damages. Curiosity and difference are viewed with suspicion, and risk itself has been pathologized as psychiatry begins to preventatively diagnose and treat a new generation of customers.

It feels like deviance is being corralled and relegated to temporary autonomous zones like Burning Man in an attempt to suppress these instincts and confine them to the margins. But, just as antibacterial soap has a tendency to select for superbugs, I am optimistic that these acts of suppression will yield a new wave of resistance. Whoever survives this attempted genocide on creativity and deviance will emerge stronger, strong enough to help transform the madness that passes for mainstream rationality into a permanent autonomous zone. In a world where violent, self-destructive, and even suicidal policies are regarded as sane, it's the captains of government and capital that need to be restrained. War criminals, environment destroyers, and compulsive usurers walk free while those who speak truth to their power are incarcerated. Our consensual reality is crazy sick and desperately needs an imagination infusion.

To anyone going to Burning Man this year, please bring back some dreams. We need your inspiring craziness in the real world.

Infiltrating the Mental Health Industrial Complex

On Being a Mental Health Patient-Professional

ELISA MAGON

Elisa Magon is a Xicanx nonbinary queer trans-femme radical social worker and mad activist. Elisa firmly believes in the feminist principle "the personal is political," and, as such, identifies herself as a survivor of childhood trauma, addiction, police brutality, and the mental health industrial complex. She received her BA in psychology and her master's in social work. She has a lifelong background in community organizing.

. . . .

Introduction

For most of my history, the two most consistent things in my life were activism and addiction. My experiences with activism and healing from addiction would greatly inform my recovery from my mental health crisis. What informed my healing and recovery consisted of three milestones of healing. The first milestone was realizing that my childhood trauma circumscribed my life's circumstances of using substances to cope with being an incest survivor and my shame surrounding my sexual orientation and exploring my gender identity. Within the first milestone, I shifted my beliefs of people who suffer from drug addiction as "addicts" to *victims* of drugs, which gave me both insight and radical compassion for those individuals.

The second major milestone was the realization that I was a victim of both police brutality and the mental health industrial complex. This acknowledgment led me to the path to resolve the shame and stigma connected with those experiences. The third major milestone was my introduction into radical mental health, which guides me to break down the division between the patient and the professional. Radical mental health is my therapeutic methodology. This is my journey of how I arrived at my clinical theoretical orientation of radical mental health and application of the model of neurodivergence.

The Patient-Professional Paradox

The mental health industrial complex (MHIC) functions on a division between mental health "professionals" on the one hand and mental health "patients/clients" on the other. Mental health professionals are composed of individuals who hold titles, such as "therapists," "psychiatrists," and "social workers," with abbreviated letters before and/or at the end of people's names, like PsyD, PhD, LCSW, or LMFT. These titles grant mental health professionals the authority to diagnose and label individuals as possessing a psychiatric and psychological disability. Patients and clients are individuals who have been diagnosed with a mental health or psychiatric disorder, such as bipolar, depression, or schizophrenia.

Supposedly, these mental health professionals are individuals who do not possess a psychiatric diagnosis or suffer from mental health problems. Mental health "professionals" are psychologically "stable" whereas mental health "patients" are psychologically "unstable." "Patients" and "professionals" are supposedly two distinct types of people. This division separating patients from professionals is rooted in hierarchies based on class, race, and ability. Supposedly, a person cannot be a patient and a professional at the same time or in the same space. But I embody both identities and experiences. On the one hand, I earned a bachelor's degree in psychology and a master's in social work (MSW) and have worked as a mental health therapist for over four years serving youth, families, and adults with severe mental illness. On the other hand, I have gone through substance abuse treatment four times from my early adolescence into early adulthood. I was introduced to "the rooms" of Alcoholics Anonymous (AA) at the age of thirteen. Shortly after obtaining my MSW, I experienced a drug-induced mental health crisis during which I was beaten and tasered by the police, and psychiatrically hospitalized against my will. "Schizoaffective disorder" is prescribed as my diagnosis. I regularly see a psychiatrist and a therapist, and I have been taking psychiatric medication ever since my mental health crisis.

I identify myself as a social worker, a case manager, a clinician, and a therapist. I align myself with the history of the helping profession of social work and psychology. Notwithstanding this, I also self-identify with the history of the mad movement, the anti-psychiatry movement, and the movement to reframe mental health issues as neurodiversity. I self-identify as neuroatypical, a mad activist, a psychiatric survivor, and a survivor of police brutality and of the MHIC. This brings me to what I would like to name as the *patient-professional*.

The patient-professional is a person who has lived experience with mental health issues, and who is in an official position as designated by a system in which they work to support patients or clients. In recent decades, the mental health care system has seen and institutionalized different types of patient-professionals in mental health care. We now see a wide variety of employment positions at different mental health clinics and programs, such as peer-support counselors, family coaches and/or advocates, and/or mental health advocates.

The mental health care system has seen the significance of how someone with lived experience with mental health issues is in a position to assist other individuals who suffer similarly. The idea is that someone who suffers from mental health issues may relate more to someone else who has lived experience with similar issues and is in recovery. The idea and institutionalization of the patient-professional begs fundamental questions about the division between these two communities of people that are epistemological and intersectional.

If the mental health industrial complex stipulates that those who are mental health "professionals" are psychologically "stable," and those who are "patients" are psychologically "unstable," then my existence as patient-professional is a paradox. To be a patient-professional is to inhabit a body, a mind, a space, and a place between the binary of the patient and the professional. It means I know what it is like being labeled with diagnosis, and I know what it is like labeling others with a diagnosis. I understand the experience of being stigmatized for possessing a psychiatric disability, and I understand the legitimate resistance of clients with whom I interact who vehemently reject the idea that they are "mentally ill." Being a patient-professional means I utilize clinical language and the terms of the biomedical model of psychiatry and contemporary psychological theory among my colleagues when talking about clients. It also means I attempt to use everyday language when speaking with clients to assist them to cope with their psychiatric disabilities. Navigating this division between the patient and the professional is a task that, I find, requires almost instinctive complexity, creativity, and nuance. But becoming a radical social worker and mad activist did not happen overnight.

Activism and Addiction

Before I experienced my mental health crisis, my world was activism and addiction. All throughout high school, I was in student clubs, such as a Latinx academic club, the Gay-Straight Alliance, and a feminist club. Through college, I took my studies and activism very seriously. My undergraduate major was psychology. I also took as many Ethnic Studies classes as I could, studying the plight of communities of color and social movements. I rigorously engaged in college campus activism through Movimiento Estudiantil Chicanx de Aztlán (MEChA), where I helped provide college campus tours for Latinx high school students; hosted Latinx-focused events and workshops on Latin American history and social movements; facilitated male allyship and gender circles; supported local community-based initiatives; and organized with other student of color organizations regarding campus culture and policies. Despite positive life lessons I learned about organizing, my life was riddled with drug addiction itself and the consequences that came as a result.

During my freshman year of high school, I was suspended for possession of marijuana. My parents then sent me into adolescent drug rehabilitation. I stayed sober until junior year of high school, but then I started smoking weed again, and more habitually. I continued to smoke into freshman year of college. Quickly, I got suspended from college for getting caught with possession of marijuana three times in the dorm rooms. After this, I was required to leave the dorms. Throughout this time, my parents suffered from seeing me reap of all of these consequences from my drug addiction.

After I graduated, I took a year off school, basically just smoking and drinking every day. Shortly around that time, my parents told me that I needed to take care of my drug addiction or move out. So, I completed adult outpatient rehab to appease their demands. However, I wasn't serious about being clean and sober at that time, and I continued to use drugs that were undetectable to the weekly toxic screen test. My parents found out I was still using drugs, and they asked me to leave, so I did. Nine months later, I was living on my own, working an overnight job, and deep in my addiction. It was not too long after that mental health symptoms began in in my life. I experienced delusions of grandeur surrounding the community organizing I was doing at that time, and I developed paranoid delusions about the police and government. I was in a manic state many times in a given week for about half a month. It was at that point that I experienced a drug-induced mental health crisis during which I was beaten up by the police, tasered three times, and psychiatrically hospitalized against my will for six days.

The process of being forcibly hospitalized really shook me. I was sent to John George Psychiatric Hospital for thirteen hours. In 2016, Fox KTVU reported on the inpatient conditions at John George through leaded video footage and anonymous interviews from staff personnel. The news report highlights that this emergency psychiatric facility was originally designed for twenty-three patients, but exceeded a capacity of seventy to eighty patients. People often slept and ate on the ground. An internal audit conducted by Alameda County Health Systems reported a staff-to-patient ratio of one to six. Staff in the interview said the ratio is even more daunting with twenty patients to every nurse and seventy patients for every doctor. These conditions made vulnerable folks even more vulnerable when, in 2005, a patient hung themselves, to which the Alameda County Grand Jury found "a failure to hire enough nurses to provide up-to-date care" in the emergency unit.[1]

I can personally attest to how the inpatient conditions there are horrendous. When I arrived, there were forty people, mostly Black and Brown folks, sleeping on chairs or on the floor waiting to be assessed and discharged. I was given a small cot to place on the floor where I slept for the night. I was also given a packaged sandwich for breakfast. Folks who were actively suicidal, delusional, and psychotic were crammed into a room half the size of home and expected to stabilize themselves. But it's hard to stabilize oneself when there are people shouting and talking to themselves all around.

Only one year previous to my psychiatric hospitalization, I was shadowing a therapist to visit a client at this same psychiatric hospital as part of my internship. Now, I *was* the inpatient. At that moment I said to myself, "Oh shit, I was trained to be professional in places like this. Yet here I am, a patient. How did I end up here?" I realized in that moment I had mentally able-bodied privilege, or that I had lost it. I had always recognized the privileges of class, skin color, and masculinity, but I suddenly saw what able-bodied privilege meant. I had never thought of myself as having mental health issues. But now I did. I was a member of society designated as a threat to myself and others. I was designated as a person who was "abnormal" and required the "care" of "professionals."

I was then transferred to a psychiatric inpatient unit. Most of my experience there was a blur because I was in an altered state. I remember getting up in the morning to eat breakfast and then spending about forty-five minutes in the outside rest area playing basketball with other inpatients or playing table tennis by myself. The living conditions at the inpatient unit were only slightly better than John George. While an inpatient, I witnessed the residential staff physically assaulting another man and forcing him to take medication. This only aggravated my altered and paranoid mental state. The most important and memorable thing that I did was request a mental health advocate. This mental health advocate provided me with support by empowering my voice as a patient. I met with this mental health advocate three times, and they helped me schedule two meetings with residential staff to make sure that I was getting out as soon as possible, and to communicate that I was being a "good" inpatient—I was displaying compliant behavior and taking my medication. This person helped me so much because they assisted me in gaining some control over my situation. I was an inpatient at this psychiatric unit for six days and then released into an outpatient drug treatment clinic. My healing began immediately after that, but it took about three years for me to really recover.

After I was released from the inpatient unit, I went into outpatient substance abuse treatment. It was in substance abuse treatment that I relinquished three secrets to my family that I realized were contributing to my addiction and my eventual mental health crisis: (1) I was an incest survivor, (2) I was bisexual, and (3) I was gender nonbinary. I remember I coordinated a family session with my drug counselor where I came out to my mother. I told my mother that I wanted to wear women's clothes and wear makeup. My parents remained silent on my gender identity for two years, and I was too afraid to bring it up. Within those two years, I went to AA meetings twice a day and worked the twelve steps. By the end of that second year, I was able to get my first job as a social worker. By three years after my mental health crisis, I told my parents that I was serious about socially transitioning. Their response was not very accepting. They told me I had to move out in three months. They told me that I had already put them through enough with my addiction. But in my mind, all I heard was, "We don't care that you are an incest survivor, or that less than six months ago you were waking us up in the middle of the night because you were having images of cutting your wrists." So, I moved out.

Within the period between my mental health crisis and disclosing to my parents about wanting to socially transition, I did a lot of introspection, not only personally for my healing, but politically for my self-empowerment.

These self-realizations were related to my experiences with childhood trauma, with police brutality, drug abuse, and being exposed to the framework and experience of neurodiversity. These self-realizations were not only major milestones of my healing, but would serve as fundamental milestones of becoming a radical patient-professional.

From Victim to Survivor to Advocate

Now that I had a clean and sober mind, I was able to reconnect with what had I learned during my undergraduate and graduate studies about trauma and drug addiction. I was able to connect with what I had learned as therapist and social worker and start applying it to myself. For example, social science research is demonstrating more and more how people who experience trauma and oppression throughout their lives are predisposed to substance abuse and mental health issues. This is true for me. I realized that my childhood trauma circumscribed my life, and made me become an alcoholic and drug addict to cope with being an incest survivor and my shame surrounding my sexual orientation and exploring my gender identity.

Within this major milestone in terms of healing related to my drug addiction there was also another layer of a learning opportunity. When watching the movie *Malcolm X* again when I was getting sober, one specific scene spoke to me: Malcolm X makes a commitment to never drink or use drugs again as a vow of abstinence against the colonizer's many tools of oppression. A light went on in my head, and I realized that drugs and alcohol are a tool of colonization, and a means to socially control people by leading them down the path of self-destruction and self-harm.

Through reflecting on my work and my Ethnic Studies background, I also watched a documentary about the Black Panthers, which portrayed a former Black Panther who took a leading role in educating the Black community about the devastating impact of drugs. He described drugs as a form of chemical warfare against his community. It was after this documentary that I began reading as much as I could about the intersections between drugs, political oppression, and communities of color. I read about the Opium Wars; the creation of crack cocaine by the Central Intelligence Agency to fund the Contras in Nicaragua; how the drug war in Third World countries is utilized as a pretext to displace indigenous peoples from their lands so corporations can appropriate their resources; and how the political pretense of the War on Drugs was leveraged to suppress the liberation movements of communities of color in the late '60s. These were all things I had already learned in my undergraduate years when I was in addiction, but now that I was clean and sober my personal experience shifted my consciousness.

I shifted from seeing myself as a drug "addict" to seeing myself as a *victim* of drug addiction. I moved beyond conceptualizing drug addiction as a disease to understanding it as a form of structural violence, and a politically motivated system to socially control people. I began to see drug victimization as a structural form of violence from this basis: (1) people experience a form of trauma that a majority of the time is both structural and interpersonal, sexual, racial, or economic; (2) they use drugs to cope with this trauma; (3) their use of drugs morphs into an addiction that then co-opts their livelihood, which results in damaging consequences; (4) society then blames them for using drugs instead of holding the root of accountability in the interpersonal/structural trauma that victimized them in the first place; and, thus, (5) the structural/interpersonal trauma that victimized them continues to reproduce itself by blaming the victim.

Instead of society-at-large facilitating a situation where survivors of trauma can resolve and reconcile their trauma on their own or with their community, through a vast complex of structural forces, drugs and alcohol are introduced into the lives of these same trauma survivors, actively suppressing their potential for healing. If people who are the most impacted by intersectional and interpersonal trauma cannot heal themselves and hold accountable those who are responsible for their victimization, then the culturally hegemonic trauma that they first, or repeatedly, experienced is never addressed. Civil rights activist and writer James Baldwin said, "The victim who is able to articulate the situation of a victim has ceased to become a victim: he or she becomes a threat." In my opinion, that's what drug victimization does: it neutralizes and prevents the potential for someone who is a *victim* of trauma to transform themselves into a *survivor* of it, which would then lead them to become an *advocate:* a person who can articulate, resolve, and fight against the oppression they have experienced all their lives. This was all true for me as an incest survivor and a queer and nonbinary trans person being in the closet.

This major milestone in my healing provided me with an opportunity to realize a few things about working with clients who suffer from drug addiction. Whenever I begin working with a client and learn they have substance abuse problems, the first question I ask myself is, "What trauma did they experience that drove them to use drugs to cope with their trauma?" I also keep at the forefront of my mind that people who are addicted to drugs are individuals who are seriously hurting on the inside. They are individuals who have experienced an event so traumatic that they use drugs to cope to hide the shame and embarrassment of that trauma, and specifically to mask the self-blame and self-hate they internalized as a result of no one addressing or taking accountability for that trauma. They feel so alone with their trauma and they feel they cannot share it with anybody. When I work with folks who suffer from substance abuse, they are fixated, legitimately so, on how they have been hurt in life. My role is to facilitate a space where they can gradually move through their hurt.

My work with folks who abuse substances is not so much to motivate them to go into substance abuse treatment. If that's what they want, then I help them achieve that goal. But if it's not their goal, then all I do is simply hold space for them and listen to their stories. Gradually, I attempt to converse with them in subtle ways to begin chipping away at those various forms of self-hate and self-blame they have internalized. My goal in talking with folks who experience substance abuse is to attempt to create some spaciousness around various internal and external factors that are often so confounded it is hard to perceive their interdependence: past traumas, current triggers, the desire to self-medicate, loss of agency. Through this process, people gradually reflect on what agency they do have in various areas of their lives.

Overcoming Shame through Structural Analysis

My second major milestone in my journey of healing was my realization of the trauma I experienced with the police the night of my psychiatric hospitalization. There is a growing conversation regarding the intersections between mental health issues, substance abuse, and state violence. We hear the stories of police murdering and assaulting folks with psychiatric disabilities or folks who are experiencing mental health crises, specifically Black folks and dark-skinned people of color. In many cases Black and Brown people are murdered because of their mere existence, and police officers perceive Black and Brown bodies as a threat. There are also other cases of police brutality where the victim of color is experiencing a mental health crisis and the police are quick to use violence, or kill them, instead of de-escalating the situation. In 2013, Black Lives Matter emerged as a movement and community, and it was in that same year that I first got clean and sober. Because of Black Lives Matter and other movements combating police brutality, I was able to reflect with heightened awareness upon my experiences of being beaten up and tasered by the police.

I realized that I was a victim of police brutality, which was hard to admit. Some people have responded to my story negatively by saying, "Well, of course you were beaten up by the police for being drunk and disorderly. You should have expected that to happen." The tone and assumption underlying this comment implies that people who experience mental health and substance abuse issues should expect violence to be inflicted against their own person and body. If it were not for these movements and conversations about police brutality, I would be overwhelmed by shame and guilt. I would think I had "deserved" to be physically assaulted by the police. But I am not obligated to think this way.

I have "swept my side of the street," as they say in Alcoholics Anonymous (AA), and I fully acknowledge my behavior of acting "erratic" while intoxicated and with psychological instability. Yes, people do experience crises wherein they may pose a serious harm to themselves and others. However, police should be trained to respond to mental health crises. Their tactical priority should be to engage in crisis de-escalation instead of violence. I did not deserve to be pummeled to the ground multiples times, repeatedly punched in the face, and tasered multiple times. I was a person in distress, and I should have been treated in a caring and nurturing way when I was most vulnerable. This realization regarding my victimization by the police was the second milestone in my healing. It was in the middle of these two milestones of healing and self-actualization that I became exposed to what would truly change the way I perceived both my own mental health and how I view my work as a social worker and therapist: the concept of *neurodiversity*.

Neurodiversity and Radical Mental Health

I don't quite remember how I found out about The Icarus Project, but I did. Through The Icarus Project, I learned about the intersections between madness and creativity. I learned about the history and traumas of psychiatric hospitalizations. I reread Michel Foucault's work on asylums and psychiatry, which I had read in undergrad, but now I returned to it with a more personal interest. I learned about reframing mental health "signs" and "symptoms" as altered states of consciousness, and as different mental and psychological ways of being in the world that should not be medicalized. This then led me to the framework of disability justice.

When I read about other people's experiences with involuntary psychiatric hospitalization, I had to also apply that hard fact to myself. I had to admit that I was not only victimized by the police but also by the mental health industrial complex. I realized that John George is not a facility that adequately treats folks experiencing crises. I learned that when I saw the inpatient staff assault a man and force medication on him, this was a standard practice within inpatient hospitals. I also read about the critiques of the dominant paradigm of psychiatry and psychology, the biomedical model. I have come to understand the biomedical model as created and funded by the pharmaceutical industry in order to make massive capitalist profits off drugging people. Lastly, I learned that mental health is in and of itself its own radical intersection, just as much as the lived experiences of race, class, or gender. Learning about radical mental health influences my work as a patient-professional in many ways, specifically with self-disclosure. I use self-disclosure as a small way to break down the division between the "patient" and the "professional."

As a patient-professional, I have to be very careful about disclosing my story and history. Rarely do I disclose my whole history. I do not mention my childhood trauma history, my experience with police brutality, or my psychiatric hospitalization. I do not disclose this because it would be inappropriate for me to do so. It would be inappropriate because my history is a lot for anyone to handle, even for me to talk about. The clients I work with are already going through enough as it is, so hearing specific details about my trauma is the last thing they need.

When I do disclose my story, I tell my clients only that I have a "diagnosis," that I take my medication, and that I am in recovery from drugs and alcohol. I do not share which diagnosis I have, or which drugs I used, or which medication I take. Most clients who are receiving services can infer from the little I tell them because they are, a majority of the time, in a similar situation, and they can connect the dots given what they have been through as well.

Right after I disclose my story, I also make sure to tell them, "Everyone's story is different, and my story may be different from yours." I say this to let them know a few things: everyone's situation is different, the way those around you support you is different, and everyone's journey from healing is different. I also disclose so little because my journey in healing has taught me that self-identification with another person is a contributor to healing, but not the only one. I never disclose my history to a client thinking that just by me telling them my story they will automatically start healing. Far from this. And I would caution anyone not to think so naively. Most importantly, I am able to disclose what little personal history I can only because my supervisor and my place of work have sanctioned it.

The traditional therapeutic/social worker model functions through the therapist being a "blank slate." As a therapist, I am supposed to be a nonperson, a person without a history. I am not supposed to disclose anything about my personal identity or history, except maybe superficial things. Therapists are trained to use self-disclosure only when it is clinically appropriate, which means when it may facilitate the client relating to the therapist in a way that can facilitate valuable insight about the client's internal world or identity. The mental health industrial complex has institutionalized the role of the "patient" and "professional" so strongly that clients do not expect their "professional" to be a person who has been through similar things.

Disclosing too much of my personal history may inadvertently damage my relationship with clients. It may damage the relationship because they may feel an urge or pull to attend to my emotional needs and provide me with emotional care. *Mutual aid* names the process through which two people who have lived experience with mental health share their experience of healing and the knowledge they have acquired through that healing. Mutual aid is when two or more people consent to engage in the process of mutual self-disclosure to facilitate each other's healing. Mutual aid is a tool of radical mental health. While self-disclosure may be a small way by which I attempt to break down the division between the "patient" and the "professional," I am mindful of the limitations of this radical approach.

The clients I work with have not intentionally entered a radical contract of mutual aid, and so disclosing to them my history untactfully may imply to them that I am inviting them into this type of process. My role is to assist clients to achieve their goals in healing, not for them to facilitate my healing or create an emotionally safe space for me. While I await the days that radical mental health—specifically the tools of mutual aid and peer-to-peer support—becomes an equal and equitable method of mental health care equivalent to the "professional-patient" relationship, those days are far from here. My attempts to disclose my story to clients are small and strategic moments where I attempt to break the division between the "patient" and the "professional." Lastly, I want to refrain from providing any concrete recommendations about when or when not to use this tactical self-disclosure. Knowing when to self-disclose is an organic process.

Beyond this small radical method of self-disclosure, my understanding of radical mental health informs my work in other ways. When I work with clients who are neuroatypical, I don't assume that they want to take medication or that they want to see a psychiatrist. I seek to build a relationship with them, offering assistance in obtaining basic needs and supportive resources, and offering a listening ear. This is a way I build rapport with them. I do mention to them that I can connect them with mental health resources such as therapy, psychiatry, and case management, but I only offer these resources to them. I don't impose or coerce them to accept these resources.

As a social worker, I was afforded the opportunity to create a brochure for the clients I work with. In this brochure, I refrain from talking about my clients' mental health issues in terms of "mental illness." Instead, I articulate the experience of neurodiversity from a strengths-based perspective. I describe neuroatypical experiences and invite them to consider if these experiences are a blessing or if these experiences are becoming too overwhelming. In this brochure, I write the following:

> Neurodiversity is a range of behaviors, attitudes, beliefs, and lifestyles experienced by individuals who some people may see as "different." These "differences" may include, but are not limited to, hearing voices, seeing things other people can't see, believing in things other people don't believe, using drugs, and sudden bursts of physical and mental energy.

> Many people experience these "differences," but are ashamed to talk about them. This shame is a response to what is called mental health stigma. Stigma causes people to feel embarrassed and ashamed of their differences. This then leads people to use drugs excessively or creates conflict with a person's family members. Some people consider these differences as hurtful because they don't want to believe, hear, or see things other people can't. Other people view them as helpful and a gift. My goal is to help you figure out what is helpful or hurtful about your differences and how I can support you in coming to resolve any conflicts in your life.

I also elaborate in this brochure the experience of how trauma impacts people to then experience a deep sense of pain and suffering, and the consequences that manifest as a result of this unresolved trauma and pain. In the small section entitled "The Power of Pain," I write:

> Pain can be overwhelming. Pain is a result of trauma. Trauma can include rape; racial and gender discrimination; parental divorce; death in the family; community violence; or witnessing a traumatic event. When trauma is

not resolved, pain causes people to be in a constant state of hypervigilance; not trusting others; difficulty establishing long-term relationships; trouble concentrating; and sacrificing significant long-term priorities for immediate gratification. Many people turn to drugs to cope with their own personal trauma. Most importantly, unresolved trauma can contribute to people making decisions in their life which can create more harm for themselves.

I also attempt to provide some hope with these descriptions of unresolved trauma and pain by writing a short section entitled "Turning Pain into Power." In it I write:

> To turn pain into power one must confront one's trauma which can be done in many ways and is not easy, and takes time. It can be done through creative ways, such as writing, art, poetry, film, or dance. We will not judge you or blame you for your pain or suffering. I am here to listen to your story as I connect you to other resources you may want or need.

I certainly recognize the limitations of this brochure, and that it is not a complete answer to all of their problems. However, I would say this brochure is one of my first "clinical interventions" when working with clients. This sets the stage for my work with them to be from a place of radical compassion and acceptance. When I give it to clients to read, I attempt to accomplish a few things.

I contextualize for clients how I approach what my potential work and services might be with them. I introduce the concept of radical mental health without saying it. I name the experience of neurodiversity and invite them to consider if their neuroatypical experiences are helpful in their lives or if they are causing stress and conflict; I let them know that I can create a safe space for them to help them figure that out. Through this brochure, I acknowledge the realities of trauma and how deep pain and suffering is the response to unresolved trauma. I also acknowledge various forms of trauma, which can be structural or interpersonal. And lastly, I invite them to consider that methods of resolving trauma are not solely restricted to therapy and psychiatry, but different forms of art and expression.

My journey in healing has taught me about the process of turning pain into power. The victimizations I experienced, which are rooted in childhood trauma, drugs, police brutality, and cis-straight supremacy, I thought, were random occurrences of bad luck. However, I have been able to understand that my experiences were part of a concerted effort of societal oppression operated through interpersonal and structural violence and trauma. I now see my role in life is to contribute to the process of healing and recovery, on personal, social, cultural, and political levels. My role as a social worker is to facilitate the process whereby the clients I support can make similar connections that I made in my life as a basis for empowerment. I will continue to navigate what it means to be a patient-professional, a mad activist, and a therapist. It is through this complex and nuanced awareness that I am best able to serve myself and the clients I work with.

NOTE

1. Simone Aponte, "2 Investigates: Leaked Video Shows Mental Patients Sleeping, Eating on John George Hospital Floor," *KTVU*, May 4, 2016, www .ktvu.com/news/2-investigates/2-investigates-leaked-video-shows-mental-patients-sleeping-eating-on-hospital-floor.

On Becoming a Politicized Healer

JACKS MCNAMARA

Jacks McNamara is a genderqueer healer, teacher, artist, and writer based in Santa Fe, New Mexico. Jacks offers somatic coaching, intuitive counseling, and wellness mentoring to clients locally and across the world via Skype. In 2002 they co-founded The Icarus Project, an international support network and participatory adventure in mutual aid and radical mental health. Jacks is the author of *Inbetweenland,* a collection of poetry, and co-author of *Navigating the Space between Brilliance and Madness,* and their life and work is the subject of the poetic documentary film *Crooked Beauty.* Jacks loves to help all kinds of amazing people heal from trauma and transform their lives. Find out more at https://jacksmcnamara.net.

. . . .

My original background is in peer-based radical mental health, which opened up my world and created my first ever network of support, but peers did not save my life. A deeply compassionate trauma therapist and a few somatically trained trauma healing coaches saved my life. Working with them gave me deep respect for those rare professionals who have cultivated both great skill and a nuanced political analysis, and set me on a path of becoming a practitioner myself. I endeavor to hold the kind of space for my clients that was held for me, in my times of greatest need, and to be one more politicized healer in a world that has far too few of us.

My official journey with mental health began at nineteen with two hospitalizations and a diagnosis of bipolar disorder, which was supposed to be the primary cause of all of my wild emotional struggles. Medications with sketchy side effects were sold as the only solution. In the following years, I visited a host of psychiatrists who treated me primarily as a chemistry experiment and an insurance liability if I ever questioned or reduced my meds.

These encounters left me with a profound mistrust of the Western disease model of mental illness and deep resentments toward practitioners operating within the parameters of the medical-industrial complex. I sought out homeopaths, acupuncturists, psychics, Buddhist priests, and self-proclaimed shamans in my quest for relief and balance. I found community through organizing with folks like The Icarus Project and the (now defunct) Bay Area Radical Mental Health Collective. The Icarus Project is a grassroots network at the intersection of mental health and social justice that provides support, education, and mutual aid to folks living with the experiences that are commonly labeled as "mental illness." I co-founded the project with Sascha DuBrul in 2002. The Bay Area Radical Mental Health Collective was a project founded in 2005 by a group of activists in Berkeley and Oakland who hosted community dialogues, skillshares, and other educational gatherings around radical mental health. In these intrepid, DIY spaces, I met others who were self-educating, trying to figure out the world of mental health, and placing our struggles within social and political contexts that understood oppression itself as one of the primary triggers for extreme states and emotional distress. We swapped stories and traded insider knowledge about remedies ranging from antipsychotic drugs to skullcap and fish oil. We wanted to change the world and survive the process.

In 2006, I witnessed my mom die a brutal death and the Pandora's box of my lifelong traumas exploded into my daily life. At the time, I had been living in an anarchist farming collective and devouring seminal books like Judith Herman's *Trauma and Recovery* in an attempt to understand some of the patterns that ran through my life. The books made so many things make sense, and also brought me to the edge of total breakdown. After my mom died, my world disintegrated. I began struggling with daily nightmares that I was failing, over and over, to save her on the last day of her life, as well as dealing with overwhelming anxiety, panic attacks, flashbacks, dissociation, suicidality, and preverbal states. Every instance of trauma I'd been through in my life—from sexual assaults to childhood abuse—came flooding out of my system and completely overwhelmed me. My friends were burned out trying to support me, and the grisly stories I needed to tell and retell were too much for them. My peers loved me but did not have the tools to help me put my pieces back together.

Things changed one night at an Al-Anon meeting almost a year after my mom's death. As I tried to tell fragments of my story, I began to unravel at the seams, crying uncontrollably and finally talking about the things that were really scaring me, including how when I visited my parents' home I smelled my mother's dying body everywhere. After the meeting, a woman who was a therapist approached me and said it sounded like I was having olfactory (scent-based) flashbacks, and that I might have post-traumatic stress disorder (PTSD). Up to that point I had just thought I was crazy, hallucinating, and bipolar. I didn't know olfactory flashbacks existed. I also thought you could only qualify for PTSD if you were a sur-vivor of acute shock traumas like war and car accidents—somehow I didn't think my variety of lifelong struggles counted, and I didn't know anything about complex PTSD. None of the dozens of mental health professionals I had seen over the years ever seriously considered that trauma, rather than biochemistry, might be at the root of many of my struggles. This stranger reassured me otherwise and gave me the name of a colleague—a skilled and gentle trauma therapist named Noelle—and sent me on my way.

Noelle changed my life. She did not see me as broken or histrionic, nor did she attribute all my difficulties to bipolar disorder. She took me seriously, held all the horrendous stories that were too much for my peers, and nor-malized my suffering as a set of understandable reactions to extreme events. She educated me, in a nonpatronizing way, about how trauma affects the nervous system and how that impact trickles down into so many aspects of our functioning, behavior, relationships, and thought processes. She made things make sense and gave me hope that people can find stability and possibly even peace after living through hell. After two months of seeing her, I started to do a lot of research about how to become a trauma pro-fessional myself. The world needs more Noelles. But I was not ready to commit to much of anything, and later in that strange summer of 2007 I left therapy to resume my habit of moving across the world in search of the next adventure that would make life livable.

Flash forward a couple years and I had moved from New York to San Francisco to England and back to the Bay Area. My last relationship had combusted in dramatic fashion, and I decided I would finally resume the hard work of healing my various traumas so I might have a chance at ever being in a healthy long-term relationship, both with other people and with myself. A dear friend pointed me toward generative somatics (gs), an organization working at the intersection of social justice and somatic transformation. The founder, Staci Haines, is a committed activist who was very open about her history of sexual abuse and the paths through which she overcame it. Her openness instantly increased my trust in the organization and the modalities it taught. I began seeing a somatic coach from gs to help with my own trauma resolution, and after ten months enrolled in the first level of their somatics and trauma practitioner training.

What is somatics? It depends who you ask—somatics has many lineages, and definitions can be overly broad—for example, any practice related to the body—or very specific. According to gs, "somatics is a path, a methodology, a change theory, by which we can embody transformation, individually and collectively." The authors are quick to emphasize that somatics is *not* just "the 'body' add-on to psycho-therapy; it is not any 'body-based' exercise; and it is not solely 'bringing your attention to your bodily sensations.'"[1] In my experience as a student, client, and practitioner, somatics is all at once a set of practices, an orientation toward embodiment, a modality of transformation, and a mysterious sort of magic that opens space for more aliveness and alignment in how we move through the world. It is profoundly healing and can be effective in working with trauma. Trauma literally shapes us on physical, psychological, spiritual, and social levels; the path of somatics can engage them all.

When I began studying somatics, I thought it would mainly be something I brought into my existing work with groups as an organizer, facilitator, and popular educator. I had reservations about the idea of working as a trauma healing coach with individuals one-on-one, partly because I didn't know if I would enjoy it, and partly because I didn't trust myself to stay stable long enough to be an ethical practitioner. I didn't want to be unreliable for clients who were in a long-term healing process. It turns out my reservations were unfounded. When I took on my first few practice clients, I discovered that I loved one-on-one work, and as I continued to commit to my own healing process, I became stable enough to be there for folks. At the time of this writing, I've been seeing clients for six years, and some of those clients have been with me for as long as four years. I've discovered that I can indeed show up week after week, year after year, and that being a practitioner is actually incredibly grounding for me. For the sake of my clients, I become my best self. I draw on every resource I have to stay centered, present, compassionate, and intuitive in our sessions. I find that our work together requires of me every thread of wisdom I've studied and metabolized, whether it's from Buddhism, Internal Family Systems, attachment theory, or somatics. Everything I have lived through becomes useful, and while I'm quite careful about what details I actually disclose from my own life and journey—I keep a very clear container with clients that our sessions are for my clients to work through their stuff, not mine—I still draw from my experience on an internal level, and find that any degree of suffering I've made it through helps me have more insight, understanding, and empathy for those with whom I work. I identify very strongly with the archetype of the wounded healer, and find that my wounds take on a whole new depth of meaning when they help me be of service to other people.

As I've followed my winding path toward being a healing practitioner, a recurrent question has been whether to go to grad school and pursue the path of licensure as a therapist, rather than remaining an alternative practitioner outside the system. The question is complicated: as a licensed therapist, I could take insurance, see clients without the means to private pay, and get a job with benefits. I would have a job title people recognize, and a searchable listing on Psychology Today. As an independent practitioner, I must remain self-employed and economically precarious, seeing only folks who can afford my sliding scale, finding clients through creative self-promotion and word of mouth. At the same time, I have an enormous amount of freedom in how and when I work, and I do not have to acquire thousands of dollars of student debt or diagnose clients using a medical framework in which I don't believe. I'm free from the *DSM-5*, clinical exams, and HMOs. I can weave energy work, bodywork, magic, and nature into my coaching practice. As my teacher Staci once said, "every session is an art project." The options are limitless.

I have attempted to pursue a master's degree in counseling twice, and each time I have found the experience alienating and overwhelming. We study conventional texts and learn a narrative of therapy developed almost entirely by white men. My professors do not self-disclose; they investigate human development and "mental illness" from an external, paternalizing orientation. This makes it hard for me to trust them. I am wary of purely theoretical knowledge with a distinctly pathologizing bent. My teachers outside academia, by contrast, have been grounded, honest, political practitioners with lived experiences of trauma, oppression, and healing. I trust them implicitly. Within academia, it has not felt acceptable to be both a peer and a professional, and I find that my life experience, activism, and years of studying healing outside the institutional context is generally discredited or misunderstood. At the moment, the jury is out on whether I will continue jumping through the hoops necessary to get a degree and a license. At the moment, I am pretty happy to be a trauma healing coach with a full and creative practice and an abundant life.

In the context of my practice, I am not a peer. I continue to have many peer relationships in my life, whether as an organizer, student, new parent, or friend. Fellow organizers from my years at The Icarus Project continue to be some of my closest chosen family, and other peer-based groups like 12-step programs have been fundamental to my recovery and transformation as a survivor. But as a practitioner, I hold a sacred space for the healing of the people who come to see me, whether in my little office or across the world via video-chat. Our time together is their time, a time in which I see them in their wholeness and their woundedness and gently guide them in finding their ways back to themselves. In my own healing process, receiving that kind of holding and guidance has been absolutely essential. I feel called to return the gift.

NOTE

1. "What Is Somatics?," Theory: Personal and Social Transformation, Generative Somatics, March 29, 2018, www.generativesomatics.org/content/what -somatics.

Apples and Oranges

L. D. GREEN

When I was 16, I went on a mental trip.
I was convinced that if I ate oranges, everyone would know I liked girls.
    But if I chose an apple instead, I would land only in boys' beds. But this
    wasn't acid—this was

psychosis.

So I wrote this—

for every queer who spent their teenage years in fear,

and especially for the ones like me, raised on the buckle of the Bible belt,
    who felt their yearning splinter like a broken mirror: I want both!

Apples and oranges ...
But by now it seems painfully obvious to me what I should have done:

Come out, join the fun!
So I moved to San Francisco. And the minute I landed north of the
    Mason-Dixon line,

I went south ... of a girl's panty line.

But somewhere between my thighs—Still—is that Oklahoma teen
    whispering—

I'm sorry! I didn't mean to! I want—The drama club king, drunk on
    Applejack. I want only his fierce funny laughter and none of that …
    soft flute player, trilling her tongue across the passion of her breath—
    and oh if that were only my neck … but I certainly can't hold both of
    you inside my hopechest—No.

I must choose *…* **between apples and oranges.**

I can't take a girl for a whirl and make a boy my toy because that would
    destroy …

the prom picture.

And I know it sounds trite, a broken record from 1995, but I have had
    eleven years of movement away from that red dirt, and I'm telling you:

the dirty blood dust left a film on my skin. A tornado took hold of my mind,
    and said: you'll never be the same again. Competing desires pulled me
    in bipolar directions, and the weathervane spun like a journey, like a
    lesson. And all I can say now to these memories, these flashes … is to
    kiss. their. wind. *and watch them fall*

into dust, into ashes.

Because an Oklahoma storm can tear the roof off your house.
And an Oklahoma town can rip you in two.

But the air is so much sweeter after that storm is through.
And it's true, my breakdown was not a hate crime.
It wasn't my body left crucified in a Wyoming field.
But in a town where crosses are taller than water towers,
without the lord as my shepherd, I could not walk out of the valley of doubt
    into a calmer plain of existence without first falling headlong into a
    nightmare madness
that stretched my soul across a fence.

And it took Haldol, it took Zoloft …

No.

It took poetry. It took punk rock.
It took Sylvia Plath, Kathleen Hanna, and a hot Jewish dyke from
    Connecticut.
It took years before I could stand on this stage and
act. out. now. *and* **call. out. proud.**

Because when I tasted the apple, I didn't taste sin …
And when I swallowed an orange slice,
my hunger was satisfied.

So I know now whatever state I'm in, it doesn't matter if it's
South, North, West, or East
When I see fruit
I see a feast.

Where Icarus Flew

KEN PAUL ROSENTHAL

Ken Paul Rosenthal is a cinema artist and mental health advocate whose work explores the geography of madness through the regenerative power of nature, urban landscapes, and archival footage from social hygiene films. His current project, *Whisper Rapture,* is a doc-opera about the life and music of cellist-vocalist Bonfire Madigan Shive (www.whisperrapture.com).

. . . .

I stood on the bridge
I howled at the stars
Tried to deposit my madness
In a bank of fog
Tried to navigate between
My brilliance and my blues
In the space where Icarus flew
In the space where Icarus flew

I'm porous and plastered
And split to the core
I'm wired to the manic static
I've hit transparent doors
I lingered in the labyrinth
'Cause I didn't have a clue
In the space where Icarus flew
In the space where Icarus flew

They say you gotta write
Or be written upon

Seems no can read me
Seems I've become withdrawn
I broke the holey tablets
That cure was much too cruel
In the space where Icarus flew
In the space where Icarus flew

I walk into the fire
I run from the rain
The world says I'm crazy
But the world's insane
Wings of wax can melt
And wings can be renewed
In the space where Icarus flew
In the space where Icarus flew

Gravity, gravity
Pounding on trees
I'll unscrew this downward spiral
With the tools god's given me
With a pen and a paintbrush
And a map that I drew
In the space where Icarus flew
In the space where Icarus flew

The eye of a hurricane
Is blind to its limbs
No medicine can levee
The storms that swell within
Got to roll with the tide
Got to rise with the moon
In the space where Icarus flew
In the space where Icarus flew

My candle burns at both ends
It will not last the night
It waxes as it wanes although
It gives a lovely light
Crooked and beautiful
It's just my flickering mood
In the space where Icarus flew
In the space where Icarus flew

In the space where Icarus flew
In the space where Icarus flew

Occupational Therapy

CASEY GARDNER

Casey Gardner is a queer poet and educator who writes both to heal and to critique the intersections between identity and culture. She teaches with both SPARC Poetry and Digital Storytellers and has been on three National Poetry Slam teams (Palo Alto 2015, Alchemy Slam 2016, and Berkeley 2017). She is currently pursuing her master's in English education at the University of California, Santa Cruz.

. . . .

One year ago
I was in the hospital.

I asked myself what I was doing here
besides keeping myself safe
from the pill bottle next to my bed.

I couldn't sleep in that place.
They checked on us every fifteen minutes.
Yelled in the hallways.
Sometimes I still smell the formaldehyde
from the blankets and think …

Am I supposed to be there now?
Is a year enough to be healthy?

That question hangs in the air when I kiss you.
You say you need time
to learn how to love yourself
before you can love me.

3 months.
3 months until I am supposed to start
seeing my future inside of you,
3 months until I move away.
3 minutes to read this poem.

Is any of this enough?

Lately I've been hearing everyone
say the same thing:

Art is not therapy.

I introduced you to poetry
because I wanted you to get better.
I started doing poetry
because I wanted to get better.

Did I get better?

I had a panic attack before I wrote this.
I did not eat or sleep enough this week,
All things the therapist told me to focus on
Before they would release me.

I promised.
That I wouldn't fall in love
with anything that wasn't myself
And now I'm so in love with you.
I cannot eat or sleep.
Even though eating and sleeping
means my anxiety stays quiet.

I came back from the hospital
just in time to jump back into my art
like a bottle of pills.

This was a cure for a while.
But can you see how the scars on my wrists
have not quite healed over?
Can you see how afraid I am of going back
like I believe that I am still
a single serving jello cup.
A morning pill regime.
Part of me is still in a room
full of 5150s reading a poem
because this is the only way
I know how to heal.

But if I could see that therapist again,
I would tell her this:

I got into grad school yesterday.
Spent 3 months in my moldy apartment
investing in my future.

A year ago, I didn't think I had a future.
Couldn't go out in public
without hearing the voices
of all of my demons
superimposed on my friends.

I made progress.
I fixed my bicycle.
Started eating fruit.

Stopped talking to people
who want to swallow me.

When my anxiety creeps into my nightmares,
I change.

Everyone thinks I am still a little crazy.
That my chewed nails and shaking hands
still mean I am sick.

But I am so different.

Like yesterday you kissed me
and I told myself
My health is more important than this.

Last night I was supposed to write a poem
Memorize it, make it ready for a stage.

But instead,
I made cupcakes.
I played music.
And I am here writing about it now
because that is more important
than any applause.

This page has held me in its arms saying
Do you love yourself today?
And that is more important
than being the best writer
Or artist.

I am my best self.
And I am better than I was yesterday.

And we are all better than we were yesterday.

Isn't that the most important thing?
Isn't that the best poem
I have ever written?

She Wasn't Crazy

KELECHI UBOZOH

She wasn't crazy, but the world had a way of making her feel so.
You trying being a Black goth girl in Stone Mountain, Georgia.
She liked vampires and Morrissey, and how the darkness wrapped around
    her like a warm familiar blanket.
She was always too sensitive and reactive.
Felt every feeling at a high voltage.
She wasn't crazy, but she said whatever the fuck she wanted.
Spilled words from her lips like red wine on white carpets.
She left many stains.
They called her Crazy K and it stuck.
She never slept.
She crawled up fire escapes to hang off the edge.
Longingly looking down, she flirted with death.
She wanted to know if she let go, if she would be free.
She imagined a place where all the people loved her.
She wasn't crazy, but when grandma, the ultimate matriarch who kissed
    her thick eyelined face and marveled at her choice of combat boots with
    fishnets, died ...
The darkness welled up and started choking her. She wanted to stop the
world and get off.
When your world ends, but you're still alive, there is something crazy
    about that.
She was thirteen when she wrote the first suicide note, it was on a post it.
She wasn't crazy, but succinct as fuck.
She wasn't crazy, just honest. She didn't want to live.

She got messy, and a friend found the note and called her mom.
All her mom could say is, why, why, why, why baby? The words left her.
    Was she crazy? But she didn't feel crazy.

They stripped her down like an animal. Took her shoelaces, put her on
    suicide watch, while she squirmed on an uncomfortable cot.
She felt crazy then.
The psych ward for kids smelled like every hospital, bleach with the stench
    of death and disappointment.
Even in this place, there was psych ward hierarchy.
They separated the kids with eating disorders from the "crazy" kids.
The frail-looking teens never made eye contact. But the other kids got it.
They all dreamed of McDonald's french fries and getting out of this sterile
purgatory, this life-size pause button.
One day little Christine tried to open the locked door, but it wouldn't
    budge. The security guard said, "we lock it to keep the crazy people out."
    She laughed uncontrollably.

In hindsight, she could see that he was right.
Because when she left the psych ward, she created a papier-mâché
mask of glitter and light.
She smiled until her eyes bugged out. She stopped
wearing liquid eyeliner and made everyone feel comfortable.
She said all the right things, and lied about the darkness.
See, all better now!
The moment she stopped telling the truth, that was when she was truly
crazy.

PART TWO

Radical Interventions: Challenging the Biomedical Model and Stigma with the Recovery Model

What Is Radical Mental Health?*

THE MINDFUL OCCUPATION COLLECTIVE

> *Stories matter. Many stories matter. Stories have been used to dispossess and to malign. But, stories can also be used to empower and to humanize. Stories can break the dignity of a people, but stories can also repair that dignity.*

—CHIMAMANDA ADICHE

Radical mental health means conceiving of, and engaging with, "mental health" and "mental illness" from a new perspective. There are many ways to understand our psychic states, flows, and differences, and there is a rich tradition of groups and individuals that have been exploring the boundaries of these experiences for many years. What follows is a list of key principles that we find woven through this diverse movement; it is not intended to be exhaustive or universal, but more to offer an overall sense of who we are, what we do, and why.

Radical mental health is about grass roots and diversity. For so long, our psychic differences have been defined by authority figures intent on fitting us into narrow versions of "normality." Radical mental health is a dynamic, creative term; one that empowers us to come up with our own understandings for how our psyches, souls, and hearts experience the world, rather than pour them into conventional medical frameworks. For example, The Icarus Project understands people's capacities for altered states as "dangerous gifts" to be cultivated and taken care of, rather than a disease or disorder to be cured or eliminated. Indeed, by joining together as a community, they believe that "the intertwined threads of madness and creativity

---

* From www.mindfuloccupation.org. Chapter 3, Creative Commons License (Attribution-NonCommercial-ShareAlike). See end of selection for full list of contributors. Booklet also published by AK Press, reprinted with gratitude.

can inspire hope and transformation in a repressed and damaged world." It follows that any realistic approach to well-being has to begin by accepting and valuing diversity. There is no single model for a "healthy mind," no matter how many years of drug treatment, schooling, or behavior modification programs we've been put through. And without differences, there can be no movement.

Radical mental health is about interconnectedness. While mainstream conceptions of mental health and illness reduce people's experiences into brain chemicals or personal histories, radical mental health sees human experience as a holistic convergence of social, emotional, cultural, physical, spiritual, historical, and environmental elements. This interconnectedness also spirals outward with the idea that we all share this planet together—humans, animals, insects, and plants—what happens in one world affects all other worlds. We don't have to see ourselves as separate beings, but rather in terms of relationships: a part of myself "overlaps" with a part of you; if you're hurt I can be hurt too. No matter how alienated we are by the world around us, no matter how out of step, depressed, and disconnected we might feel, We Are Not Alone. Our lives are supported by the lives of countless other beings, from the microbes in our eyelashes to the people who plant our strawberries. The world is so much more complicated and beautiful than it appears on the surface. A premise of radical mental health, then, is not only that we are not left to deal with everything on our own, but that things that support our well-being can come in many different forms (they do not just have to be psychological or pharmaceutical).

The growth and strength of individuals and communities comes from our interconnectedness—we struggle and celebrate together, always.

Radical mental health is about emotional/embodied expertise. Although careful to not overly romanticize suffering or different mental states (obviously, some can be very painful and disruptive, or even fatal) we see the beauty and expertise in all of our feelings. Radical mental health is about survival—not "survival of the fittest" or survival through teeth gritting, but survival through chaos and exploration. It means observing how others support themselves—things that might seem self-destructive from afar—with compassion and understanding. Radical mental health is about opening up doors for conversation; about taking shame out of the equation. It is not about trying to fit into narrow definitions of "normal," which are always wrong anyway, because every culture, every group, every place might have its own normal. Radical mental health is about using your lifetime to learn about yourself, your loved ones, and strangers too, and envisioning and moving toward societies and ways of living that better support us all. It is about making worlds that recognize "breaking down" as a meaningful, important part of life that must be attended to, tended to, and not necessarily fended off. Radical mental health is about listening to and learning from the expertise of our feelings and bodies.

Radical mental health is about new languages and cultures. Language is powerful. It can open the world up like sunrise and it can block out the sky like prison walls. We have other people's language in our heads and on our tongues. The medical authorities offer us all kinds of words to talk about ourselves and the troubles we have, like "depression" and "psychosis." Sometimes these words help us look back on our lives with a new way of understanding what was going on, but too often these words end up putting us in sad, separate boxes where we feel like there's something wrong with us and we can't connect to anyone else. Words like "disorder" and "disease" offer us one set of metaphors for understanding the way we experience our lives through our unique minds and souls, but it is such a limited view. We think in language, constantly filtering all our perceptions through the available structures of words and metaphors in our brains—in many senses the available metaphors create our reality. If we can change the metaphors that shape our minds, we can change the reality around us. We need to get together and find language for our stories that makes sense to us; to unlearn social conditioning about what it means to be "sick" and "healthy." We should feel empowered to create words that better reflect our personal experiences. Some of us have reclaimed the terms *mad* or *madness* as no longer negative, but rather, as a proud statement of survival.

Radical mental health is about challenging the dominance of biopsychiatry. The biomedical model of psychiatry, or "biopsychiatry," rests on the belief that mental health issues are the result of chemical imbalances in the brain. It is an idea that is wrapped up in the same ideology of the marketplace that has cut our social safety nets and fragmented our communities—that is, that the problems and solutions of our lives are located solely in the individual. More and more, the belief that our disease is in our brains has desensitized us to the idea that our feelings and experiences often have their roots in social and political issues. If we are going to do anything to change the mental health system (along with the decaying economic system!) we need to begin by simply acknowledging how fundamentally flawed the current, medicalized model is—how it privileges "specialists," "professionals," and "scientists" in such a way that can undermine the expertise of personal experiences, local communities, and alternative models of well-being. In addition, a clearer distinction must be drawn between the usefulness of some modern psychiatric drugs for some people at some times, and the biopsychiatric program that shrinks our minds into brains, and our feelings into chemical reactions. Above all, radical mental health urges us to talk publicly about the relationship between social and economic injustice, the pharmaceutical industry, and our psychic well-being. As such, it is about redefining what it actually means to be "mentally healthy" not just on an individual level, but on community and global levels.

Radical mental health is about options. Some may assume that radical mental health is simply "anti-psychiatry." However, most of us take far more complicated, diverse, and nuanced viewpoints. Radical mental health may mean accepting some of the things that mainstream, medicalized models suggest for our well-being, while discarding some of the things we may not find useful, helpful, or positive. In practice, this means supporting people's self-determination for personal, ongoing decision-making, including whether or not to take psychiatric drugs, and whether or not to use diagnostic categories. Importantly, this support is done with an acknowledgment that the pressure to make more medicalized choices is significant in our society, and as such that these carry considerably more influence than, and often shout over, alternatives. In addition, while medical tools may sometimes be useful in the short term, some diagnoses turn our experiences into chronic incurable sickness, and their treatments come with their own problems that cannot be ignored. As such, radical mental health often includes taking a "harm reduction" approach (promoting strategies to reduce harmful consequences) with regard to people's use of psychiatric diagnoses and drugs. Radical alternatives to mainstream approaches celebrate multiple options and diverse forms of expertise. They value, for example, peer support, listening, dialogue, mutual aid, activism, counseling, spirituality, creative activity, community engagement, politicization, and access to more marginalized healing methods.

Radical mental health is about politics and social justice. Radical mental health understands how the tools of psychiatric intervention are embedded in broader relations of power. People in power benefit from controlling and silencing how our psyches/bodies/souls speak about an unjust world. They also see these tools as part of a powerful, global medico-industrial complex that profits from framing our experiences as chronic illnesses that require lifelong treatment. Participating in radical mental health activism might include denouncing how the pharmaceutical industry gains from creating new diagnostic categories, and agitating on a major scale for changes among mental health institutions, professionals, government policies, and insurance companies. A radical mental health lens could also mean looking at the history of psychology with a skeptical eye and researching how definitions of madness vary across time and space, how they are socially produced and have political (as well as personal) consequences. For example, the psychiatric establishment has a history of diagnosing entire groups of people who were queer, Black, women, poor, gender-variant, and/or trans, sick, and abnormal, therefore justifying forms of violence and exclusion that maintained the dominance of whiteness, cis-patriarchy, and heteronormativity.

Radical mental health then, is about returning the pathologizing gaze to our crazy-making world. Our struggles for mad justice intersect with others challenging oppressive social relations, including anti-racist, feminist, queer, decolonization, disability, antiwar, decarceration, anti-corporate, public education, and other grassroots community movements.

Radical mental health is about questioning and imagination. Radical mental health questions authorities and critiques accepted knowledge.

It draws attention to the ways that diagnostic categories and treatment regimes can be based on assumptions about science and expertise that deny the subjective and political nature of all knowledges, especially those assumptions that are embedded in powerful social and corporate structures that have a vested interest in pushing illness models of madness. Radical mental health, then, might mean critiquing some of the assumptions underpinning mainstream approaches to our psyches. For example, the concept that being a "productive member of society" means the production of certain goods, or performing certain types of jobs, even though these may serve our unjust economic structure over individual or community well-being. In addition, radical mental health is about imagining what could be. Our psychic experiences are seen as an important source of desire and possibility; a (sometimes distressing, sometimes delightful) place of learning and revolution that can be squashed or hardened when approached solely through a medical lens of fear, risk, or danger.

We need to reclaim our dreams and scheme up ways to make them happen. We need to share everything we've figured out about how to be a human being. We need to love ourselves as we are—crooked and intense, powerful and frightening, unruly and prone to mess around in the dirt—and understand that weeds are simply plants who refuse to be domesticated and displayed. We need to write new maps of the universes we share in common and find ways to heal together.

Radical mental health is about working within, and without, the bigger mental health systems. Radical mental health activists have a diversity of perspectives toward hospitalization, medication, and diagnoses. Most of us are not dogmatic about these issues, although we make a critical distinction between an individual's informed consent and a critique of the psychiatric establishment and the pharmaceutical industry. Perhaps the most radical aspect of radical mental health has to do with questioning authority and the production of knowledge. We challenge the exclusive voice of formal expertise, and demand that our stories and experiences be considered alongside the voices of professional mental health service providers, profiteers, and institutions. Along with the disability rights movement, we insist: **Nothing about Us without Us.**

We recognize that there are many people who work in mainstream mental health settings who are deeply committed to anti-oppressive practices, who are end users of mental health care, who are traumatized by working in profoundly unjust and under-resourced systems, and who aim to share hope and support with the people most victimized by those systems. As such, while being in some ways "cogs" in a highly flawed system, they (we) are also allies in any systemic change. We need each other. For radical shifts to a monstrous, complex structure can occur only through dialogue and movement across multiple forms, people, and sites.

Dandelion Roots

There are so many of us out here who feel the world with thin skin and heavy hearts, who get called crazy because we're too full of fire and pain, who know that other worlds exist and aren't comfortable in this version of reality. We've been busting up out of sidewalks and blooming all kinds of misfit flowers for as long as people have been walking on this earth.

So many of us have access to secret layers of consciousness—you could think of us as dandelion roots that gather minerals from hidden layers of the soil that other plants don't reach. If we're lucky, we share them with everyone on the surface—because we feel things stronger than the other people around us, a lot of us have visions about how things could be different, why they need to be different, and it's painful to keep them silent. Sometimes we get called sick and sometimes we get called sacred, but no matter how they name us, we are a vital part of making this planet whole.

It's time we connect our underground roots and tell our buried stories, grow up strong and scatter our visions all over the patches of scarred and damaged soil in a society that is so desperately in need of change.

Credits, Contributors, Co-Conspirators

This booklet was lovingly created by a community of authors, editors, designers, artists, and other contributors. Some of this material was remixed from existing sources, while other works were created especially for this booklet. To contact us, please write to info@mindfuloccupation.org.

Collaborative authoring and editing: Aki Imai, Becca Shaw Glaser, Cal Moen, Eric Stiens, Jonah Bossewitch, M. Osborn, Rachel Liebert, Sarah Harper, Sascha Altman DuBrul.

What's There to Be Proud Of?*

PATRICK CORRIGAN

Pat Corrigan's twenty-five-year career has led to positions as Distinguished Professor of Psychology at the Illinois Institute of Technology and as principal investigator at the National Consortium on Stigma and Empowerment (www.ncse1.org). He has been married to Georgeen Carson for more than thirty years; they live in a Chicago suburb and have two children, of whom they are immensely proud. They have a golden retriever named Cleo and like to travel together. Pat has seen more than ten psychiatrists, has been hospitalized for mental illness, has learned to master his symptoms, and has come out proud.

· · · · · · · · · · · · · · · ·

Nervous breakdowns, failures, hospitals, broken promises, cracked relationships: what is there to be proud of? I don't come easily to the notion that pride defines the experience of many people who identify themselves with mental illness and in recovery; it has been a twenty-year journey for me. However, I am certain Honest, Open, and Proud is an important vision for many. In this essay, I review evidence that supports my beliefs: some that reflects my research, some that represents my lived experience. This research has led me to create an evidence-based practice program called Honest, Open, and Proud, which was registered with the National Registry of Evidence-Based Programs and Practices (NREPP), a past effort of the Substance Abuse and Mental Health Services Administration (SAMHSA). At the scientist level I know pride is a meaningful product of recovery. At the personal level, I have experienced accomplishment and am more authentic by disclosing about my mental illness with dignity.

---

*This is an edited reprint from the Coming Out Proud curriculum (www.HOPprogram.org).

I have been studying the stigma of mental illness for more than fifteen years, having written six books on the topic as well as more than one hundred peer-reviewed articles. I head the National Consortium on Stigma and Empowerment, which has been supported by the National Institute of Mental Health (NIMH) for fifteen years. I am a licensed clinical psychologist who has set up rehabilitation programs for people with mental illness in order to help them with vocational, independent living, and health goals. During this time, I have also been beaten by the stigma of mental illness. I am a person who has struggled with and often has been overcome by significant symptoms of depression and anxiety. I know what it means to be crippled by panic on one hand—overwhelmed by stress, not being able to calm down—and overwhelming sadness on the other, literally glued to my chair and unmotivated. I have tried a variety of meds for more than twenty-five years, some helpful, others that cause wicked side effects. I know the embarrassment of going to an emergency program and having to recount my history to the psychiatry resident for the tenth time. I know the shame of being hospitalized, having my teenage children, Abe and Liz, visiting Dad, terribly confused by what was happening. My parents are blue-collar tradespeople; the mental hospital was as foreign to them as a trip to Singapore. I attended conferences for years on mental health and stigma, knowing the issues applied to me, but not standing up and out as a person with mental illness. Stigma is not just a scholarly thing for me; it's personal.

What Is Stigma?

Stigma is stereotype, prejudice, and discrimination. Public and self-stigma hamper the lives of many people with mental illness. Public stigma occurs when the population endorses stereotypes about mental illness (people are dangerous, incompetent, and responsible for their mental illness) and discriminates as a result. Many of the employment, independent living, and health goals of people with mental illness are blocked by a public that endorses prejudice. Employers do not want to hire people with mental illness or provide them reasonable accommodations. Landlords do not want to rent quality units or provide access of full support systems. Health care providers offer a lower standard of treatment. Research on this last point is particularly sobering. A study by Ben Druss from Emory University examined the practice of primary care providers in the Veterans Administration. Druss tested the degree to which veterans were referred to cardiologists if they presented with symptoms consistent with heart trouble. He found that 100 percent of patients were referred to a cardiac care clinic unless the primary care doctor knew the patient had a mental health history. In that case, only about 50 percent of patients labeled with mental illness were referred. These were not uneducated people discriminating against individuals with mental illness; these were physicians who should be fairly well educated about psychiatric disorders. This was not an irrelevant result but rather a case of life and death!

Public stigma concerned me personally. The Illinois Department of Professional Regulation asked about mental health history when I applied for my license in 1990. "Yes or no? Have you ever been diagnosed with mental illness?" I was not going to admit my history, fearing the licensing board might throw up hurdles. I could not practice in the state without the license. (Might I be risking action by the state admitting my response to the 1990 application?) Nor did I let my colleagues know. Although wounded healers are common metaphors for mental health professionals, I was aware colleagues look askance at the psychologist who cannot manage his illness. I also knew about the gallows humor that punctuates our practice. Being overwhelmed by the troubles of our clients, some professionals laugh them off with dark humor. I've personally heard professionals say: "That's just a case of the nuts running the nut house." Colleagues who were out with their mental illness were often butts of these kinds of jokes.

Self-stigma occurs when some people internalize the stereotypes of mental illness, applying those stereotypes to themselves. Self-stigma harms peoples' sense of self-esteem and self-efficacy, leading to the "why try" effect. Why should I try to get a job; someone like me is not worth it. Why should I try to live in my own apartment; I am not able. Why should I try to be a psychologist; I can't handle it. Think of self-stigma's implication for someone who is already depressed and anxious. It deepens the sense of shame that accompanies the illness. "Why try" was *the* hurdle in my life; believing I could not handle graduate school or professional jobs, I would drop out precipitously, often after only a week or two. I want to describe the depth of this problem. I dropped out of Creighton University medical school after a semester. Med school was a lifelong dream that was crushed under the demands of gross anatomy, biochemistry, and embryology. I dropped out of the PhD program in clinical psychology at Illinois Institute of Technology after a summer session. I dropped out of a National Science Foundation–funded PhD program in the philosophy of science at the University of Chicago after one week. I dropped out of an NIMH postdoc at the University of California, Los Angeles, after a year. I almost quit my first faculty position at the University of Chicago medical school after one week. I dropped out of a faculty position at Northwestern University after a year. While my wife and friends were accomplishing their goals, I was at the curb sheepishly looking on, very doubtful about my future.

Erasing stigma is not enough. We also must promote affirming attitudes: (1) people with mental illness recover—that is the rule, not the exception; (2) people with mental illness can achieve their goals; (3) mental health services should be dominated by hope. If there was a sad irony to my education, it was the lesson I learned about serious mental illness and expected poor prognosis. I learned in my class on abnormal psychology that illnesses like schizophrenia were defined by "a progressive downhill course." The expectation for people with this diagnosis was that they would end up on the back ward of a state institution, catatonic and unable to care for themselves. The kind thing, so we were told, was to prepare people and their families for this inevitability, to help them mourn their irretrievable losses. We stole hope from them! Sometimes the logic was circular. If a person diagnosed with a serious mental illness recovered, then they were never seriously ill to begin with.

Recovery is a vision of hope and accomplishment that has replaced the wrongheaded notions of poor outcome. Programs need to foster belief in recovery: inject hope right back where it belongs. Recovery did not emerge from the professional and research community. People with lived experience of mental health issues gave voice to its wisdom. I remember, as a second-year psychiatry professor in 1992, listening to Andrea Schmook tell her story of recovery and accomplishment and thinking her story was impossible. Andrea was a person with serious mental illness who had been hospitalized many times. After seeing her, however, I thought Andrea never had a serious mental illness. I falsely believed that people with the real serious diagnosis are unable to do more than work a few hours a day on a janitorial crew. But I also observed the infectious spread of her messages. Others with lived experience quickly embraced recovery, moving it from pipe dream to predominant vision of our time. Researchers, as we often do, came along later showing recovery is a factual reality. Long-term follow-up studies where people with serious mental illness were tracked for twenty years or more found a rule of thirds. A third of this group pretty much got over their mental illness like a respiratory infection, recovering and going on with life. A third managed their illness just fine when adopting the same kind of chronic disease strategies one might consider for addressing something like diabetes. Most of the last third were able to accomplish their goals when they received the kind of evidence-based treatments that comprise a competent treatment system: self-determined medication management along with supported employment, education, and housing.

Advocates need to take a step beyond affirming attitudes to promote affirmative behaviors. Most countries in the Western world now have some version of the Americans with Disabilities Act (ADA), which bans discrimination against people diagnosed with serious mental illness. Woe to the employer, landlord, or primary care provider who withholds rightful opportunities to someone because of a psychiatric label. Equally important to the ADA are provisions for reasonable accommodations. Employers, for example, need to adapt work settings so people are able to complete their job. These are affirmative behaviors. We expect employment settings to be set up so people in wheelchairs can easily access their desk or workstation. Accommodations for people with mental health issues have been slower in coming and harder to define. In fact, the ADA was in place for five years before the US Equal Employment Opportunity Commission formally stated the law applied to people with "psychiatric disabilities, not just physical disabilities." It now seems reasonable for work supervisors to consider requests from employees to move to quieter spaces, or to allow employees to adjust work periods to attend therapeutic appointments or interventions. More progressive versions of reasonable accommodations might include on-site job coaches for the interested employee, coaches who help the person adapt to in-the-day stresses, providing prompts or feedback to specific coping skills. I set up and evaluated this kind of program in Peoria, Illinois, where, for example, job coaches dropped in on a worker at a local Walmart, providing support and meeting with the supervisor in an effort to make sure all parties were satisfied. Affirmative behaviors and reasonable accommodations are not charity; they are the rightful expectations of people with mental health issues.

How Do We Erase Stigma and Promote Affirmation?

Americans, like people in most Western countries, believe education is the secret to changing social behaviors. Drug Abuse Resistance Education (DARE) is a prominent example; this program teaches children life behaviors so they have the skills necessary to avoid drug abuse in later years. My children, Abe and Liz, attended DARE at Churchill School during second and third grade. In a similar vein, education programs have been established to address other social concerns. Among these are programs meant to address the stigma of mental illness by contrasting myths with facts. Below are some examples of the educational materials developed for myth versus fact.

> Myth: People with mental illness choose to have their symptoms because they have weak character.

> Fact: Most mental illnesses are medical illnesses. People do not choose to be depressed.

The NIMH started the Decade of the Brain project in 1990 partly to tear down the stigma that rests on this myth. Mental illness is a brain disorder.

Proponents believed members of the general public exposed to this message would be less likely to blame individuals for their mental illness.

How well do education programs work? Contrary to what might be expected, findings about DARE are consistently negative and sobering; research from Harvard, the California Department of Education, and the American Psychological Association concluded DARE had no meaningful effects on drug behavior, such that the US Surgeon General in 2001 declared DARE to be an ineffective program, at times leading to a boomerang effect where impact on drug use might worsen. How about education against stigma: mental illness is a brain disorder. What is its impact? While research consistently shows the message decreases blame, it too yields a rebound effect. Members of the general public who learn mental illness is a brain disorder believe individuals with psychiatric illness do not get better. The latter belief is the more damning. Employers will not hire and landlords will not rent to people who are not getting better.

Contact is the alternative approach to challenging public prejudice and discrimination. Members of the general population who have contact with people in recovery show significant reductions in stigma. Recovery stories meant to tear down stigma usually have four components:

1. On-the-way-down messages: experiences with mental health symptoms and barriers faced

2. On-the-way-up rejoinders: despite my mental health issues I have accomplished goals

3. Stigma experiences: despite my recovery I have been victimized by public prejudice

4. Call for change: we need to stop the stigma to promote full opportunity

To determine the impact of contact versus education, my research group completed a summary of the more than seventy research studies on the approaches to stigma change in 2012. Results showed that contact with people in recovery is twice as effective as education in reducing prejudicial attitudes and discriminatory behaviors immediately following the intervention. In addition, analyses showed follow-up effects to contact are still obvious up to a month later, whereas any benefits to education return to baseline at follow-up. Let us understand the take-home message here. Power to change stigma lies in the hands of people with lived experience of mental health issues, not "experts." I have a much bigger impact on the public when I share my personal experiences of illness and recovery than when I pull out my books and talk as a professor.

Contact also seems to positively impact self-stigma. Many people who identify and interact with peers who openly discuss their mental health issues typically show less depression, more hope, and better self-esteem. Our research showed people who are out and share their stories exhibit personal empowerment and pride. For myself: I did not ever believe that I was hiding my story or have a sense of shame or something I needed to carefully guard. In part, the support of my wife and parents combated this problem. But a noticeable change occurred when I did start to disclose my story. I felt fuller, like the world was seeing me now, warts and all. I liked the complete "me" being out there.

Honest, Open, and Proud

Disclosure hits stigma and promotes recovery with a double punch. First, it weakens self-stigma. People who share their stories about their mental illness have better health and well-being. Second, it erases public stigma. Contact is the tool that undermines prejudice and discrimination. This leads to what I call the atomic bomb for erasing stigma. When we realize that our co-workers, neighbors, and fellow faith-based community members have mental illness and are in recovery, prejudices will be snuffed out. Contact needs people who are out with their mental illness.

Coming out proud? Is pride a fair word here? After all, I dropped out of school (four times), got hospitalized, had side effects, and disappointed my family. Is this an accomplishment to wear on my sleeve with honor? Depression and anxiety, what's to be proud of? Let's consider these questions from lessons learned from other marginalized and oppressed groups. Social justice advocates now realize people of color from diverse ethnic or racial backgrounds should embrace their identity and heritage. Earlier, in the 1950s, for example, some wrongly preached a vision of color blindness, that Americans should ignore skin color and view everyone similarly. This was mostly an attempt to promote the white majority while suppressing Blacks. We learned since then that Black pride is the better way to promote justice for this group. African Americans learning about their background come to cherish their history and embrace their group. Similarly, Latinos, Asians, Native Americans, and Pacific Islanders are all urged to know their culture and honor its roots. Women's empowerment leads to feminist studies. Proponents of gay rights recognize the need for the LGBTQ+ community to embrace each other with pride.

Does that hold for mental illnesses, or are things fundamentally different with us? Unlike people of color, the LGBTQ+ community, or women, isn't the number one goal of being a part of the depressed group to get out of it? When I am sad, without hope, and suicidal, I will do *anything* to erase the pain. When I started my career in mental illness—my sophomore year at Creighton University—I hurried to the counseling center in the administration building seeking the magic bullet to make the pain go away. If I become symptomatic again, I will do most anything to make it stop; I've taken my share of medication cocktails over the years, some with fairly significant side effects. I remember having to slowly walk down the stairs of Union Station one evening certain that I would fall because of the jitters from lithium. I would do so again if it would make the depression end. Mental illness? No, no, that's not me.

But somewhere along the way something changed. Mental illness became part of who I am. I am Pat Corrigan, a son, husband, father, psychologist, Irishman, Chicagoan ... and person with mental illness. When and how mental illness got added to the list I am not sure. But many people at some point include some aspects of mental illness and recovery in pictures of themselves. Not everyone does so; I would still expect most of the people I meet early in psychotherapy to believe their symptoms will remit and they will go on with life untouched. Most of the research suggests they are right. However, there are other people who, as a result of their illness, corresponding treatments, and reactions of others add mental illness and recovery to the self-statements that define who they are.

So, I am a person with mental illness. Is this something to be proud of? Definitions of pride include two components: accomplishment and authenticity. Accomplishments are defined by external criteria as well as personal goals. I was proud when I came in first for my age group at the Morton Grove 5K race. Are there accomplishments related to my mental illness for which I am proud? I've earned a doctorate in psychology and authored or edited more than a dozen books, and I am a distinguished faculty member at my university (one of only twelve among the four hundred faculty). The victories inherent in overcoming my depression and anxiety trump those accomplishments manifold. I remember being physically crushed and bent over when I got out of the hospital in 2005. I had two children in school and had to get back to work. A marathon seemed less daunting than the hurdles here. What happened if I could not hack it? What if the chairman of the department found I was missing meetings and appointments? I got through it, though, with the help of dad, also my family and good care from Dr. McSay. But my dad was amazing. He was struggling with emphysema at the time and had to ride a scooter hooked up to an oxygen bottle in the front basket. Every morning he picked me up at home and drove me to my office. He then sat in the room next to mine watching daytime TV and reading the *Tribune;* every half hour he would knock on the door and ask how I was. He took me to lunch and then home in the evening. He took me to medical appointments and to the pharmacy. He did this full time for two weeks and then slowly decreased the support. This was among the toughest times in my life. As I write this now, my heart beats fast reminding me how hard this was. Getting back on my work feet surpassed all the challenges of grad school and moving up faculty rank.

We have to be careful with ideas of pride and accomplishment. It might suggest people with mental illness need to meet some kind of hurdle to claim accomplishment: beat their symptoms entirely to score a success. For many, symptoms and barriers do not disappear totally. I personally must still be mindful of stressful events (usually at work) where anxiety spins out of control. Hence, we should not hang the victory of recovery on some kind of artificial criteria like three months without depression, or two years without hallucinations, or back to full-time work, or living by oneself in an apartment. Enlightened views of recovery base the experience on a renewed sense of hope and personally meaningful accomplishment. Accomplishment is meeting one's personally defined goals. For example, people with schizophrenia do not have to graduate college to be a success. Perhaps an associate's degree, or a certificate, or an adult education course, or a class at the local park district captures their personally defined goal. People with bipolar disorder may continue to struggle with euphoria and disinhibitions, but do so in ways that do not throw their life off kilter: no longer getting arrested or finding credit card bills well past their limit. People with depression do not have to go back to an executive position full time. Perhaps working fewer hours a week, or finding a less demanding job, or volunteering meets their goals. As previously stated, accomplishment is meeting one's personally defined goals.

Pride is also an issue of authenticity or embracing who you are. I am fourth-generation Irish American. My great-grandfather came over to the Chicago suburbs about one hundred years ago. I am fairly far removed from my Irish roots. But I am proud of being Irish American, especially every March 17 when Chicago dyes the river green. It is who I am, a part of my story that stands out for me. People who know me over time hear me sing "Danny Boy" or share stories about one of my trips to the ole sod. My favorite among these was a few years ago when I was in Dublin for Saint Patrick's Day. That is a holiday of pride for the Celts.

I share an extra personal admission about authenticity. I am a trained operant and cognitive therapist with views about good therapy based on Skinner and Beck. I once ran a training center for Illinois, visiting state hospitals to set up token economies. Words like authenticity scared me, always seeming mushy and of no real value in helping people meet real-world goals. "Authenticity" scared me until I tried to make sense of who I am—why do I need to add experiences of illness and recovery to my stories of family and professional accomplishments? Authenticity for me is the full picture, nothing hidden. I admit that in weak moments authenticity still seems a little flaky to me as a therapy goal, something an existentialist (my God) might pursue rather than an evidence-based clinician. But as a human and friend and peer, authenticity—putting it out there who I am—has immense worth.

The Honest, Open, and Proud Program

Although coming out proud and/or disclosure has advantages, we still need to be wise about disclosing. Disclosing about living with a mental illness clearly has its risks; if not, I could have skipped the past several pages about the nasty effects of prejudice and discrimination. Although I believe coming out is a good decision for some, it might not work for others. People need to make the decision carefully. To paraphrase a US Supreme Court judge, it is hard to stop the clanging bell. Once you are out, it is hard to go back in. I would like to think others would receive my story respectfully and with acceptance. But, I also know aspects of my story are juicy tidbits; excellent gossip is also likely to occur. Did you hear Professor Corrigan was once locked up in the psych unit at Evanston Hospital? For this reason, we developed the three lessons of the Honest, Open, and Proud program.

First, program participants weigh the pros and cons of disclosing: what are the benefits and the risks of sharing one's story with others? Many of us live in a compartmentalized world: for me, what happens at work can be fairly segregated from home and church. Hence, cost and benefits need to be considered by the setting. For example, program participants might be instructed to list the pros and cons of disclosing about their mental health issues at their work. My work list includes many benefits. I get to align myself with peers whose courage I admire. I share a more complete story about myself. I do not have to worry about other people discovering my secrets. I have been out publicly for about five years, so few risks are now on my list. Occasionally, I am concerned a colleague will disapprove of my disclosure. I don't particularly care about their disapproval of me, only that they might discount my science. "Corrigan's research is not rigorous because he is biased." I also have a more complex concern: I don't belong in the cadre of heroes who are out. "I have not faced 'real' mental health issues like my heroes from the ex-patient movement. My depression does not compare to someone hearing voices, I have never attempted suicide, and I was hospitalized only once. I have not earned the right to step out with those who have had greater challenges."

I am also concerned whether coming out is self-serving. Sometimes it seems that the net of mental illness and recovery includes everyone. Depression and anxiety are not rare; almost everyone has stories of overwhelming sadness, stress, and exhaustion at times in their life. They handle it quietly and with dignity, seemingly not needing to be on a platform to tell their story. I come from a stoic family where public displays are not encouraged; I recall that when I was a child, my parents never discussed with relatives how my brother, Mike, and I were doing in school or extracurricular activities, even though we both were fairly successful. Perhaps my public disclosures are self-congratulatory pats on the back.

I loathe pity, absolutely hate it. I therefore do not want to tell my story if people sympathize with me. I remember in a men's group at church once telling my story when Bob DuCharme clapped me on the shoulder and said, "Wow, Pat. You really deal with a lot. I'm impressed with everything you have done." I was ashamed and angry. "I didn't tell you this, Bob, so you would pity me." As I sit at my desk and write this now, I wonder from where these reactions come. Perhaps it reflects the stoic, Irish male I have learned to be, the person who does not like the limelight for its own sake. Perhaps it also reflects my need to open myself to the good wishes and support of others. I learned a bit more about myself while on the coming out journey.

Second, program participants consider different ways of disclosing. Some people are still not prepared to tell their story because the costs of disclosure at a specific setting far outweigh the benefits. They choose to keep it a secret. Others want to come out loud and proud, believing the more people who know their story, the more stigma will be crushed, and opportunities may open. They choose to shout their story from the rooftops. A third group is in between these extremes; they are cautious and selectively disclose. The Honest, Open, and Proud program includes strategies people might use to test the waters before sharing their stories with selected people.

Third, participants learn how to craft stories that meets their goals. There are two elements to this task.

1. People who decide to come out need to consider their goals ahead of time. People might disclose at work to obtain reasonable accommodations from supervisors, identify peers at work with similar challenges, or feel the relief of no longer hiding an important part of themselves. There are no right or wrong goals, but there is benefit to discussing one's expectations with peers in the program, obtaining feedback so the person is not sadly disappointed by their subsequent disclosure. "I thought Sharon, my co-worker, would be friendly and invite me to socialize on weekends. But she didn't."

2. People should decide what, of the many facets of their lives, might they disclose. "What do I want my co-worker to know about me?" Once again, discussing this with program peers prior to actually disclosing at work can diminish disappointments. For example, Sherry wants to tell people she tried to kill herself by hanging. Bert, a program peer, wonders whether that is a bit more information than necessary. Like goals, there is no right or wrong decision here, only the wisdom of considering one's story before sharing with others.

People should not feel compelled to tell any aspect of their story. There is no first principle on what should or should not be discussed. Generally, we suggest people coming out should not report issues that are still traumatizing or stressful for them. Most of the stressors that led me to being overwhelmed with anxiety and depression were work related. I dropped out of school and jobs because I felt the demands of the situation overwhelmed my ability to cope. "How come everyone else in med school can handle the ceaseless hours of anatomy and biochemistry? What's wrong with me?" The only way I got a doctorate in psychology was to attend a professional school part time and at nights when I could control the demands. One thing I will not discuss publicly now is current stressors at work, things that potentially might overwhelm me. They are current and raw. Admitting them will cause me more harm than benefit.

Solidarity

I learned a lot about solidarity from Abe and Liz's attitudes about the LGBTQ+ community. Abe has a T-shirt that sums it up nicely: "Gay? Fine by me." This is not so in terms of mental illness. I learned in graduate school that people should not adopt a patient identity. They should overcome their symptoms, be cured, and move on. Normalcy is the goal; pass for everyone else. I believe, however, that solidarity is a vision for coming out proud.

"I stand with mental illness." The message has several parts. Clearly there is ownership and solidarity because "I" join people with mental illness. I decide to get up out of my chair and move next to those out with their mental illness. Memorable pictures from the civil rights movement show whites stepping up and joining Blacks as they march across the Selma bridge or to the Woolworth's lunch counter together. Standing and marching are active. "I stand with mental illness" has an important double meaning. The person exhibiting the message may be saying, "I have a mental illness too." I stand here publicly showing the world. I do so proudly. The coming out proud movement seeks to upset the status quo.

Going Forward

I have said it before and I will say it again. I will do just about anything in my mental health recovery with Dr. McSay to keep the depression and anxiety from overwhelming me again. I am blessed by a wife and family who have provided infinite support and have beat my symptoms accordingly. I am sixty-three now and have a better mastery of things and, like in the past, hope my depression and anxiety are gone. I know, however, that it could rear its ugly head despite my efforts. I also know that I have been marked by my experiences with symptoms, treatments, and recovery, a mark that has proudly influenced my identity and my story. I am privileged to live in a community that has honored me by disclosing my story. I have a hope that someday everyone else will feel similarly safe and honored.

Treating Trauma through the Imagination
Therapeutic Effects of Simulation and Mimetic Induction

ALISHA ALI AND STEPHAN WOLFERT

Alisha Ali, PhD, is an associate professor in the Department of Applied Psychology at New York University. Her research examines the mental health effects of oppression, including violence, racism, discrimination, and trauma. She has studied community-based and arts-based interventions that address mental health issues in a range of marginalized populations such as male and female military veterans, residents in domestic violence shelters, clients in poverty transition programs, and immigrant/refugee women. She is co-editor (with Dana Crowley Jack) of the book *Silencing the Self across Cultures: Depression and Gender in the Social World*, published by Oxford University Press.

. . . .

Stephan Wolfert, MFA (Actors' Equity Association, Screen Actors Guild; US Army, 1986–93), is an army veteran and founder of the DE-CRUIT military veterans program. Stephan received his Master of Fine Arts from Trinity Repertory Company in Providence, Rhode Island. On Broadway, Stephan created and directed the military segments for Twyla Tharp and Billy Joel's Tony Award–winning production *Movin' Out* and has been a character coach for Cirque du Soleil's *Mystère*. He also co-created a touring Shakespeare company for Trinity Repertory Company and directed and taught acting Shakespeare at Cornell University and at Antelope Valley College, California.

. . . .

The treatment of trauma is emerging as one of the most complex and multifaceted challenges in the mental health field. For large numbers of individuals living with the aftermath of trauma and with ongoing trauma, the pathway to psychological health and wellness is a constant struggle and one that must be negotiated between options offered through the medical paradigm and through "alternatives" that are too often inaccessible from a financial perspective and under-studied from a scientific perspective. In response to such challenges, the DE-CRUIT treatment program was developed. This program was designed to meet the needs of military veterans who have experienced trauma. Since its inception, the program has expanded in part through our scientific partnership that has allowed for the collection of outcome data demonstrating its effectiveness.

In this chapter, we will outline the key therapeutic aspects of the DE-CRUIT program, with a particular focus on the ways that the program uses the human capacity for *imagination* as a psychotherapeutic element. We will also describe some of the components of the program that our scientific examination has revealed as particularly helpful for the military veterans who have gone through the treatment. Our overarching theme in this analysis is that creativity and imagination are essential ingredients of psychological health that are absent from the traditional medical model that dominates psychiatric care—ingredients that our work indicates are life transforming and even in some instances lifesaving for military veterans trying to transition back into civilian life.

The DE-CRUIT Program

I (Stephan Wolfert) began the DE-CRUIT program after discovering firsthand the healing power of Shakespeare's plays, particularly in relation to the veteran experience. The plays are full of soldiers, military veterans, and family members of veterans. I encountered Richard III purely randomly and during the depths of my traumatic stress experience—recovering from witnessing the loss of a close friend who was killed during a routine training run. Richard III and Shakespeare's other military veterans spoke to me in an elevated language about the exact suffering I was experiencing. The world of Shakespeare—structured in accordance with the Elizabethan Great Chain of Being—was a world of hierarchy and rank that I, as a member of the military world, understood instinctively. I learned that veterans from centuries ago suffered in much the same way that I have. And I learned that the ways that the military had "wired me for war" in basic training had shaped me profoundly—and yet, I had never been "rewired" in order to function in the civilian world. This process of *rewiring* is the heart of the DE-CRUIT program.

DE-CRUIT is delivered as seven three-hour weekly sessions in a format that parallels group psychotherapy. Groups of veterans come together each week and study the Shakespearian monologue form, thus learning about the timelessness of the psychological trauma they and other veterans have experienced over the ages. They then compose their own personal trauma monologues that document the trauma event that has affected them the most. This can be a pre-military, military, or post-military trauma—an important feature of the program, given that our previous research has shown that many veterans identify pre-military trauma as their most significant trauma experience (Ali, Wolfert, McGovern, Aharoni, and Nguyen, forthcoming). Each veteran will then "hand off" their personal monologue to a fellow veteran in the group who will rehearse and perform that monologue for the entire group, thereby honoring the suffering of their comrade in the group. Each veteran is also assigned a Shakespearian monologue to practice and rehearse; the monologue is selected for them based on an algorithm that matches the content of the monologue to the primary trauma they have identified as the event that has most affected them.

After the weeks of practicing and rehearsing together, the DE-CRUIT program culminates in a final performance for other veterans, friends, family, and other civilians. For this culminating performance, each veteran will perform their personal trauma monologue as well as their assigned Shakespearian monologue. This performance is designed to capture the process of *communalization of trauma*, which psychiatrist Jonathan Shay (1995) identifies as crucial to the healing of trauma for military veterans. The audience bears witness to the veterans' pain, the fellow veterans in the group support each other through the performance and through the articulation of personal suffering, and together the entire group contributes to the process of sharing, feeling, and healing.

The Therapeutic Power of Imagination in the DE-CRUIT Program

Our empirical examination of the DE-CRUIT program has shown that it significantly reduces symptoms of post-traumatic stress and depression in veterans who take part in the treatment (Ali and Wolfert 2018). We have also found significant increases in self-efficacy and significant improvements in heart rate variability and EEG function in the participating veterans (Ali and Wolfert 2018). Since analyzing these outcome variables, we have reflected on the question of what makes this treatment program so effective for healing veterans' trauma. We have identified key therapeutic elements that center around the theme of *imagination*. Below we outline three types of imagination that intersect in the treatment process of DE-CRUIT to contribute to its effectiveness in supporting veterans' psychological growth and recovery.

Imagination and Trauma

The DE-CRUIT program is informed by principles of drama therapy—specifically the use of drama therapy for the treatment of trauma (Ali and Wolfert 2016; Sajnani and Johnson 2014). As such, its creative elements comprise aspects of aesthetic distance in which veterans write about and perform their experiences of trauma through a process that *simulates* the suffering that they have undergone while not being in the actual suffering itself. This process of simulation is central to healing because it reflects the firsthand encounter with trauma while also creating an external object (in the form of a written monologue) that can be examined at a safe distance. Beyond this, seeing one's story of trauma performed by a fellow veteran allows one to forgive actions (e.g., the killing of innocent civilians during combat or the death of a comrade) when acted by another soldier that one could not forgive oneself for. This experience demonstrates the simulative process of healing in which the imagination provides an outlet for both representing and reflecting upon trauma.

Imagination and Neurodiversity

In many ways, the narratives in Shakespeare's plays follow plotlines and trajectories that are not linear or simplistic. Rather, they mimic human beings' inner world of divergent forms of consciousness, and they traverse the line between reality and unreality. This form of narration instills in us an experience of both knowing and not knowing the stories and characters because varying elements of the stories are both familiar to us and foreign to us. We call this process *mimetic induction,* based on Oatley's (2001) description of Shakespeare's use of mimesis or the simulative power of narration that allows the reader or viewer of the story to imagine themselves in the narrative (i.e., "That is me") while also being aware of being outside of the narrative (i.e., "That is not me"). This balanced perspective is therapeutic because it provides a means for us to imagine ourselves in a story and to ask ourselves what we would choose to do if faced with the same circumstances.

In the DE-CRUIT program, the use of Shakespeare provides stories in the form of complex narratives representing characters that are sometimes otherworldly (e.g., ghosts). Because the emotional impact of viewing or reading about these otherworldly beings and entities is experienced at the same level of realization as viewing traditional characters (such as princes and kings), the unreal in Shakespeare's plays feels as emotionally powerful as the "real." Such representation privileges different, diverse, and unusual ways of thinking, in much the same ways that proponents of neurodiversity privilege perspectives that arise from extreme mental states (Hall 2016). As such, part of the psychotherapeutic effect of DE-CRUIT resides in the ways that diverse and unusual experiences in Shakespeare reflect the inner worlds of those who have experienced trauma and psychological distress. This process provides traumatized veterans with a means of feeling connected to the material and also with a way of feeling understood and known.

Imagination and Incompatible Truths

The healing capacity of the DE-CRUIT program also lies in the ability of Shakespeare's verse to capture contradictory experiences simultaneously. This element is essential for reflecting the realities confronting military veterans because so much of their experience is defined by being both killers and victims all at once. Many veterans who enter the program describe the struggle with the mismatch between being treated as a hero while feeling like a murderer. Several of Shakespeare's military characters describe a similar experience. For example, Richard III's nightmare monologue is a speech of contradictions between being a military veteran who is a vilified killer and but also not a bona fide murderer. He states: "What do I fear? Myself?... Is there a murderer here? No. Yes, I am." The monologue continues with this description of contradictions: "I rather hate myself for hateful deeds committed by myself! I am a villain: yet I lie. I am not." These contradictions simulate the veteran experience of being labeled a hero while often feeling a coward.

This simulation is healing for traumatized veterans because it provides a "way in" for entering the complexity of their suffering—a suffering that rejects idealized notions of heroism while also forging a path to self-forgiveness by showing that the one-dimensional image of a hero who has not suffered is not realistic or possible (Wolfert and Ali, forthcoming). The ability of Shakespeare to represent co-occurring contradictions is thus liberatory for the military veteran who has struggled with apparently inconsistent ideas of heroism and victimhood.

Reflections and Future Directions

As we reflect on the future of the DE-CRUIT program, we see many potential challenges. For instance, we know that most military veterans will not seek any kind of professional help or support for their traumatic stress. While this is partly due to the belief that psychological suffering is a sign of weakness, also persistent is the reality that most available treatments are simply not responsive to the needs of veterans: medications, traditional individual psychotherapy, and exposure therapy (i.e., the "treatments of choice" offered to most veterans) run the risk of contributing to the isolation and pain experienced by veterans (Caplan 2011; Shay 1995), largely because they do not make use of the group connection that can be shared by veterans based on the sense of unit cohesion that is instilled during military training and that bonds veterans together—even those who have not served together in combat (Freud 1921). This bond is what allows the DE-CRUIT veterans to support each other during the process of rehearsing and ultimately performing Shakespeare in front of an audience—something very few of them ever expected to do in their lives.

Another challenge is that treatment offerings that use creativity or the arts in any form are rarely offered to veterans in any setting. We hope to use our outcome data to reach audiences of policy makers and other decision makers to expand offerings of creative approaches for helping veterans and as a way of redefining the "evidence base" to include findings documenting the effectiveness of these approaches. As such, our partnerships between research, practice, and communities of veterans are crucial to our efforts to provide alternatives to the over-medicalized framework that has unduly shaped veterans' services in the United States.

We also believe that the creative arts can be a viable treatment approach for other traumatized populations. We aim to expand the DE-CRUIT method to offer it to women in domestic violence shelters and to other survivors of abuse. We have recently adapted DE-CRUIT for use with low-income high school students in New York City to assist them with planning their educational and career goals. We plan similar adaptations with the hope that the DE-CRUIT approach can help the healing of trauma across populations who deserve treatment options that honor both the depth of their suffering but also their capacity for psychological growth and creativity.

References

Ali, A., and Wolfert, S. 2016. "Theatre as a Treatment for Posttraumatic Stress in Military Veterans: Exploring the Psychotherapeutic Potential of Mimetic Induction." *The Arts in Psychotherapy* 50: 58–65.

————. 2018. "From Victimization to Empowerment: Using Communalized Narration to Address Military Sexual Trauma." Paper presented at the Annual Meeting of the Association for Women in Psychology, Philadelphia, March 8–11.

Ali, A., Wolfert, S., McGovern, J., Aharoni, A., and Nguyen, J. Forthcoming. "A Trauma-Informed Analysis of Monologues Constructed by Military Veterans in a Theatre-Based Treatment Program." *Qualitative Research in Psychology*.

Caplan, P. 2011. When Johnny and Jane Come Marching Home: How All of Us Can Help Veterans. Cambridge, MA: MIT Press.

Freud, S. 1921. Group Psychology and the Analysis of the Ego. London: Norton.

Hall, W. 2016. *Outside Mental Health: Voices and Visions of Madness*. Portland, OR: Madness Radio Press.

Oatley, K. 2001. "Shakespeare's Invention of Theatre as Simulation That Runs on Minds." *Empirical Studies of the Arts* 19: 27–45.

Sajnani, N., and Johnson, D. R. 2014. *Trauma-Informed Drama Therapy: Transforming Clinics, Classrooms, and Communities.* New York: Charles C. Thomas.

Shay, J. 1995. *Achilles in Vietnam.* New York: Simon & Schuster.

Wolfert, S., and Ali, A. Forthcoming. "Re-Humanization through Communalized Narrative for Military Veterans." In *The Crisis of Connection: Its Roots, Strategies, and Solutions,* edited by N. Way, A. Ali, C. Gilligan, and P. Noguera. New York: New York University Press.

Underground Transmissions and Centering the Marginalized

Collaborative Strategies for Re-Visioning the Public Mental Health System

SASCHA ALTMAN DUBRUL

Sascha Altman DuBrul is the co-founder of The Icarus Project and the author of *Maps to the Other Side: The Adventures of a Bipolar Cartographer*. He is currently the recovery specialist and trainer for OnTrackNY and the ACT Institute through Columbia's Center for Practice Innovations. His interests lie at the intersection of the public mental health system and the mad underground (http://mapstotheotherside.net).

. . . .

The purpose of this paper is to lay the intellectual foundation for the development of a new generation of mental health support services. These services will both model cooperation between clinicians and the growing Peer Specialist Workforce in the public mental health system and actively encourage the proliferation of a vibrant, independent peer-led movement that has the power to creatively influence the current culture of mental health services. This grassroots movement would express its influence *both within and outside of* the public mental health system with a common set of core principles based on self-determination and social justice.

In this paper I argue that the current peer specialist movement struggles with the co-optation of its original principles that grew out of the civil rights–inspired psychiatric survivor movement of the 1970s (Penney

2016). Like many other oppressed groups throughout history, a challenge faced by members of this growing movement is the widespread assumption of incompetence, in this case by virtue of our psychiatric diagnoses. I believe that for the growing peer recovery movement to be effective in changing the language and culture of mental health, we need to put at the center of concern *those who most suffer from systemic oppression* and have a strong collective analysis reflected in our action. To do this we have to align ourselves with the contemporary Movement for Black Lives and the growing North American social justice movements for human dignity (Movement for Black Lives 2016). At the heart of this vision is the understanding that those labeled "mad," "traumatized," "disabled," or "addicted" do, in fact, have the potential to be the most powerful leaders for profound social transformation, since we directly have experienced the very maladies that are affecting our society. I believe that by embracing this shifting power dynamic and developing effective strategies for collaboration between clinicians and those most affected, we have the potential to make profound changes in our mental health system, paving the way for healing some of the critical wounds in our society.

Historical Context

For much of its history, the mental health system has been designed by experts in the field without the critical perspective of those who use the services themselves. It is not surprising therefore that today the dominant paradigm in the public mental health system is the *biopsychiatric model* (Lewis 2010). Biopsychiatry examines mental health solely through the lens of brain chemistry, excluding social, political, and economic factors of distress and disease. It rose to dominance in the 1980s during the Reagan era of neoliberal economic policy and incorporated the increasing use of the *Diagnostic and Statistical Manual (DSM),* a seemingly objective catalogue of mental pathologies that has grown to be hugely influential in the diagnosis and medication of vast numbers of North Americans today (Moncrieff 2008). Even in the current trends in psychiatry that focus on neuroscience, neuropsychotherapy, and the plasticity of the brain, the focus remains on individual brain chemistry, with no attention or recognition given to the impact of socioeconomic factors (Lewis 2017).

This biopsychiatric paradigm has left little room for alternate views of health and wellness. It privileges the knowledge of scientists and experts and belittles the resources of local communities, families, and alternative health care practitioners (Thomas et al. 2005). It reduces human emotions and behavior to chemicals and neurotransmitters (Horwitz and Wakefield 2007) and reinforces the divide between the "consumers" and the "providers" of mental health services, further stripping agency from users of services in taking leadership in their own healing. The role of trauma in patients' suffering is de-emphasized, perhaps because it would lead to too harsh an indictment of larger social factors (Herman 1997). Where to begin with addressing these issues in our field?

Key Terms

Dandelion Vision/Underground Transmission. With the understanding that lasting change happens from below, the dandelion vision uses the pioneer plant as a metaphor for describing the way ideas come from the cultural "underground" and influence the dominant culture.

Dangerous Gifts/Mad Gifts. A potential re-visioning of the language of mental illness, the idea is that our differences might be seen as gifts rather than diseases. While some in the movement objected to the language of "danger" when describing mental illness, the language of "mad gifts" is a re-vision.

Dialogism—as opposed to Monologism. A term from Open Dialogue practice with its origins in the Russian philosopher Mikhail Bakhtin. In a literary text it refers to different tones or viewpoints, whose interaction or contradiction is important to the text's interpretation. In family therapy practice it refers to the importance of different viewpoints coming together to help illuminate the whole.

Intentional Peer Support (IPS). A training modality that grew from the informal practices of grassroots peer support, IPS is a theoretically based, manualized approach with clear goals and a fidelity tool for practitioners. This approach defines peer support as "a system of giving and receiving help founded on key principles of respect, shared responsibility, and mutual agreement of what is helpful" (Mead 2003). Intentional Peer Support understands that trauma is central to the experience of emotional distress that often results in psychiatric labeling. It is an explicitly survivor-controlled, nonclinical intervention with primarily intrapersonal and social benefits.

Mad Maps/Transformative Mutual Aid Practices (T-MAPs). Transformative Mutual Aid Practices (T-MAPs) are community-developed workshops that provide tools and space for building a personal "map" of resilience practices and local cultural resources. Each participant collaborates with the group to complete a personalized booklet (or "T-MAP") of reminder documents that can be used as a guide for navigating challenging times and communicating with the important people in their lives. Through a mix of collective brainstorming, creative storytelling, theater games, art/collage making, and breath/mindfulness practices, the group is guided through a process to develop greater personal wellness and collective transformation.

Peer Specialist. In the mental health system, "peer support" is offered by an individual who identifies as having "lived experience" with trauma, psychiatric diagnosis, and/or extreme emotional states (Western Mass Peer Network 2014). The peer specialist role initially developed out of the movement for human rights in the mental health system in the 1970s (Chamberlin 1978) and grew in power with the rise of the mental health recovery movement (Fisher 1994).

Personal Journey: From Peer to Clinician amid the Recovery Movement

The context of this paper is the growing peer specialist movement in mental health (Salzer et al. 2010) and the understanding that, if given the right set of tools and circumstances, it has the potential to be a potent catalyst in creatively evolving the culture of the public mental health system. From my background as a mental health patient, beginning with my institutionalization as a teenager, to working for many years on creative peer-support models outside the traditional mental health system, through my experience as a social work student at the Silberman School of Social Work, and now as a clinical intern on the Parachute NYC Manhattan mobile treatment team, I will attempt to reflect on the relationships between peers and clinicians and some strategies for growing a vibrant and more effective mental health system in New York City and beyond.

The Icarus Project

For more than a decade I co-developed and helped run an organization that was created to empower people, like myself, who had ended up in the mental health system and had been diagnosed with a "serious mental illness." The Icarus Project was created with the lofty mission of changing the language and culture of what is considered mental health and to empower those who saw themselves as "sick" by appreciating the potential gifts they could offer to the larger society (DuBrul 2014). We began as a website community, published a handful of crowdsourced books that were used as organizing and empowerment tools around the country, hosted art shows and workshops, and, with years of grassroots organizing and the help of some private funding, developed into an international network of peer-based support and activist groups (Bossewitch 2016). The Icarus Project proudly worked outside the traditional mental health system because all of us had directly experienced oppression at the hands of it, including forced treatment, belittling of our life experiences, and the existential sense of disempowerment that develops from being told repeatedly and condescendingly of our biologically based "dysfunction" and "disease."

The Icarus Project was determined to develop an alternative to the reductionist biopsychiatric model and traditional hospital-based care. Unlike earlier movements for change in the mental health system (Frese and Davis 1997), we were inclusive and strategic in our organizing strategy: we opened up spaces for many different perspectives and embraced self-determination and harm reduction. Everyone was welcome to participate, whether they used diagnostic language to refer to themselves or rejected the mainstream language, whether they used psychiatric medications or chose not to take drugs. We also very much took advantage of internet technology and quickly became a magnet for creative people who were alienated by mainstream society. Our gatherings and publications were full of art celebrating our life experiences (Fletcher 2015). *The key passion that brought us together was a desire to actually change the narratives we used to talk about ourselves and each other, and to envision a community where people's differences could not only be embraced but given space to shine.*

According to Bossewitch (2016) in his recent Columbia University dissertation "Dangerous Gifts: Towards a New Wave of Mad Resistance":

> The Icarus Project represents a new wave of resistance, one that shifts from the ontological questions of the definition of disease and illness, to the epistemological questions of whose stories and voices are considered in the production of psychiatric knowledge. *This insistence on full-fledged participation in one's own healing, and more importantly, in healing by and through community, represents a new modality of protest that goes beyond the discourse of human rights and individual choice.* It is a modality of protest that meshes well with our "decentralized networked-era culture" and offers a path for taking direct action in the context of mental health." (italics mine)

It was this sense of being actors in our lives, and creating new ways of living for ourselves and others, that propelled us forward and gave us a sense of purpose and community. It was a sense of outsiderness, a distrust of larger narratives about the world, that allowed us to stay out of mainstream discourse and practice alternative ideas.

Silberman School of Social Work

After twelve years of working outside the system as a peer, I made the fateful decision to go back to school and become a clinician. My personal journey led me back to my hometown of New York City as a student at Silberman School of Social Work. As a first-year student in the One-Year Residency (OYR) program, I found myself immersed in theories to help guide me in the process of thinking like a social worker.

In our Clinical Practice Lab class we were given the opportunity to think deeply about the process of direct service work from exploration to termination (Hepworth et al. 2016; Berzoff 2011), had practice writing biopsychosocial evaluations (Engel 1980), and engaged with contemporary systemic models like ecological systems theory (Berkes 2008). In my other clinical classes I absorbed the teachings of ego psychology (Goldstein 1995), object relations (Fairbairn 1952), self psychology (Kohut 2009), and attachment theory (Bowlby 2005).

In my first-semester Human Behavior and the Social Environment (HBSE) course, we were introduced to *Pedagogy of the Oppressed*, by Paulo Freire (1970), in which he argues that knowledge isn't neutral; it is the expression of historical moments where some groups exercise dominant power over others. This idea was further elaborated in our Clinical Practice Lab with the study of critical race theory (Ladson-Billings 1998), which argues that liberalist claims of objectivity, neutrality, and color blindness actually normalize and perpetuate racism by ignoring the structural inequalities that permeate social institutions. These were ideas I had thought about but by reading and discussing them in school with others some alchemical process took place that gave me more personal power to articulate my understandings. Being part of a larger institution lent power to the theories.

While all of the social and clinical theories were very rich in ideas, my real learning happened with my fellow classmates. Every student in our program was required to take a two-semester course called Clinical Practice Lab. Practice Lab was partly an attempt to create an environment where students could discuss issues of oppression openly—the intersections of race and class and gender and how they impact the clients we work with as well as ourselves. Because the OYR program was designed for people already working full time in the profession, the majority of my fellow students were women of color, Black and Latina, all with full-time jobs on the front lines at places like the Administration of Children's Services (ACS), Office of Alcoholism and Substance Abuse Services (OASAS), homeless shelters, and the juvenile justice system.

Many of my fellow students had children waiting for them at home after we finished our night classes. My real teachers at social work school ended up being my fellow classmates, discussing institutional oppression.

As a middle-class white man whose experiences in organizing have been in majority-white spaces, I found those nights in Clinical Practice Lab to be critical to my social work education.

Our first year at Silberman coincided with the murders of Eric Garner and Michael Brown, verdicts that catalyzed the Black Lives Matter movement with protests erupting in cities all over the country calling for the accountability of police.

Here is something I wrote on social media at the time:

> Just to be real: so many of my fellow students at social work school are mothers and tonight in class when we talked about the #EricGarner verdict and the #BlackLivesMatter movement three Black moms in a row started crying and talking about how terrified they are for their little boys' lives because of the police and this racist society we live in. These are women I've been learning and studying and writing papers and sharing stories with all semester and it was so painful to see their fear and rage and helplessness rise up, the looks of horror on their faces, so scared for their children's lives. Those of us who don't have to suffer this racist bullshit on a daily, those of us who don't have children of color who might just get picked up or shot by cops just for walking down the street, we need to educate ourselves and talk to other white folks to make sure they understand just how bad it is out there for so many of our fellow citizens. We need to put ourselves on the line and be in active solidarity with our brothers and sisters who suffer under the oppressive weight of this country's brutal and divisive history. This growing popular movement that's erupting in the streets is long overdue and I sure hope we can learn from the lessons of our past and do it better than our parents and take care of each other along the way. #collectiveliberation. (Sascha Altman DuBrul Facebook page)

The Need for Mentorship

One of the most important reasons I decided to go to social work school was that I desperately wanted mentorship—supervision from people wiser and older than me. After many years of navigating roles of unofficial authority in The Icarus Project, without any kind of system of ethics holding me and others accountable, I longed for clearer boundaries and the power and camaraderie of a professional group. I was grateful to find a profession, unlike other schools of therapy, where an analysis of oppression was incorporated into the healing practice and worldview. I also saw that if I wanted to have an effect on the larger culture I would need to be able to understand how people were being trained to be healers. I wanted to understand what it meant to play the role of a mental health "clinician."

My timing was fortuitous because just as I decided to work inside the system, the Peer Specialist Workforce began to grow and evolve in ways that are allowing me to bring my particular set of experiences to the table in a vocal and creative way.

What Is a Peer Specialist?

In the mental health system, a "peer specialist" is someone who has been hired because they have personal experiences with trauma, psychiatric diagnosis, and/or extreme emotional states (Western Mass Peer Network 2014). Their "specialist" status is given as an acknowledgment of hardships they have endured that cannot be taught in a training program. While peer support for people with specific medical conditions, like diabetes and cancer, focuses on coping with physical illness, peer support in the mental health system has always been associated with feelings of powerlessness within the mental health system and with activism promoting human and civil rights and alternatives to the traditional medical model (Chamberlin 1978).

The idea that someone who has been through their own mental health journey can help another person is potentially revolutionary in a system that has always relied on the authority of doctors and other clinical staff. The realization that "peers" who have struggled with mental divergence and stigma have the ability to help in ways that clinicians cannot creates a potential opening in a formally closed system: an opening that allows for a formally impossible shift in perspective. The peer role is the role of a change agent in a system needing to evolve beyond historically hierarchical relationships.

It is important to state that in the mental health context the term "peer" does not simply refer to someone who has had a similar experience as another person. In practice, peer-to-peer support is primarily about *the nature of the relationship between two people*: a mutuality that isn't possible in a traditional clinician role because of built-in power imbalances.

Conflicting Forces

The peer specialist or certified peer specialist (CPS) role in the North American mental health system is in the process of evolving, and there are many forces, some of them conflicting, that are attempting to shape its growth. There are now more than twenty-five thousand peer specialists working in North America (Wolf 2018). It has been said that the value system of the peer movement is at odds with the medical model and there are strong forces of co-optation (Penney 2016). A compelling argument can be made that cutting costs lies at the heart of the mental health system's embrace of the recovery movement. Some (Braslow 2013) compare the peer movement to deinstitutionalization: a way to cut funding for mental health services by having lower-skilled people paid lower salaries to do the same jobs. That said, the peer movement's growth around the country has paved the way for fundamental shifts in the way mental health not only is treated, but even the way it is socially conceived.

The peer specialist movement or peer recovery movement holds all of these complexities as it develops and matures, and its history will naturally affect the dynamics between peers and clinicians in the mental health workforce.

ThriveNYC—An Example of the Use of Peer Specialists

Early in 2015 mayor Bill de Blasio's administration announced a plan called "ThriveNYC," an effort to overhaul New York City's mental health care system with a package of fifty-four initiatives costing $850 million over four years. According to NY1: "[ThriveNYC] relies heavily on peer counselors, who are not mental health professionals but are already entrenched in underserved communities" (Billups 2015). Peer specialists play an important role in the vision of ThriveNYC: "Peers are a critical component of any plan to address the mental health challenges facing New Yorkers. Drawing from both lived experience and specialized training, *Peer Support Specialists have a unique ability to engage people whose needs might not be fully recognized and understood by the traditional health care workforce.*" (City of New York 2015, 61, italics mine)

According to the report: "As of January 2016, New York State is providing coverage for peer support services delivered by professionally certified Peer Specialists to adults enrolled in Health and Recovery Plans. Coverage for these services is expanding to include children beginning in January 2017. *To facilitate the expansion of these pivotal services that is being driven by these changes in State payment practices, the City will invest in the training of additional peer specialists.* This training will equip individuals who have lived experience with mental illness and substance use to take on workforce positions in the health care system and obtain their NYS Peer Specialist Certification. *The City will graduate 200 peer specialists from this program per year beginning in Fiscal Year 2017.*" (City of New York 2015, 63, italics mine)

Visionary Peer Leadership—Parachute NYC

In my second year of social work school I was given an internship at the Manhattan mobile treatment team of Parachute NYC, a cutting-edge project that has a staff mix of peers and clinicians. In 2012 the Fund for Public Health in New York, Inc., in partnership with the New York City Department of Health and Mental Hygiene's Division of Mental Hygiene, launched Parachute NYC, a citywide approach to providing a "soft landing" for people experiencing a psychiatric crisis. It is an experimental model of family therapy influenced by the Need-Adapted Treatment Model (NATM)/Open Dialogue and Intentional Peer Support (IPS) with the aim of shifting the locus of care from hospitals to community integrated care (Sadler 2015).

The team I work on is a mix of peer specialists and clinicians (three social workers, three peer specialists, a family therapist, and a psychiatrist.) We work with people who have been diagnosed with psychotic disorders and have recently been in the psychiatric hospital. But unlike a traditional medical model, we are trained to allow unpredictability and an acceptance of multiple, potentially contradictory voices.

It is a working environment marked by creativity and a tolerance of uncertainty. The egalitarian and respectful relationship between the peers and clinicians on our team is striking considering how much the power differential exists between the two groups in traditional mental health contexts. While the culture at my internship definitely has something to do with the particular individuals, I think the environment that has allowed these dynamics to flourish is created by the healing modalities and treatment models the staff have all been trained in. It gives us a common language to use and a set of guidelines that lend themselves to opening up minds and informing actions.

Importance for Social Work Practice and Education

As seen from the literature, the peer recovery movement on its own easily falls prey to the hierarchies of the mental health system. My exploratory research points in the direction that programs such as Parachute NYC hold out the hope for a socially just and effective mental health system, taking the best aspects of different worlds and adapting them to work in an evolving system. I also propose that the social work field, because of its commitment to social justice, is uniquely situated to growing this strategic development of the peer specialist and clinical roles.

Education and Evolutionary Relationships

It is clear that the peer recovery movement is having an effect on the social work landscape economically. In order for this to be a positive effect there needs to be an embracing of what I refer to as the peer/clinician evolutionary relationship. I propose the development of an explicit study of how social workers and peer specialists can collaborate. According to the literature cited above, there is a long way to go. Given the opportunity, the peer perspective has the ability to play a critically important role in making the social work profession more relevant and effective in mental health service provision.

Social Work Education

Since 2014 the Silberman School of Social Work has offered a course dedicated to giving social workers tools to examine intersecting oppressive dynamics about race, class, heterosexism, and ableism. There are similar classes in social work schools around the country. That said, there is a striking lack of awareness in most social work curricula dedicated to issues of oppression that relates to mental health diagnosis. Poole et al. (2012) use the term "sanism" to describe the ways the social work profession belittles the experience of people who have struggled with psychiatric diagnosis.

I propose that to stay relevant in a shifting and evolving mental health framework, social work students around the country be provided a curriculum that engages the possibility of peers and clinicians working together in egalitarian ways, as has been addressed in this report. Initially this could take the form of guest speakers, readings, and discussion in seminar classes, to eventually an elective class in the Health and Mental Health Field of Practice. Furthermore, there are many students of social work who have struggled and continue to struggle with their own "lived experience" related to trauma, psychiatric diagnosis, and/or extreme emotional states. Rather than continuing to perpetuate the shame and discrimination that keeps transformative conversations from happening, the social work field could lead the way in making space for those of us who, by our own personal experiences, have the ability to help evolve the current mental health system.

This research is grounded in an understanding that the mental health system has caused an enormous amount of harm to both individuals and society, and that ironically much of what gives peers their power is a shared understanding of ways they have been failed by the mental health system and society. This research is important not just because the peer movement is growing but because peers themselves have an opportunity to shift the culture of the mental health system in a positive direction. Whether they have the power to do this will depend on a number of factors, one of them being their healthy working relationships with clinicians.

Conclusion

From the beginning, both liberatory and co-optive forces have been at play within the peer movement, with the growth of peer specialists within the mental health system as well as alternative models of peer support outside of it. There are opportunities to change how mental health is addressed in our society: from an isolating, consumer-based biomedical model to one that is holistic, transformative, and socially contextualized. Transformation of the mental health system from within is dependent both on how clinicians are able to respect the expertise of peers and how peers and clinicians are able to form mutual, collaborative relationships. It is also dependent on the energy of a mental health movement outside the system that intersects with other liberation movements and brings transformative mental health praxis into all spaces of society.

References

Alanen, Y. O. 2009. "Towards a More Humanistic Psychiatry: Development of Need-Adapted Treatment of Schizophrenia Group Psychoses." *Psychosis* 1 (2): 156–66.

Alexander, M. J. 2015. "Crisis as Opportunity: The Parachute NYC-Approach and Participant Outcomes." Presentation at the 143rd APHA Annual Meeting and Exposition, October 31–November 4, 2015.

Berkes, F. 2008. "Commons in a Multi-Level World." *International Journal of the Commons* 2 (1): 1–6.

Berzoff, J. 2011. "Why We Need a Biopsychosocial Perspective with Vulnerable, Oppressed, and At-Risk Clients." *Smith College Studies in Social Work* 81 (2–3): 132–66.

Billups, Erin. 2015. "Thrive NYC: An $850 Million Overhaul of the City's Mental Health Services." NY1, November 24, 2015. www.ny1.com/nyc/all-boroughs/health-and -medicine/2015/11/23/thrive-nyc-an-850-million-overhaul-of-the-city-s-mental -health-services.html.

Bossewitch, J. 2016. "Dangerous Gifts: Towards a New Wave of Mad Resistance." PhD diss., Columbia University.

Bowlby, J. 2005. *A Secure Base: Clinical Applications of Attachment Theory.* London: Taylor & Francis.

Braslow, J. T. 2013. "The Manufacture of Recovery." *Annual Review of Clinical Psychology* 9: 781–809.

Cain, N. R. 2000. "Psychotherapists with Personal Histories of Psychiatric Hospitalization: Countertransference in Wounded Healers." *Psychiatric Rehabilitation Journal* 24 (1): 22.

Chamberlin, J. 1978. *On Our Own: Patient-Controlled Alternatives to the Mental Health System.* New York: McGraw-Hill.

———. 1990. "The Ex-patients' Movement: Where We've Been and Where We're Going." *Journal of Mind and Behavior* 11 (3): 323–36.

City of New York. 2015. *ThriveNYC: A Mental Health Roadmap for All.* https://thrivenyc .cityofnewyork.us/wp-content/uploads/2018/02/ThriveNYC-3.pdf.

Davidson, L., Bellamy, C., Guy, K., and Miller, R. 2012. "Peer Support among Persons with Severe Mental Illnesses: A Review of Evidence and Experience." *World Psychiatry* 11 (2): 123–28.

DuBrul, S. A. 2014. "The Icarus Project: A Counter Narrative for Psychic Diversity." *Journal of Medical Humanities* 35 (3): 257–71.

Engel, G. L. 1980. "The Clinical Application of the Biopsychosocial Model." *American Journal of Psychiatry* 137 (5): 535–44.

Fisher, D. B. 1994. "Health Care Reform Based on an Empowerment Model of Recovery by People with Psychiatric Disabilities." *Psychiatric Services* 45 (9): 913–15.

Fisher, D. B., and Chamberlin, J. 2004. *Consumer-Directed Transformation to a Recovery-Based Mental Health System.* Boston: National Empowerment Center.

Fleischer, D. Z., Zames, F. D., and Zames, F. 2012. *The Disability Rights Movement: From Charity to Confrontation.* Philadelphia: Temple University Press.

Fletcher, Erica. 2015. "Mad Together in Technogenic Times: A Multi-Sited Ethnography of The Icarus Project." PhD diss., University of Texas Medical Branch at Galveston.

Frese, F. J., and Davis, W. W. 1997. "The Consumer-Survivor Movement, Recovery, and Consumer Professionals." *Professional Psychology: Research and Practice* 28 (3): 243–45.

Gates, L. B., and Akabas, S. H. 2007. "Developing Strategies to Integrate Peer Providers into the Staff of Mental Health Agencies." *Administration and Policy in Mental Health and Mental Health Services Research* 34 (3): 293–306.

Goldstein, E. 1995. *Ego Psychology and Social Work Practice.* New York: Simon & Schuster.

Hepworth, D. H., Rooney, R. H., Rooney, G. D., and Strom-Gottfried, K. 2016. *Empowerment Series: Direct Social Work Practice: Theory and Skills.* Nelson Education.

Herman, J. L. 1997. *Trauma and Recovery.* New York: Basic Books.

Horwitz, A. V., and Wakefield, J. C. 2007. The Loss of Sadness: How Psychiatry Transformed Normal Sorrow into Depressive Disorder. New York: Oxford University Press.

Icarus Project. n.d. "Mission, Vision, and Principles." Accessed August 6, 2016. http://theicarusproject.net/mission-vision-principles.

Kaufman, L., Brooks, W., Bellinger, J., Steinley-Bumgarner, M., and Stevens-Manser, S. 2014. *Peer Specialist Training and Certification Programs: A National Overview—2014 Update.* Austin, Texas: Texas Institute for Excellence in Mental Health, University of Texas at Austin.

Kohut, H. 2009. *How Does Analysis Cure?* Chicago: University of Chicago Press.

Ladson-Billings, G. 1998. "Just What Is Critical Race Theory and What's It Doing in a Nice Field like Education? *International Journal of Qualitative Studies in Education* 11 (1): 7–24.

Lewis, B. 2010. *Moving beyond Prozac,* DSM, *and the New Psychiatry: The Birth of Postpsychiatry.* Ann Arbor: University of Michigan Press.

———. 2017. "A Deep Ethics for Mental Difference and Disability: The 'Case' of Vincent van Gogh." *Medical Humanities* 43 (3): 172–76.

Lindy, D. C. 2014. "Parachute NYC: An Innovative Approach to Serving People with Psychosis in New York City." Presentation at the 142nd APHA Annual Meeting and Exposition, November 15–19, 2014.

Macias, C., Aronson, E., Barreira, P. J., Rodican, C. F., and Gold, P. B. 2007. "Integrating Peer Providers into Traditional Service Settings: The Jigsaw Strategy in Action. *Administration and Policy in Mental Health and Mental Health Services Research* 34 (5): 494–96.

Mead, S. 2003. "Defining Peer Support." parecovery.org/documents/DefiningPeerSupport_Mead.pdf.

Moncrieff, J. 2008. "Neoliberalism and Biopsychiatry: A Marriage of Convenience." *Liberatory Psychiatry: Philosophy, Politics and Mental Health* 9: 235–56.

Movement for Black Lives. n.d. "A Vision for Black Lives: Policy Demands for Black Freedom, Power, and Justice." Accessed August 6, 2016. https://policy.m4bl.org.

National Institute of Mental Health. 1990. *Clinical Training in Serious Mental Illness.* DHHS Publication No. ADM 90-1679. Washington, DC: US Government Printing Office.

Nevo, I., and Slonim-Nevo, V. 2011. "The Myth of Evidence-Based Practice: Towards Evidence-Informed Practice." *British Journal of Social Work* 41 (6): 1176–97.

Ostrow, L., and Adams, N. 2012. "Recovery in the USA: From Politics to Peer Support." *International Review of Psychiatry* 24 (1): 70–78.

Penney, D., and Prescott, L. 2016. "The Co-optation of Survivor Knowledge: The Danger of Substituted Values and Voice." In *Searching for a Rose Garden: Challenging Psychiatry, Fostering Mad Studies*, edited by Jasna Russo and Angela Sweeney. Monmouth, UK: PCCS Books, 50–61.

Pernice-Duca, F. M. 2010. "Staff and Member Perceptions of the Clubhouse Environment." *Administration and Policy in Mental Health and Mental Health Services Research* 37 (4): 345–56.

Poole, J., Jivraj, T., Arslanian, A., Bellows, K., Chiasson, S., Hakimy, H., Pasini, J., and Reid, J. 2012. "Sanism, 'Mental Health,' and Social Work/Education: A Review and Call to Action." *Intersectionalities: A Global Journal of Social Work Analysis, Research, Polity, and Practice* 1 (1): 20–36.

Sadler, P. 2015. "Systems Implications of Parachute NYC—Back to the Future: Moving to Home and Community Based Services." Presentation at the 143rd APHA Annual Meeting and Exposition, October 31–November 4, 2015.

Salzer, M. S., Schwenk, E., and Brusilovskiy, E. 2010. "Certified Peer Specialist Roles and Activities: Results from a National Survey." *Psychiatric Services* 61 (5): 520–23.

Seikkula, J. 2008. "Inner and Outer Voices in the Present Moment of Family and Network Therapy." *Journal of Family Therapy* 30 (4): 478–91.

Solomon, P. 2004. "Peer Support/Peer Provided Services Underlying Processes, Benefits, and Critical Ingredients." *Psychiatric Rehabilitation Journal* 27 (4): 392–401.

Teghtsoonian, K. 2009. "Depression and Mental Health in Neoliberal Times: A Critical Analysis of Policy and Discourse." *Social Science and Medicine* 69 (1): 28–35.

Thomas, P., Bracken, P., Cutler, P., Hayward, R., May, R., and Yasmeen, S. 2005. "Challenging the Globalisation of Biomedical Psychiatry." *Journal of Public Mental Health* 4 (3): 23–32.

Tolliver, W. F., Hadden, B. R., Snowden, F., and Brown-Manning, R. 2016. "Police Killings of Unarmed Black People: Centering Race and Racism in Human Behavior and the Social Environment Content." *Journal of Human Behavior in the Social Environment* 26 (3–4): 279–86.

Turner, J. C., and TenHoor, W. J. 1978. "The NIMH Community Support Program: Pilot Approach to a Needed Social Reform." *Schizophrenia Bulletin* 4 (3): 319–49.

Walker, G., and Bryant, W. 2013. "Peer Support in Adult Mental Health Services: A Meta-synthesis of Qualitative Findings." *Psychiatric Rehabilitation Journal* 36 (1): 28–34.

Western Mass Peer Network. 2014. "Declaration of Peer Roles." www.westernmassrlc.org /images/stories/Declaration_of_Peer_Roles_2014.pdf.

Western Mass Recovery Learning Community. n.d. "Our Defining Principles." Accessed August 6, 2016. www.westernmassrlc.org/defining-principles.

Whitaker, R. 2010. *Anatomy of an Epidemic: Magic Bullets, Psychiatric Drugs, and the Astonishing Rise of Mental Illness in America*. New York: Crown Publishing Group.

Dangerous Gifts

A New Wave of Mad Resistance

JONAH BOSSEWITCH

Jonah is an educator, a technologist, and an activist who currently works at the Mental Health Association of New York City as the director of software architecture. Jonah studied communications at Columbia University and in 2016 defended his doctoral dissertation, "Dangerous Gifts: Towards a New Wave of Psychiatric Resistance," an ethnographic study of significant shifts in the politics of psychiatric resistance. He has been organizing around radical mental health issues for over a decade and cares deeply about the environment, social justice, and privacy. He earned a masters in communication and education at Teachers College, Columbia University, in 2007 and graduated *cum laude* from Princeton University in 1997 with a BA in philosophy. He blogs at www.alchemicalmusings.org.

. . . .

In August 2007 *The Onion*, a satirical publication with a track record of clever and incisive sociocultural observations, ran a story with the headline "Woman Overjoyed by Giant Uterine Parasite." The story describes the patient's happiness about the "golf ball–sized, nutrient-sapping organism embedded deep in the wall of her uterus." It also describes how this "endoparasitic ailment" is a "disorder [that] strikes without prejudice across racial, ethnic, and class lines," and its symptoms can include "nausea, vomiting, constipation, irritability, emotional instability, swollen or tender breasts, massive weight gain, severe loss of bone density, fatigue, insomnia." The author sustains a pitch-perfect deadpan tone for over five hundred words and describes the clinical dark sides of the creature "writhing restlessly inside her … robbing her of her strength and stamina." All this is juxtaposed with the patient's exuberance over the "miracle" and her excitement over telling her parents about the parasite. The readers are left to figure out for themselves that she's pregnant.

E. B. White famously claimed that explaining a joke is like dissecting a frog. "Humor can be dissected, as a frog can, but the thing dies in the process and the innards are discouraging to any but the pure scientific mind" (White 1941). While we might kill this joke through serious examination, it brilliantly captures an essential issue at the theoretical heart of the controversies surrounding mental health and wellness. This *Onion* story is one of my favorite illustrations of the challenges we face when untangling facts from values. In purely factual terms, *The Onion*'s clinical description of pregnancy is accurate. However, the framing of the pregnant woman's condition, and the cynical and deprecating attitude applied to the shared underlying facts, succinctly illustrate the power of the narrator and the dominant narrative. Most humans throughout history have greeted pregnancy as a cause for celebration, even though it carries some negative consequences, including, in premodern history, childbed fever and early death for the mother. Healthy pregnancies are not typically categorized as "disorders," even though the symptoms caused by pregnancy could very well be construed as such. Babies can feel like a disease that causes suffering, but in another narrative, the one that is culturally normed, that suffering leads to something beautiful. Through humor, *The Onion* illustrates the power of language and the ways that narratives shape and distort consensual reality.

The production of psychiatric knowledge currently shares many absurdities with the portrayal of pregnancy in *The Onion*. Psychiatry is wedded to an epistemology that is rooted in an outdated philosophy of science, clinging to a diminished conception of objectivity and wielding scientific authority as a trump card that the psychiatric-pharmaceutical establishment uses to shut down and short-circuit debate. Psychiatry is wedded to an impoverished vocabulary and refuses to acknowledge the validity of alternative descriptions and understandings of experiences. Psychiatrists insist that their diagnostic language is the privileged or even the sole legitimate way to give an account of, and an explanation for, mental reality. Laboratory data in the forms of neuroimaging, genetic sequencing, and bio/blood chemistry are offered as conclusive evidence that patients are broken and need to be fixed. These measurements are wielded to bluntly assert the necessity of psychiatric diagnoses and treatment while lived experiences are denied entry to the arena of valid evidence. The stakes here go beyond the binaries of illness or wellness—it is essential to acknowledge the real phenomena of emotional trauma, suffering, crisis, and illness. The substantive controversies are about where these lines are drawn, who is involved in drawing them, and how we should decide what to call people on either side of the line.

The anthology you are reading now collectively tells the story of an emerging wave of mental health activists, what I call the "mad underground," who challenge the assumptions underlying this drawing of lines. Mirroring similar trends in the civil rights and disability rights movements, a new generation of mad activists is struggling to assert their right to substantively engage in the conversation around our own identities and self-care. We want to participate in the production of the knowledge that governs our diagnosis and treatment, and we are questioning the very language and narrative frames used to talk about our mental health and wellness. Our arguments, made explicitly and embodied in our stories, represent a dramatic shift from the anti-psychiatry, psychiatric survivor, and consumer movements that preceded them. We assert our prerogative to narrate our own identities using our own language, and demand that experts acknowledge our subjective experiences alongside objective measurements. Our struggle echoes the enduring standoff between empiricism and phenomenology, as we strive for our experiences to be recognized as integral to the formation of psychiatric knowledge, and not simply ignored or dismissed as unscientific. We insist our experiences, captured in our stories, should be admitted as

first-class evidence in "evidence-based" research, a claim whose implications extend far beyond the realm of psychiatric knowledge construction
and mental health policy.

Participatory Paradoxes

Over the past decade the politics and rhetoric of activists organizing
around mental health issues have begun to shift dramatically. These shifts
have been simultaneously subtle and stark. Crucially, some elements of the
movement have moved away from a purely oppositional, head-butting critique of the psychiatric-pharmaceutical alliance, and their demands have
begun to focus on questions of voice. Channeling the spirit of the disability rights movement, this new generation of the mad resistance has taken
up the cry Nothing about Us without Us.

James Charlton cataloged the centrality of this phrase to disability
rights in his book *Nothing about Us without Us: Disability Oppression and
Empowerment* (1998). Charlton first heard the expression invoked by
leaders of the South African disabled people's group in 1993, who claimed
to have heard it used earlier by an Eastern European at an international
disability rights conference (Charlton 1998, 2). Two years later he saw a
front page headline in the Mexico City daily about thousands of landless
peasants marching under the banner *Nunca más sin nosotros* (Never again
without us), and adopted *Nothing about Us without Us* as the working title
of his book.

Charlton quotes Ed Roberts, a leader of the international disability
rights movement: "If we have learned one thing from the civil rights
movement in the U.S., it's that when others speak for you, you lose"
(Driedger 1989, 28), and traces the impulse behind the expression
Nothing about Us without Us to the Civil Rights Era, embodied in
works such as *Our Bodies, Ourselves: A Book by and for Women* (Boston
Women's Health Book Collective 1973) and in the widely used Civil
Rights slogan Power to the People.

On the surface the proposition Nothing about Us without Us seems
like a timid assertion, easy to satisfy. However, it has proven to be one of

the most radical demands a movement can make. It has radical implications for the ways in which human conditions are investigated and addressed. It also challenges the binary distinction between objectivity and subjectivity and calls into question the possibility of objective knowledge devoid of context.

The short phrase Nothing about Us without Us contains two occurrences of the word *us,* each with distinct meanings. The first occurrence of *us* refers to a group identity that is created and imposed by sociopolitical forces external to the group. The second occurrence of *us* refers to a group identity that has been reclaimed by the group itself, demanding their own participation in the co-construction of their own world. The second *us* challenges the very categories that underlie the first *us,* a complex feedback loop that negates an externally imposed identification and replaces it with the solidarity of self-identification. This feedback loop is common across groups engaged in identity politics, as an aspect of their identity is initially defined by others only to be reclaimed and redefined by their own advocacy.

Mad folk have traditionally occupied a paradoxical place in public discourse. By definition they are branded "irrational" and are categorically precluded from having a voice in rational public debate. In an age when people of all sorts insist that their understandings of themselves and their problems matter, how can this constituency find their voices, sustain them, and make them persuasive? Who will accept their legitimacy and listen? This problematic has shaped mental health activism throughout its history, amplifying the dynamics around "credibility struggles" that Stephen Epstein details in his analysis of AIDS activism (1996). Layered on top of the distrust of established experts, mad activists struggle to assert their own credibility. This struggle mirrors the struggles of other marginalized groups, such as women, children, African Americans, and LGBTQ+ people, who have needed to assert their own humanity, arguing for their right to speak and be heard prior to advocating for their specific issues. This emerging wave of mad resistance has begun to confront this impasse directly.

Mad Voices

In the first decade of the twenty-first century, the mad underground reinvented psychiatric resistance with a politics that deeply resonated with trends in activism and participatory culture, supported by a new generation of communications technologies. The Icarus Project, a leading organization at the forefront of this shift, developed hybrid models of peer support and direct action that were accelerated and amplified by new communicative possibilities. They mobilized around free and open-source communications platforms, and constructed architectures of participation that supported their existing commitments to access, advocacy, transparency, expression, engagement, and community building. They foregrounded their personal stories, resisting the dehumanizing power of statistics and studies, and asserting the validity and importance of their lived experiences. I call this modality of activism "narrative advocacy," a form that is expressed in part of this anthology. This rhetorical style reflects an important trend in activism exemplified by social movements including the Arab Spring, Occupy Wall Street, Black Lives Matter, and #MeToo, all of which emphasize storytelling, insisting on the dignity of their subjects and using a barrage of personal stories of rank-and-file activists to advocate for change.

Challenging psychiatric methods and paradigms, questioning the validity of pharmaceutical research, and protesting the political processes that shape mental health policy is nothing new. Activists have struggled for decades (Crossley 2006), if not centuries (Foucault 1965; Whitaker 2003), to resist the imposition of the category of mental illness for the maintenance of hierarchical societies. *Madness and Civilization* (1965) presents the historical role of mad folk as society's outsiders and identifies "power" as the mechanism that determines who is mad and who is sane. The horrors that the mad face at the hands of power are extensive and varied. From forced sterilization to insulin-induced comas, ice baths to rotational therapy, electroshock to lobotomies, and, of course, confinement and chemical swaddling. The narratives in this anthology provide a much richer account of these tortures than statistics ever will. Foucault recommends studying sites of resistance to better comprehend the machinery and contours of power, a strategy that is evident throughout this book.

In the modern period, cultural theorists such as Bradley Lewis and Jonathan Metzl have exposed the entrenched ideological and commercial interests that aggressively promote the dominant narratives that flatten minds into brains and reduce feelings to chemical reactions (Lewis 2006; Metzl 2010). In the 1990s, a wave of psychiatric resistance first self-identified as the mad pride movement emerged, advancing a more nuanced critique of mainstream perspectives on mental illness than earlier generations of anti-psychiatry activists and the consumer/survivor/ex-patient (c/s/x) movements (Coleman 2008; Morrison 2005; Crossley 2006). This emergence marked a break from the orthodox psychiatric survivor movement that came before them.

Like the gay/queer pride movement, whose name and politics directly inspired them, mad pride activists focused more on identity politics than human rights discourses. As the second-wave feminists argued, "the personal is political," and this reframing of the issues opened up powerful new avenues of critique (Hanisch 1969). This new wave of criticism did not entail any particular dogma around hospitalization, medication, or labels, but was rooted in challenging authority and the means by which knowledge is produced (DuBrul 2014). What has opened up as a result is a whole field of linguistic contestation. The term "mad pride" is problematic, embraced by some and rejected by others in our movement. Currently, there is no recognized term identified with the new wing of the movement, aside from the generic "radical mental health movement"—I call us the "mad underground." This book is an important step in helping to coalesce around a shared identity.

The radical epistemology captured in the mantra Nothing about Us without Us succinctly represents this unnamed transformative shift (Charlton 1998). Instead of simply resisting forced drugging and electroshock therapy, this new wave of mad resistance affirms an epistemology that diverges from the conventional medical model. We embrace liberation politics and stage direct actions that attempt to transform the language used to describe the mentally ill. We aspire to develop languages of compassion, celebrate our "dangerous gifts" through creative expression, and facilitate safe spaces for people to share our experiences and subjective narratives. Building on the work of earlier generations of activists who advocated for individual treatment choices and informed consent (Oaks 2006), we encourage active participation in our healing communities, and insist that our voices and stories be heard and respected alongside those of experts and professionals. We believe that we are the experts on our own lives, and psychiatry needs to act in consultation with us on decisions governing our treatment and our health.

The transformational shift in this emerging wave of resistance can be construed as a shift from advocating for a particular ontology to advocating for a new epistemology. More than a discursive face-off disputing the nature of reality, the disagreement focuses on the question of how to approach controversies and establish consensus. For example, many anti-psychiatrists and psychiatric survivors in the 1970s have argued (and still continue to argue) that there is no such thing as mental illness. The newly emerging wave of mad resistance operates on a different plane. We are more concerned with ensuring that all of the relevant stakeholders have seats at the tables of power, where our voices can be included in the production of psychiatric knowledge. First and foremost is the primacy of our own voices in the understanding of our situation and the co-creation of our stories. Crucially, our insistence on co-constructing our own identities and narratives underlies our platforms, critiques, and actions.

Medical Authorities

The psychiatric-pharmaceutical establishment rarely acknowledges challenges to their authority, but their messaging reinforces and relies on the validity of a form of scientific objectivity that can definitively distinguish between sickness and health based on observable criteria. Mainstream patient literature often explains mental illness by drawing an analogy between mental illness and diabetes, or other chronic ailments that require medical intervention (National Alliance on Mental Illness, n.d.). This comparison once again advances the notion that patients are sick and there are no lasting cures—only chronic treatments of symptoms requiring lifelong medication, despite many of the documented health risks that psychiatric drugs introduce (Whitaker 2010).

The parameters of normal and illness are defined in the *Diagnostic and Statistical Manual (DSM)*, a book published by the American Psychiatric Association (APA) whose influence extends far beyond psychiatry, throughout medicine, therapeutic services, insurance claims, and health policy. There are important differences between the diagnoses in the *DSM* and classic physiological illnesses. First and foremost, many of the diagnoses in the *DSM* lack consensus on whether the conditions described are *illnesses* deserving medical intervention or *patterns of behavior* that deviate from societal norms. Furthermore, psychological and emotional distress is incredibly complex and varied, and its causal roots are multivariate and remain shrouded in uncertainty. Some physiological disorders have clearly defined symptoms, whose underlying causes are theoretically grounded in well-established models, and can be directly measured. Others, such as chronic fatigue syndrome (Institute of Medicine 2015), irritable bowel syndrome (Ohman and Simrén 2010), or Morgellons discase (Pearson et al. 2012) currently defy simple explanation, and Western medicine struggles to treat. Psychiatry's approach toward mental distress more closely resembles the treatment of these poorly understood syndromes than the treatment of a well-defined illness such as diabetes. We still don't understand enough about mental distress to compare it with confidence to anything other than another mystery.

Diabetes is a metabolic disorder that is believed, with support from a variety of empirical observations, to be caused when the pancreas fails to create enough insulin to break down glucose, causing increased glucose levels in the blood (American Diabetes Association, n.d.). A network of beliefs and accompanying evidence have confirmed this interpretation of symptoms such as increased thirst, hunger, fatigue, blurred vision, and headaches. Psychiatry, on the other hand, is still searching for a causal model, and the *DSM*'s attempts to carve out analytic categories and constructs are regularly called into question. Some argue that many of the diagnoses in the *DSM* are actually "catch-all" categories. For example, the grab bag of symptoms associated with schizophrenic diagnoses arises from a variety of disparate causes, which may each benefit from differential treatments (Zimney 2008). Despite investing hundreds of millions of dollars into decades of research, psychiatric researchers have yet to produce a test validating psychiatric diagnosis (Valenstein 2002). In 2005 the president of the American Psychiatric Association, Steven Sharfstein, backpedaled on the profession's longstanding claim that mental illnesses are caused by chemical imbalances (Hickey 2014) and admitted that "brain science has not advanced to the point where scientists or clinicians can point to readily discernible pathologic lesions or genetic abnormalities that in and of themselves serve as reliable or predictive biomarkers of a given mental disorder or mental disorders as a group" (American Psychiatric Association 2003). The use of the term "readily discernible" hedges the profession's uncertainty about their lack of supporting evidence for the chemical imbalance hypothesis, without disavowing it entirely. In recent years, psychiatric researchers have begun to favor the language of "information processing errors" over "chemical imbalance," reflecting the dominant metaphor for understanding brain functions as computations (Rabinbach 1992). Sharfstein later wrote that "[psychiatry] must examine the fact that as a profession, we have allowed the biopsychosocial model to become the bio-bio-bio model" (2005).

The biomedical model of emotional distress attempts to definitively state the nature of this distress in objective terms. Many on the receiving end of these diagnoses feel that this claim of objectivity inhibits their ability to locate meaning in their condition by reducing it to a medical label. Despite the widespread claim that labels are purely instrumental, shorthand for doctors to communicate with each other, labels can deeply influence people's identities. Diagnostic labels make some people feel powerless and objectified, like they are "a mood disorder with legs" (Rosenthal 2010). There are always elements of a psychological state that cannot be captured by physiological measures. Diagnostic labels often ignore individual and intergenerational trauma, structural oppression and inequality, and a range of social, cultural, political, spiritual, and psychological lenses for understanding complex conditions. Some people I met described feeling that labels stripped them of their agency, absolving them of responsibility for behaviors associated with their condition or dooming them to fulfill their diagnosis. The objective authority of labels also discourages people from exploring alternative explanations for their conditions. Language matters in defining the reality of subjective states and is central in the formation of identity and meaning.

Doctors, academics, and journalists have written extensive accounts of disturbing trends in pharmaceutical expansion, and here I will only reference this history in broad strokes. In 2004, Marcia Angell, an American physician, a Harvard lecturer, and the first female editor-in-chief of the *New England Journal of Medicine*, published a book titled *The Truth about the Drug Companies: How They Deceive Us and What to Do about It*. She described watching the drug companies stray from their original mission to discover healing drugs and become "vast marketing machines" with "nearly limitless influence over medical research, education, and how doctors do their jobs." David Healy is an Irish psychiatrist and researcher who studies the relationship between antidepressants and suicide, as well as conflicts of interest between pharmaceutical companies and academic researchers. *Pharmageddon*, his most recent book, forcefully argues that drug companies' drive for profits has led them to overhype the benefits of their products and downplay their risks, often with deadly consequences (2012). Most provocatively, Peter Gøtzsche, a Danish physician and researcher, and former sales representative for AstraZeneca, convincingly compares the pharmaceutical industry to organized crime syndicates in his book *Deadly Medicines and Organised Crime: How Big Pharma Has Corrupted Healthcare* (2013). Drawing on published studies and numerous anecdotes, he describes an "extraordinary system failure caused by widespread crime, corruption, bribery and impotent drug regulation." These books are just a sampling from the long list of works detailing pharma's bad faith (Kassirer 2005; Goldacre 2012). Taken together they demonstrate the urgency for industry regulation to correct this behavior, and a complete reexamination of how psychiatric knowledge is assembled and evaluated; the lack of any meaningful policy reform helps explain the rise in organized resistance.

Incorporating a range of diverse stakeholders in the production of psychiatric knowledge would help illuminate the narrowness of current assumptions and give voice to alternative ways to conceptualize and support existential diversity, suffering, and crisis. This position does not amount to radical relativism or endorse the idea that anything goes. Instead, it challenges monocultures of knowledge production and demands that diverse pluralities participate in the judgments that society enforces around values and norms. The systematic denial of the role of value judgments in the production of psychiatric knowledge needs to be interrogated and challenged. The pretense of atheoretical "views from nowhere" needs to be exposed, laying bare its underlying biases and ideologies. To be sure, our capacity for reconciling difference is woefully lacking, but the precondition to begin this process starts with listening.

Unleashing Patient Power

The mad underground is not the first movement to advance the case for patient power. Briefly examining the recent history of a few closely related movements reveals the genealogy of our struggle and greatly informs the work. The similarities and differences of these analogous arguments suggest strategies and alliances.

The trope of patient empowerment was forced onto the mainstream agenda through the largely successful activism of the international direct action group AIDS Coalition to Unleash Power (ACT UP) (Halperin 1995; Epstein 1996; Gould 2009). In the early 1980s, when the scourge of AIDS erupted in the United States, the government and pharmaceutical corporations were negligent in responding to the urgent needs of the afflicted. ACT UP formed to demand patient empowerment, and contingents within the group began conducting scientific research, drafting policies and protocols, and ultimately became leading experts on their own condition. They formed their own support groups, pooled their resources to collectively purchase experimental drugs that were not yet approved in the United States, and staged vivid protests and direct actions, such as die-ins and the creation of alternative sexual education material. While ACT UP demanded new attention, research, and drugs from the pharmaceutical industry, and mental health activists are not especially interested in the development of new pharmaceuticals—one might say that they are demanding *less* attention—there are interesting parallels in the underlying ideology of their demands.

In his sociological account of the history of AIDS research and treatment, Stephen Epstein describes the interactions between traditional "insiders" and "outsiders" of scientific (and medical) knowledge production (1996). He argues that AIDS activists transformed themselves from a "disease constituency" to an "alternative basis of expertise" whose contributions were especially evident in the politics of treatment. These activists played a key role in altering the way that biomedicine is conducted, challenging the morality of double-blind, placebo-controlled studies and influencing the ways the FDA approves and speeds drugs through the approval process. Epstein claims that the AIDS crisis mobilized a critique of the medical-industrial complex, calling it to task for its lust for profit and control over patients'—and especially women's—bodies.

> The AIDS epidemic has magnified these various misgivings about doctors and researchers. Indeed, in the face of death and disease, popular ambivalence about biomedicine has undergone a peculiar amplification: distrust has been accentuated, but so has dependence. Despite their suspicion of expertise, people in advanced industrial societies typically expect doctors and scientists to protect them from illness and death. Yet, half a decade into the epidemic, researchers had not found an effective cure or vaccine. Scientists insist this is not surprising given the "normal" rate of progress in biomedical investigations. Nevertheless, the failure of experts to solve the problem of AIDS quickly, as they were "supposed to," has led to a "credibility crisis." This in turn has opened up more space for dissident positions, both among scientists and doctors and within the lay public. (Epstein 1996, 7)

ACT UP's activism represents one way that an *us* has made itself heard. In this case, the infected *us* accepted their designation as sick and became directly involved in fighting stigma, improving treatments, and searching for a cure. Some AIDS activists learned the languages of experts and began participating directly in policy work and epidemiology research. Others asserted their expertise based on their lived experiences and insisted that they should ultimately decide the degree of risk they were willing to take with experimental treatments. Their response accepted the medical model, though they vigorously contested the pejorative and moralizing judgments of gay lifestyles and demanded agency in deciding appropriate risks when pursuing a cure. Their acceptance of the medical model was likely a function of the stark brutality of the progression of HIV and the widespread illness and death it caused.

New Normals

The radical epistemology captured in the mantra Nothing about Us without Us is a recurring theme that has also shaped advocacy across defining struggles within the disability rights movement. In the past few decades, a variety of subcultures within the disability rights movement have spawned a range of responses to the credibility crisis, challenging the underlying assumptions of the externally imposed *uses*. These responses vary in their acceptance of the language used by medical experts to describe and categorize the group, and often involve contestation over labels, as well as treatment. In contrast to the ACT UP activists, many disability activists question the medical model of disability, challenging frameworks that define disability as an "impairment" and that glorify "normal." Being diagnosed with HIV was universally considered a scourge, and no one claimed it represented an alternative lifestyle, as with some so-called disabilities. Throughout these sites of contestation, we witness the value of democratic meaning-making as these groups assert their identity in their own terms. This dynamic is most visible in the feedback loop that flows from the second, participatory *us* back to the first, externally imposed *us*, as the group reclaims the power to name themselves and their concerns, prioritizing these concerns according to their own values.

Listening to the Deaf

In the 1970s James Woodward, a professor of sociolinguistics and the co-director of the Centre for Sign Linguistics and Deaf Studies at the Chinese University of Hong Kong, introduced the distinction between *deaf* and *Deaf*: "use the lowercase deaf when referring to the audiological condition of not hearing, and the uppercase Deaf when referring to a particular group of deaf people who share a language—American Sign Language—and a culture" (1982). Deaf culture represents a rich history and tradition, with distinct languages, norms, and values, and Woodward's distinction was widely adopted within Deaf communities. Paddy Ladd coined the term "deafhood" in the subtitle of his book *Understanding Deaf Culture: In Search of Deafhood*, attempting to "define the existential state of Deaf 'being-in-the-world.' Hitherto, the medical term 'deafness' was used to subsume that experience within the larger category of 'hearing-impaired' ... so the true nature of Deaf collective experience was rendered invisible. Deafhood is not seen as a finite state, but as a process by which Deaf individuals come to actualize their Deaf identity." (Ladd 2003, xvii)

Many in the Deaf community have fiercely defended their culture, most famously in the controversy surrounding cochlear implants (Tucker 1998). The use of cochlear implants, especially in prelingual children, has been construed as an existential threat to the Deaf community, who question the effectiveness and morality of this invasive treatment, especially since the procedure is performed on children who are incapable of informed consent. Children with cochlear implants are often outcast from both the Deaf and hearing communities since the implants do not function well enough for them to learn spoken language naturally, and they are deprived from learning sign language. Even if the implants worked flawlessly, Deaf activists would oppose them since they vehemently deny the pathologizing of their condition, arguing that deafness is a difference, not a deficiency. Preventing children from participating in Deaf culture deprives them of their agency and is systematically destroying Deaf culture. People without hearing impairments or who lost their hearing later in life are often surprised to encounter these perspectives, confident in their belief that hearing impairment is a deficiency. They are largely unfamiliar with the richness of Deaf culture and are unaware that many people are fighting to preserve it. Deaf advocacy loudly demonstrates the importance of listening to a diversity of voices before rushing to judgment around other people's experiences.

Anything but Neurotypical

Ari Ne'eman is the founder of the Autistic Self Advocacy Network (ASAN), a group founded in 2006 that believes that autism is a neurological difference, not a disease that needs to be cured. Their website states that "ASAN was started by autistic adults who were unhappy with the prevailing public dialogue on autism, believing that the autism world would be better served by ending the misguided search for a 'cure' and focusing on empowering and supporting autistic people and all people with disabilities to live the lives we wanted." Ne'eman was diagnosed with Asperger's syndrome as a child and was frustrated that his schooling seemed focused on "normalizing" his behavior, not helping him thrive on his own terms (Hall 2009). In 2009 he was appointed by President Obama to serve on the National Council on Disability, which makes recommendations to the president and Congress on disability issues (Diament 2010). ASAN uses the term "neourodiversity" to describe people on the autism spectrum. They call "normal" people "neurotypical" and resist attempts to pathologize autistic behaviors. Similar to Deaf activism, ASAN emphasizes difference instead of a normative deficiency, and advocates for acceptance of neurodiversity instead of forcing all human experience into a rigid mold. Unlike many mental health activists, ASAN activists embrace the neurobiological causes of their differences and are not threatened by a reductionist account of their condition. ASAN faces criticism for minimizing the suffering of more extreme autistic cases, which are characterized by self-harm and an inability to take care of one's own basic needs. However, their advocacy is another example of the growing trend of advocating for diverse perspectives and respecting the value of lived experiences.

> It was only when I started to read what other people were saying about us that it began to carry a meaning. And at first a very negative, frightening meaning. People do not talk about welcoming autistic people to their communities. People talk about fear and tragedy and burden. Initially it was very frightening. My saving grace was connecting with other autistic adults and finding out that there was this larger community of autistic people who weren't willing to just passively accept how the world defines us.... We founded ASAN, in part, because there was, and is, an extensive public conversation about autism that includes everyone except the people most impacted: those on the autism spectrum.... In the parent and provider community there's more emphasis on trying to cure or fix us, and that's not something we consider a priority. (Heim 2015)

Ne'eman's account describes the formation of an *us*, a community of people diagnosed with autism who resist accepting society's definition of them. They actively engage in conversations around how they should be understood and treated, once again illustrating the importance for society to listen to the very people they are trying to help. Their priorities are often surprisingly different from those imagined by well intentioned, would-be saviors.

Abnormal Growths

The passage of the Americans with Disabilities Act (ADA) in 1990 extended the antidiscrimination protections of the 1964 Civil Rights Act to America's disabled. The academic field of Disability Studies emerged in the 1980s, and the Society for Disability Studies was formed in 1986. Disability Studies was established as a "division of study" by the Modern Language Association in 2005, and it is now a field of graduate or undergraduate study in over thirty-five US universities (Simon 2013). In an essay titled "Constructing Normalcy," which opens Routledge's canonical

Disabilities Studies Reader, Lennard Davis argues that the "application of the idea of a norm to human bodies creates the idea of deviance" and that "the conflation of disability with depravity expressed itself in the formulation of the 'defective class'" (2006). With a series of literary examples, he argues:

> [The normal] is a configuration that arises in a particular historical moment. It is part of a notion of progress, of industrialization, and of ideological consolidation of the power of the bourgeoisie. The implications of the hegemony of normalcy are profound and extend into the heart very heart of cultural production.... One of the tasks for a developing consciousness of disability issues is the attempt, then, to reverse the hegemony of the normal and to institute alternative ways of thinking about the abnormal. (Davis 2006, 15)

Questioning normal, and especially the structures and processes that determine it, is a central concern for Disability Studies. The field favors understanding disability as a social construct over understanding it according to the traditional medical model of impairment and handicap (Bickenbach et al. 1999). Disability scholars emphasizes that disability is a porous state and everyone will be disabled at some point in their lives, either through injury, old age, or disease. Those who are not currently disabled are sometimes referred to as "temporarily able-bodied."

Disability activists share many concerns with mad activists, although they have not formed a stable coalition (we should!). Apart from their different subcultures and histories, some disability activists continue to harbor "sanist" attitudes, and shy away from associating with mentally diverse. Conversely, many mad activists are uncomfortable with the "disability" label, just as many in the Deaf and neurodiverse communities are. They do not view their difference as a disadvantage; rather, they consider it a valued capacity, or a dangerous gift. Mad activists also face forms of oppression differentiating their issues from those of the mainstream disability rights movement. The mad contend with state-sponsored coercion in the form of involuntary commitment and forced medication, and are habitually scapegoated as violent offenders. Despite the uniqueness of these issues, there are more similarities than differences between the movements, and solidarity is growing alongside awareness of each other's concerns. The expansive growth of mental illness diagnosis and treatment has extended the relevance of these issues, and a significant portion of Disability Studies now engages in what has also been called Madness Studies.

The emerging wave of mad resistance is situated in these cultural and theoretical contexts, and mad advocacy has begun to embrace these moves toward patient empowerment and self-identification. The kinds of claims exemplified by ACT UP and Deaf and neurodiverse activists create an essential backdrop for understanding the emerging radical mental health movement. Many of the arguments made by the new wave of mad resistance apply with equal force to the disabled, or to otherwise marginalized groups. Closely studying the power dynamics around the mad *us* offers crucial insights into the formation of medical, scientific, and professional expertise, the validity of lived experience as evidence, and the power of narratives in the construction of identity. Society's process for defining normalcy is one that affects the mad, the disabled, the marginalized, and the temporarily able-bodied and able-minded alike.

Transcending Dualities

Critics have engaged the controversies surrounding psychiatric diagnoses on multiple conceptual fronts, provoking debates about the integrity of the rhetoric, science, and politics. The work of Stuart Kirk and Herb Kutchins, professors of social work, questions the science, statistics, and proofs claimed by the small committee of psychiatric researchers who authored *DSM-III* and *DSM-III-R*. *The Selling of* DSM: *The Rhetoric of Science in Psychiatry* (1992), published by an academic press, and *Making Us Crazy:* DSM: *The Psychiatric Bible and the Creation of Mental Disorders* (2003), a trade book, expose the workings of these backroom proceedings, and describe their success in transforming psychiatry's central problem from one of "validity" to one of "reliability," the measure of multiple doctors agreeing on the same diagnosis. Reliability is a narrower, technical problem for researchers to solve, one that effectively redefines a diagnosis as valid if multiple doctors agree on the diagnosis. As Bradley Lewis shows in *Moving beyond Prozac* (2006), the discourses around psychiatric controversies encompass multiple perspectives beyond the rhetorical and scientific. The *rhetorical critiques* are theory-laden challenges to the ideological frames that are constructed and mobilized to describe the issues. The *scientific critiques* accept (or bracket) the dominant research paradigms and concentrate on questioning the validity of the research claims, on their own terms. Finally, the *political critiques* question governance and processes such as the construction of the research agenda, the voices involved in formulating policy recommendations, corruption, conflicts of interest, and aggressive marketing practices that influence behavior and perception. These dimensions often overlap and are difficult to disentangle completely in debate or analysis.

The political plane is where questions of diversity and inclusion are activated in the context of crafting a purposeful process for building consensus, resolving conflicts, and constructing knowledge. The consideration of politics, in this sense, is largely absent from the work of Kirk and Kutchins and is the operating beachhead for the emerging wave of mad resistance, represented in this book.

The new wave of activists represented in this anthology often engage these controversies on all of these planes simultaneously, as the assertion Nothing about Us without Us embraces a range of rhetorical, scientific, and political moves. Their focus on enriching the language we use to define mental well-being and distress represents a deliberate effort to participate in the co-construction of their own reality. Their arguments are often motivated and amplified by dubious science, greedy corporations, and corrupt doctors and policy makers. The emerging wave of mad resistance is fundamentally about applying this political maxim to the full range of psychiatric discourse and making explicit their demands for a participatory voice.

It is useful to contrast this emerging position with other strands of psychiatric resistance, which often leads to opponents butting heads with little chance for reconciliation. For example, the mind-body problem, a philosophical quandary about the nature of and relationship between the mental and the physical, is one site of rhetorical contention that stands between some psychiatrists and psychiatric survivors. Arguments on both sides of this debate effectively assume dualism, although these are rarely the explicit terms of debate. Dualism is the metaphysical position that postulates that physical and mental phenomena are distinct, though they somehow influence each other. Reductionist psychiatrists cast their arguments in terms implying that the flows of neurotransmitters and the firing of neurons uniquely determine states of mind, but not vice versa. Similarly, the arguments of orthodox anti-psychiatrists suggest that they deny the impact of biochemistry or neurophysiology on their minds, and they vehemently resist biological explanations of their behavior (with the notable exception of psychiatric drugs, which they blame for detrimental effects on their minds and bodies). These largely unexamined, and, at times, incoherent positions creep into the discourse, even when the participants deny their dualistic dispositions.

A commitment to monism, a theoretical alternative to dualism, presents a substantive challenge to both the orthodox biomedical model of mental illness and orthodox anti-psychiatrists. Monism entails that all behaviors are correlated with corresponding states of mind, and similarly, changes in our brains are also correlated with changes in mind, so that mind and brain are dual aspects of the same phenomena. Unfortunately, the mind-body problem has remained unsolved for millennia, and adopting these positions results in untenable standoffs. Transcending dualism addresses only part of the conflict. To fully embrace a more democratic epistemology, we must also transcend the theoretical questions themselves and pragmatically consider their political implications, bracketing the theoretical frames, for now.

The act of categorizing a state of mind/brain and its corresponding behaviors as pathological is never devoid of subjective inflection and will always involve value judgments and interpretations of behavior that can never be isolated in a pure form. While an fMRI image may be used to demonstrate *correlations* between states of brain and states of mind (crucially, not the necessary consequences of these brain functions), an fMRI will never be able to conclusively demonstrate that a person suffers from a "psychiatric disorder." The act of categorizing certain behaviors as deviant or pathological will always involve subjective value judgments. Analytical distinctions carve up the world in particular ways, grouping data together and fitting them to preconceived patterns. Whenever something is counted, something else is omitted, and behavioral descriptions are forever imprisoned in language, comprised of words that are intrinsically bound to shades of semantic senses, embedded in networks of meaning that are inherently social.

Psychiatric facts are inextricably woven among sociocultural values. A patient, whether treated as a mind, brain, or unified whole, can never be diagnosed independently of our collective judgment of the subject's behavior and disposition. Both minds and brains exist in social entanglements—divorcing the diagnosis of a patient from his or her psychosocial context effectively locates an individual's pathology inside their skull, without acknowledging the influence and impact of their environment. In theory, a full-service treatment team might consider the patient's psychosocial context, but this contextualization is not typical in practice, as market forces, insurance codes, and psychiatric cultural norms incentivize diagnoses that are devoid of context. Laboratory diagnostics will never be able to tell us what behaviors to pathologize or determine the threshold for "normal," since we as a society co-construct these values. Is the patient suffering from a uterine parasite, or blessed with child? Is the patient suffering a psychotic break or struggling to navigate their dangerous gifts?

The human condition is richly varied, and there are limitless ways for us to find meaning in our experiences. To insist that there is only a single way to make sense of someone's life story requires generous helpings of arrogance and stubbornness (Fadiman 1997). Once we recognize the inextricable coupling of psychiatric facts with sociocultural values, the imperative to include more voices in the production of psychiatric knowledge ought to be self-evident. Under the status quo, a small group of primarily white, middle-aged men, most of whom have medical degrees from Western societies, are responsible for defining a normal range of human consciousness, what constitutes healthy experiences, and how to support and treat people who are suffering (Kirk and Kutchins 1992). Historically, the team that has drafted this defining document has omitted psychologists, psychoanalysts, social workers, philosophers, humanists, social scientists, patients, families of patients, as well as mental health activists of various stripes (Lewis 2006). While *DSM-IV* and *DSM-5* committees have made some gestures toward including more mental health professionals outside of psychiatry, as well as minorities and international representation, these additions have been ad hoc, and not part of a deliberate philosophy of inclusion. It is easy to recognize the fundamental flaws in this arrangement and how diverse perspectives are essential for a more comprehensive and reliable understanding.

The moral imperative for diversity of input is not the only argument for inclusion. Recent sociological findings have demonstrated that diversity enhances organizational creativity and innovation, while homogeneity stifles it (Burt 2004; Stark 2009). Identifying and questioning assumptions, crafting compromises, and designing innovative alternatives are some of the reasons why diversity and inclusion are so important. The mere inclusion of diverse actors does not ensure a fair outcome, and processes and procedures must be deliberately adopted that maximize the possibility of fair outcomes. Sometimes positions are irreconcilable, and compromise may feel like everybody loses, but the difficulty of achieving absolute fairness should not stop us from trying to improve the current situation.

Mediated Realities

The controversies surrounding the psychiatric-pharmaceutical complex are tangled and emotionally charged. We will not resolve them all in any one volume. What we can insist, along with the new wave of mad resistance, is that the exploration of these questions and controversies should not be reserved for the medical establishment. Alongside the voices of lived experience, the traditional human, social, and life sciences can and should bring the full force of their disciplines to bear on these questions.

Media and Communications Studies are positioned to offer unique and valuable perspectives on these issues (Peters 2009). These environments are undergoing revolutionary changes, and correspondingly, so are identity formation and social interaction (Castells 1996). James Carey writes that "communication is a symbolic process whereby reality is produced, maintained, repaired, and transformed" (1992, 23). Both McLuhan's and Carey's interdisciplinary approaches for studying media and communications as culture suggest a powerful stance for interrogating the representations of pharmaceuticals and mental illness in advertising, popular culture, and the press. McLuhan believed that "ideally, advertising aims at the goal of a programmed harmony among all human impulses and aspirations and endeavors," a claim that applies to psychiatry as easily as advertising (1964, 227). As more authoritative judgments are made through the interpretation of records gathered through institutional surveillance, diagnostic constructs and practices are subtly changing in response to this new form of scrutiny. Psychoactive drugs distort, deflect, and otherwise alter phenomenological experiences in ways that can be productively analyzed as a form of mediation. Just as traditional media mediate communications between senders and receivers, psychoactive drugs modulate cognitive and perceptual apparatuses, and effectively mediate experiences of reality. Like traditional media, these drugs shape our experiences, perspectives, and behaviors—our ways of seeing and being in the world.

Much like familiar elements of our mainstream media ecology such as advertising and the press, psychiatric diagnoses and psychotropic drugs directly mediate and shape our experience of reality. They also literally mediate our behaviors, perceptions, desires, and expectations. An entire generation is growing up inhabiting a perpetually drugged-out existence, as their constitutive environment is regulated by drugs that sedate bodies and turn minds sluggish. Our youth's ways of seeing and being in the world are being actively shaped by diagnostic labels and mind-numbing drugs. Scholars, journalists, educators, and activists must work together to marshal all the methods at their disposal to comprehend and contain this burgeoning epidemic, where, by one measure, an astonishing one in five children are now considered mentally ill (Merikangas et al. 2010).

Coda: Surveillance Psychiatry and the Mad Underground

In the past decade we have begun to glimpse what happens when Psychiatry meets Big Data. The FDA has approved a drug embedded with sensors that digitally monitors you and notifies your treatment team if you have taken it—the first drug outfitted with this technology is the antipsychotic Abilify (aripiprazole). Facebook has deployed artificial intelligence tools designed for the "proactive detection" (and intervention protocols) for users deemed to be at risk for suicide. And computer scientists are claiming they can diagnose depression (Reece and Danforth 2016) based on the color and saturation of photos in your Instagram feed and predict manic episodes (FAD Study 2014) based on the time and frequency of your social media updates.

These stories should be understood as part of a bigger pattern that is emerging around diagnosis and treatment. Large, centralized, digital social networks and data-gathering platforms have come to dominate our economy and our culture, and technology is being shaped by those in power to magnify their dominance. In the domain of mental health, huge pools of data are being used to train algorithms to identify signs of mental illness—a threat I call "surveillance psychiatry." Electronic health records, data mining social networks, and even algorithmically classifying video surveillance will significantly amplify this approach. Corporations and governments are salivating at the prospect of identifying psychological vulnerability and dissent.

The emphasis on treating risk rather than disease predates the arrival of big data, but together they are now ushering in an era of algorithmic diagnosis based on the data mining of our social media and other digital trails. Although they will carefully use the language of suicide and violence prevention, the lines between politics and harm reduction are not so clear. When algorithms are interpreting our tweets to determine who is crazy, it will become increasingly difficult to avoid a diagnosis, even if we carefully watch what we say. This environment will severely inhibit people's willingness to seek support and is creating an atmosphere where people are conditioned to report behaviors that appear different or abnormal.

To be clear, reducing suicide is good. However, this same infrastructure is already being used to police the boundaries of normal behavior—proactively detecting all forms of deviance, dissent, and protest. A nuanced critique, informed by people with lived experience, needs to shape the development of these systems, since context is everything. We need to spend more resources understanding how and why people become suicidal, and the long-term consequences of treatment by our health care systems, alongside the focus on short-term interventions.

It is crucial to connect the dots between the abstract threats of government and corporate surveillance and the immanent threats of psychiatric profiling and early interventions. The reality of preemptive and coercive psychiatric interventions demonstrates how big data is transforming authority's confidence in prediction, and how it is used to justify preventative measures. The stakes will vary depending on your status and race, but these records, and the stigma they carry, will affect your ability to be approved for insurance or a loan or admitted to school. Society's treatment of those in emotional distress serves as a harbinger of our collective future, unless we take steps to prevent these outcomes. As the stories in this anthology testify, the mad have always been oppressed and discriminated against, and the way we treat them is a stark warning of what portends for all of us.

The best way I can imagine to overcome the threat of psychiatric surveillance is by peeling back the assumptions that underlie psychiatric diagnosis and unmasking the power structures that define the normal range of the human experience. Resisting the encroachment of psychiatric power can best be achieved by listening closely to voices from the mad underground and amplifying them through the power of new media. The same technologies that enable authority to track and diagnose us are also being used by the resistance to network and organize. Mental health activists who are deeply reflective about their own psychosocial well-being also have much to teach the rest of us when it comes to using the internet purposefully, to enable greater freedom, not control.

In the face of these dystopic visions, there is still hope. The mad underground, a thriving network of mental health activists represented by the contributors to this book, is developing innovative strategies for resisting psychiatric domination and creating new models of community-driven emotional support. By listening to their voices and understanding their visions we can diffuse the menacing time bomb of big-data surveillance psychiatry before it explodes, putting the depths of our emotions in the realm of public consumption and subjecting us to new forms of oppression.

Dangerous gifts have subversive potential. These gifts can transform society and help us see past the consensus reality that the surveillance state yearns to control. Just as pregnancy can be understood as a distressing condition that yields something beautiful, someone traversing an altered state may navigate distress as part of the process of birthing something beautiful—a piece of art, a better version of themselves, a scientific breakthrough, or other forms of creative expression. Our collective challenge is explaining to the world that what we need is greater compassion and understanding, not fixing or swaddling. We are not broken. Our birth pangs may be painful, but we can truly thrive when showered with loving and nonjudgmental support.

References

American Diabetes Association. n.d. "Diagnosing Diabetes and Learning about Prediabetes." Accessed July 5, 2015. www.diabetes.org/diabetes-basics/diagnosis.

American Psychiatric Association. 2003. "American Psychiatric Association Statement on Diagnosis and Treatment of Mental Disorders." Press release. American Psychiatric Association. Accessed September 4, 2015. http://web.archive.org/web/20070614091656; www.psych.org/news_room/press_ releases/mentaldisorders0339.pdf.

Angell, M. 2004. *The Truth about the Drug Companies: How They Deceive Us and What to Do about It.* New York: Random House.

Bickenbach, J. E., Chatterji, S., Badley, E. M., and Üstün, T. B. 1999. "Models of Disablement, Universalism and the International Classification of Impairments, Disabilities, and Handicaps." *Social Science and Medicine* 48 (9): 1173–87. http://doi.org/10.1016/S0277-9536(98)00441-9.

Boston Women's Health Book Collective. 1973. *Our Bodies, Ourselves: A Book by and for Women.* New York: Simon & Schuster.

Burt, R. S. 2004. "Structural Holes and Good Ideas." *American Journal of Sociology* 110 (2): 349–99. http://doi.org/10.1086/421787.

Carey, J. W. 1992. *Communication as Culture*. Boston: Unwin Hyman.

Castells, M. 1996. *The Rise of the Network Society*. Malden, MA: Blackwell.

Charlton, J. I. 1998. *Nothing about Us without Us: Disability Oppression and Empowerment*. Berkeley: University of California Press.

Coleman, G. 2008. "The Politics of Rationality: Psychiatric Survivors' Challenge to Psychiatry." In *Tactical Biopolitics: Art, Activism, and Technoscience*, edited by Beatriz da Costa and Kavita Philip. Cambridge, MA: MIT Press.

Crossley, Nick. 2006. *Contesting Psychiatry: Social Movements in Mental Health*. London: Routledge.

Davis, L. J. 2006. "Constructing Normalcy." In *The Disability Studies Reader*, 2nd ed., edited by Lennard J. Davis. New York: Routledge.

Diament, M. 2010. "Senate Confirms Controversial Autism Self-Advocate to National Disability Council." *Disability Scoop*, June 22, 2010. www.disabilityscoop.com/2010/06/22/neeman-confirmation/9133.

Driedger, D. 1989. *The Last Civil Rights Movement: Disabled People's International*. New York: Macmillan.

DuBrul, S. 2014. "The Icarus Project: A Counter Narrative for Psychic Diversity." *Journal of Medical Humanities* 35 (3): 257–71.

Epstein, S. 1996. *Impure Science: AIDS, Activism, and the Politics of Knowledge*. Berkeley: University of California Press.

Fadiman, A. 1997. *The Spirit Catches You and You Fall Down: A Hmong Child, Her American Doctors, and the Collision of Two Cultures*. New York: Farrar, Straus and Giroux.

FAD Study. 2014. "Facebook Use in Affective Disorders." Accessed June 23, 2015. http://thefadstudy.com.au.

Foucault, M. 1965. *Madness and Civilization: A History of Insanity in the Age of Reason*. New York: Pantheon Books.

Goldacre, B. 2012. *Bad Pharma: How Drug Companies Mislead Doctors and Harm Patients*. London: Fourth Estate.

Gøtzsche, P. 2013. *Deadly Medicines and Organised Crime: How Big Pharma Has Corrupted Healthcare*. London: Radcliffe Medical Press.

Gould, D. B. 2009. *Moving Politics: Emotion and ACT UP's Fight against AIDS*. Chicago: University of Chicago Press.

Hall, W. 2009. "Autism Self Advocacy: Ari Ne'eman." *Madness Radio*, October 14, 2009. www.madnessradio.net/madness-radio-autism-self-advocacy-ari-neeman.

Halperin, D. 1995. *Saint Foucault: Towards a Gay Hagiography*. New York: Oxford University Press.

Hanisch, C. 1969. "The Personal is Political." In *Notes From the Second Year: Women's Liber-ation: Major Writings of the Radical Feminists*, edited by Sulamith Firestone and Anne Koedt. New York. 1970. Accessed July 19, 2015. www.carolhanisch.org/CHwritings /PIP.html.

Healy, D. 2012. *Pharmageddon*. Berkeley: University of California Press.

Heim, J. 2015. "Just Asking: Ari Ne'eman, Co-Founder of the Autistic Self Advocacy Net-work." *Washington Post*, March 5, 2015. www.washingtonpost.com/lifestyle/magazine /just-asking-ari-neeman-co-founder-of-the-autistic-self-advocacy-network /2015/03/05/ccb87f44-b2e1-11e4-854b-a38d13486ba1_story.html.

Hickey, P. 2014. "Psychiatry DID Promote the Chemical Imbalance Theory." *Mad in America*, June 6, 2014. www.madinamerica.com/2014/06/psychiatry-promote-chemical -imbalance-theory.

Institute of Medicine. 2015. *Beyond Myalgic Encephalomyelitis/Chronic Fatigue Syndrome: Redefining an Illness*. Washington, DC: The National Academies Press.

Kassirer, J. 2005. *On the Take: How Medicine's Complicity with Big Business Can Endanger Your Health*. Oxford: Oxford University Press.

Kirk, S. A., and Kutchins, H. 1992. *The Selling of DSM: The Rhetoric of Science in Psychiatry*. New York: Aldine de Gruyter.

———. 2003. *Making Us Crazy: DSM: The Psychiatric Bible and The Creation of Mental Disorders*. New York: Free Press.

Ladd, Paddy. 2003. *Understanding Deaf Culture: In Search of Deafhood*. Clevedon, UK: Mul-tilingual Matters Ltd.

Lewis, B. 2006. *Moving beyond Prozac, DSM, and the New Psychiatry: The Birth of Postpsy-chiatry*. Annotated edition. Ann Arbor: University of Michigan Press.

———. 2011. *Narrative Psychiatry: How Stories Can Shape Clinical Practice*. Baltimore: Johns Hopkins University Press.

McLuhan, M. 1964. *Understanding Media: The Extensions of Man*. New York: McGraw Hill.

Merikangas, K. R., He, J., Burstein, M., Swanson, S. A., Avenevoli, S., Cui, L., Benjet, C., Georgiades, K., and Swendsen, J. 2010. "Lifetime Prevalence of Mental Disorders in US Adolescents: Results from the National Comorbidity Survey Replication—Ado-lescent Supplement (NCS-A)." *Journal of the American Academy of Child and Adolescent Psychiatry* 49 (10): 980–89. http://dx.doi.org/10.1016/j.jaac.2010.05.017.

Metzl, J. 2010. *The Protest Psychosis: How Schizophrenia Became a Black Disease*. Boston: Beacon Press.

Morrison, Linda. 2005. *Talking Back to Psychiatry: The Psychiatric Consumer/Survivor/Ex-Patient Movement*. New York: Routledge.

National Alliance on Mental Illness. n.d. "What Is Mental Illness?" Accessed July 5, 2015. http://www2.nami.org/Content/NavigationMenu/Inform_Yourself/About_Mental_ Illness/By_Illness/What_is_Mental_Illness_.htm.

Oaks, David. 2006. "Unite for a Nonviolent Revolution in the Mental Health System: What 30 Years in the mad movement Have Taught Me." Talk delivered at Open Minds: Cultural, Critical and Activist Perspectives on Psychiatry, September 23, 2006, New York University. Accessed August 21, 2015. www.mindfreedom.org/about-us /david-woaks/davidoaksopenforum2006conftalk.pdf/view.

Ohman, L., and Simrén, M. 2010. "Pathogenesis of IBS: Role of Inflammation, Immunity and Neuroimmune Interactions." *Nature Reviews Gastroenterology and Hepatology* 7 (3): 163–73. http://doi.org/10.1038/nrgastro.2010.

Onion. 2007. "Woman Overjoyed by Giant Uterine Parasite." August 27, 2007. www.theonion .com/article/woman-overjoyed-by-giant-uterine-parasite-2266.

Pearson, M. L., Selby, J. V., Katz, K. A., Cantrell, V., Braden, C. R., Parise, M. E., et al. "Clinical, Epidemiologic, Histopathologic and Molecular Features of an Unexplained Dermopathy." *PLoS ONE* 7 (1): e29908. http://doi.org/10.1371/journal.pone.0029908.

Peters, J. D. 2009. "Broadcasting and Schizophrenia." *Media, Culture and Society* 32 (1): 1–18. http://doi.org/10.1177/0163443709350101.

Rabinbach, A. 1992. *The Human Motor: Energy, Fatigue, and the Origins of Modernity.* Berkeley: University of California Press.

Reece, A. G., and Danforth, C. M. 2016. "Instagram Photos Reveal Predictive Markers of Depression." ArXiv:1608.03282. http://arxiv.org/abs/1608.03282.

Rosenthal, K. P., dir. 2010. *Crooked Beauty.* (Motion picture).

Sharfstein, S. S. 2005. "Big Pharma and American Psychiatry: The Good, the Bad, and the Ugly." *Psychiatric News* 40 (16): 3–4. http://doi.org/10.1176/pn.40.16.00400003.

Simon, C. C. 2013. "Disability Studies: A New Normal." *New York Times,* November 1, 2013. www.nytimes.com/2013/11/03/education/edlife/disability-studies-a- new -normal.html.

Stark, D. 2009. *The Sense of Dissonance.* Princeton, NJ: Princeton University Press.

Tucker, B. P. 1998. "Deaf Culture, Cochlear Implants, and Elective Disability." *Hastings Center Report* 28 (4): 6–14. http://doi.org10.2307/3528607.

Valenstein, E. 2002. *Blaming the Brain: The Truth about Drugs and Mental Health.* New York: Free Press.

Whitaker, R. 2003. *Mad in America.* Cambridge, MA: Da Capo Press.

———. 2010. *Anatomy of an Epidemic: Magic Bullets, Psychiatric Drugs, and the Astonishing Rise of Mental Illness in America.* New York: Random House Digital.

White, E. B. 1941. *A Subtreasury of American Humor.* New York: Coward-McCann.

Woodward, J. 1982. *How You Gonna Get to Heaven if You Can't Talk with Jesus: On Depathologizing Deafness.* Silver Spring, MD: T. J. Publishers.

Zimney, E. 2008. "Living under the Umbrella Diagnosis of Schizophrenia." Everyday Health, April 30, 2008. Accessed July 5, 2015. www.everydayhealth.com/schizophrenia/webcasts/living-under-the-umbrella-diagnosis-of-schizophrenia.aspx.

The Intersection of Mental Health, Communities of Color, and Suicide

KELECHI UBOZOH

Recently, I was invited to Sacramento to address the Mental Health Services Oversight and Accountability Commission's public hearing on suicide prevention. This oversight body makes key statewide policy decisions on how mental health services in California are funded. Specifically, the commissioners were interested in hearing about my personal experience as a suicide attempt survivor, my research on suicide in communities of color, and culturally responsive strategies for prevention and intervention that may address suicide in diverse communities.

During my presentation, I told the commissioners that while there are many things communities of color share, each community has a unique way of handling mental health and trauma. Therefore, I could not speak on behalf of all of these diverse communities, but instead I would speak from my own experience as a Black woman and suggest to include more diverse voices in the overall conversation. Below is my response to the questions raised, and recommendations for policy makers on suicide prevention approaches in communities of color in California. However, I believe this is relevant to a needed nationwide conversation on suicide prevention with marginalized groups.

More attention needs to be paid to how suicide/suicide attempts are experienced in communities of color. For many reasons, suicide is underreported in communities of color. There is a widespread misconception among many mental health professionals and researchers that suicide is not a problem in Black communities. However, this is *not true*. Recent studies show that nationwide, suicides among Black children under eighteen are up 71 percent in the past decade, rising from 86 in 2006 to 147 in 2016, the latest year such data is available from the Centers for Disease Control and Prevention.[1]

The truth is, we don't talk about suicide in the Black community, and if we do there can be consequences. When I was struggling as a teenager with suicidal ideations and eventually attempted, I heard a lot of problematic messages from my community. *Black people don't have mental health issues. We don't try to kill ourselves. Get over yourself. Stop being so dramatic. Pull yourself up by your bootstraps. Pray it away. Take it to Jesus. Mental illness is a "white problem."* None of these messages were helpful. Eventually I started pretending that everything was okay so that I wouldn't disappoint anyone or be rejected by my community. There is a huge myth that the mere mention of suicide plants the idea of suicide in someone's head. This is not true, but could be one of the many reasons why people would want to avoid the conversation altogether. People are also afraid of saying the wrong thing. However, I know that because of the silence around suicide many people suffer in isolation.

Blue Suicide

Most of the time Black people are missing in the data around suicide, and "traditional research" does not always accurately capture our stories. During my work as a researcher and peer advocate, I interviewed Black communities in San Bernardino County with the African American Mental Health Coalition about suicide and mental health recovery. Young Black men told me stories of losing their friends to *blue suicide.* They explained that because they grew up in the church, and because faith-based communities warn of the "spiritual consequences" of suicide (e.g., eternal damnation), friends and family members who were struggling with thoughts of self-harm opted to intentionally antagonize police officers as a means to dying. This is called *blue suicide.* This concept came up across many interviews, because this neighborhood had lost several Black community members (mainly young Black men) to *blue suicide.* Community members shared that someone on the outside looking in would categorize these deaths as homicides, which demonstrates how suicide in the Black community is underreported. We have to get more culturally responsive approaches to data collection for communities of color to accurately reflect what's really going on.

Trauma and the Label of Strong Black Women

For many Black women, like myself, there is a disbelief that we are struggling because we are "so strong" and "present well." According to a recent *New York Times* article, Black women are more likely than white women to have experienced post-traumatic stress disorder resulting from childhood maltreatment and sexual and physical violence, and are more likely to have stress related to family, employment, finances, discrimination, and/ or racism. Yet fewer than 50 percent of Black adults with mental health needs receive treatment. Barriers include mental health stigma and shame. Black women also prefer Black mental health care providers, and there are not enough.[2] Many of us suffer silently, because we have to keep our families together, hold it down at work, and show up for our communities. Even though many of my Black sisters have experienced trauma, discrimination, and racism, many are more focused on taking care of others, and not their own self-care. If we could shift the paradigm that asking for help is a strength not a weakness, we might be able to reduce suicide attempts. *However, when we are ready to reach out for help, the help needs to be there ready for us.* When I was struggling with suicidal thoughts after a traumatic experience, I sought help at a psychiatric hospital. Unfortunately, the staff thought that because I was able to articulate my suicidal thoughts and depression, I couldn't be struggling. They were "culturally irresponsible." They ignored my mental health crisis, because I didn't look or act like some cast member of a Lifetime movie. I, like many Black women, "present well" and look put together. This means my pain often goes unseen. Shortly after being dismissed from needing care for being too "high functioning," I was sent back to this very hospital after a suicide attempt: the very thing I was trying to prevent.

How Communities of Color Present in a Crisis

For many communities of color, mental health and crisis present differently. What someone may view as "angry" or "aggressive" might actually be trauma. There is a high correlation/connection between trauma and suicide attempts and deaths by suicide (youth and adults). There is also a high correlation between experiencing racism and traumatic stress. Because of a myriad of reasons (e.g., implicit bias) if communities of color cannot access mental health services because they aren't presenting in a way that is recognized by providers, they are at risk for receiving mental health services in emergency room settings or in the criminal justice system. Trauma-informed approaches across the life span can address the issues driving suicidality. Trauma-informed approaches first acknowledge trauma and respond by fully integrating knowledge about trauma into policies, procedures, and practices to actively resist re-traumatization.[3] Trauma-specific treatments such as eye movement desensitization and reprocessing (EMDR), somatic experiencing, and Intentional Peer Support teach a trauma-informed relational approach. Additionally, supported decision-making and collaborative approaches to care are needed. I've personally benefited from trauma-informed therapy. I used to think recovery meant not ever being in a dark place again. I was wrong. Recovery, for me, is about the choices you make when you are in those spaces. For me, healing was developing boundaries, seeking trauma-informed therapy, removing toxic people from my life, increasing connection, poetry, and singing. I have created a safety net to catch myself.

Recommendations for Policy Makers

As a mental health advocate who has benefited from connecting with mental health advocates statewide, I thought it would only be appropriate to include them in this conversation about what should be considered in the suicide prevention plan. The following are culturally relevant strategies for prevention and intervention that may more effectively address suicide and suicide attempt in diverse communities. Thank you to all of the peers, family members, therapists, crisis intervention service providers, suicide prevention hotline workers, suicide attempt survivors, and suicide loss survivors who contributed to this response.

CULTURALLY RELEVANT STRATEGIES FOR SUICIDE PREVENTION

- **Consider employing culturally specific mental health ambassadors to support suicide prevention planning.** While there are many things that communities of color share, each of these communities has a unique way of dealing with mental health and trauma. Include people from these diverse communities as mental health ambassadors and connectors to learn more about what works for them (e.g., art and healing, culturally specific practices).

- **Involve the voices of suicide attempt survivors and suicide loss survivors.** Each county should have consumers and family members representative of their "isolated and underserved" communities involved in suicide prevention planning. It is important in communities of color to also authentically engage suicide attempt survivors of color (e.g., clear roles and responsibilities) to mitigate the experience of "tokenization."

- **Develop culturally specific suicide prevention outreach tools that feature communities of color.** Suicide prevention needs faces of color and messages that will speak to these diverse communities. PSAs, social media, billboards, radio ads can help normalize the conversation and let people know that suicidal ideation is something that many people experience. Include messaging that says they are not the only one or not alone and resources for help, and ensure these messages are available in many languages.

- **Create opportunities for people of color (POC) with lived experience or survivors to connect and share their experiences** in safe spaces like support groups. This may help decrease stigma and isolation, increase knowledge of wellness tools, and normalize the conversation around suicide in diverse communities.

- **Alternatives to 911.** For many communities of color, calling police can escalate situations, and many may avoid seeking help through this venue. Can the suicide prevention plan build networks of mutual aid and crisis support from the community? This should include outreach materials that provide information on alternatives to 911.

- **Strengthen discourse and 5150 education for law enforcement.** A careful assessment is needed when writing a 5150.[4] Sometimes an individual may appear to be a harm to themselves or others because they are intoxicated, which can lead to a 5150. In other cases, where individuals are suffering in silence and hopelessness and potentially a rapid cycling in and out of psychiatric hospitals, their needs are not addressed, and they are not given the support they need. Oftentimes putting people on 5150 and placing them in a locked psych unit exacerbates the issues. What can we learn as a community around this topic?

- **Recognize that "outcome-based/evidence-based practices" are not always responsive to what consumers need in the moment.** Develop culturally responsive research that includes what is working right now and what consumers need from people on the front line, such as crisis, warm line, and hotline workers. (A warm line is an alternative to a crisis line that is run by peers.) Involve consumers in how they measure their own success.

- **Increase overall capacity for county crisis support services.** Statewide, crisis support services like warm lines, hotlines, crisis text, and crisis clinical services are seeing a severe increase in both need and calls (e.g., Alameda County Crisis Support Services had 457 calls in January, and in March of 2018 had 832 calls). In order to meet the needs of these services (many of which are volunteer run), these nonprofits need more human resources, funding, and sustainability approaches to attract and maintain staff. Additionally, these groups need bilingual and bicultural staff to respond to the linguistic needs of diverse communities to provide a better option than tele-interpreters.

- **Strengthen data collection on suicide deaths by incentivizing partnerships with coroners' offices.**

- **Financially incentivize and hire more diverse peers and other behavioral health providers.** This also includes members from the LGBTQ+ communities.

- **Partner with primary care doctors and faith-based congregations/leaders** on how to recognize early warning signs and connect their members with mental health support. Learn from existing national and local models like Mental Health Friendly Communities (training for faith leaders).

- **Create clinical support training for first responders like EMS/ EMT and ER nurses** who often interface with mental health consumers after a suicide attempt but don't have training on how to triage or support them.

- **Provide information and resources to family/friends/loved ones helping someone who is suicidal.** Providing support to the loved ones of those who are suffering is important. We need to educate and be more supportive of family members, caregivers, and friends who are supporting the individual who is at risk for suicide. Include wellness and self-care resources for the families that may be experiencing secondary trauma.

- **Develop several options for suicide prevention trainings.** Provide options for brief training on suicide prevention, from "what to say to someone who is suicidal" to more intensive training like "assessment tools." Ensure trainings are free to the community, and host suicide prevention trainings for adults and youth of color.

- **Establish Statewide Peer Respite Centers.** Many mental health consumers are traumatized by their experiences in hospital settings. Peer respite centers can offer a homelike environment that can be an alternative in a crisis. Consider investing in crisis respite programs to divert from the emergency rooms, and decrease reliance on inpatient locked facilities.

- **Integrate the Zero Suicide** model in all inpatient hospital programs.

- **Partner with universities to integrate mandatory intensive and robust suicide prevention training** into the curriculum for all providers interfacing with mental health consumers, including clinical interns. Trainings should include the intersectionality of systematic oppression, classism, racism, sexism, historical trauma, transphobia, and homophobia as risk factors for suicide. Provide ongoing support for providers' professional development.

- **Provide more education and training on assessment for suicide risk; ensure it includes cultural considerations**. More educational support around assessment for suicide risk is needed. Individuals at risk for suicidal ideation, intention, or completion of suicide look different. There are cultural differences in relation to religious beliefs about dying and worldviews related to individuals' racial identity. This will aid clinicians in providing more thorough assessments as well as other service providers and officials who may come into contact with an individual who is at risk. Suicide is preventable, and it starts with how we assess for suicide risk.

We have to normalize the conversation about suicide in diverse communities and create a culturally informed safety net to catch people. If we create a responsive mental health system and also decrease the stigma of suicide, maybe more people will speak out when they are in pain. Maybe more people will stay. It is a difficult and worthwhile fight, but I trust that each community has its own solution within. If policy makers are truly interested in investing in the mental health of diverse and marginalized communities, they need to trust that these communities have wisdom and follow their lead into tangible results.

NOTES

1. Justin Wm. Moyer, "Researchers Unclear Why Suicide Is Increasing among Black Children," *Chicago Tribune,* March 8, 2018, www.chicagotribune.com /lifestyles/health/ct-black-childrens-suicide-20180308-story.html.

2. Inger E. Burnett-Zeigler, "The Strong and Stressed Black Woman," *New York Times,* April 25, 2018, https://www.nytimes.com/2018/04/25/opinion /strong-stressed-black-woman.html?smprod=nytcore-iphone&smid =nytcore-iphone-share.

3. United States Department of Health and Human Services, Substance Abuse and Mental Health Services Administration, Value of Peers, *Peers Supporting Recovery from Mental Health Conditions,* Bringing Recovery Supports to Scale Technical Assistance Center Strategy, November 20, 2017, http://SAMHSA.gov.

4. California police code for involuntary psychiatric hospitalization.

AFTERWORD: MENTAL HEALTH IN THE AGE OF PERPETUAL CRISIS

L. D. GREEN

Kelechi and I began this project not long before Trump was elected. At the risk of dating this book, I do want to say a few words about how all of our mental health has been impacted in the time of this book coming together, and hopefully look forward to a future where our political and environmental climate will heal—radically. Whenever you are reading this book, consider this note as a message in a bottle from November 2018. We are currently in an age of perpetual crisis, and I pray that ends soon.

Not only is Trump the individual slashing budgets for mental health care in alarming and frightening ways, but the cruel hypercapitalism, racism, sexism, homophobia, transphobia, xenophobia, and just plain evil his regime represents—and rises from—is fueling the mental health crisis. In the age of Trump, people's comfort with showing hatred, and committing violent acts, is rising in a perpetual toxic wave of ignorance and brutality. Children are torn from their families. Marginalized bodies and minds are under siege in heightened ways—people of color, undocumented folks, Muslims, queer and trans* folks, women, Jewish folks, and more. It's a painfully frightening world for many people right now: "Last fall, the American Psychological Association found that almost two-thirds of Americans listed 'the state of the nation' as their primary source of stress, above both money and work."[1] Those who were sensitive to begin with are suffering more, and we are seeing the result of that. More people are in physical and mental anguish than ever, and the role of the "mad" as agitators and advocates has never been more urgent. The world now more than ever needs the "dangerous gifts" of the neurodiverse; the world needs our mad rage, brilliance, creativity, and yes, lack of patience, to fight for a better future for us all.

Let's also discuss why calling Trump himself "mentally ill" for the purpose of maligning him is offensive. Whether we choose to use the term "mental illness" to describe our experience, or if we prefer "mental health struggles" or "neurodiversity," I stand with people who claim "mental illness" as the most humane and accurate description of their lived experience, and putting that suffering in the same breath to describe a fascist demagogue is beyond unfair—and it's also inaccurate. Further, it erodes years of mental health advocacy progress to begin using "mentally ill" as a synonym for "evil" rather than as a phrase that should garner empathy and compassion.

Even to call him a "madman" is risky. For one, there is the mad pride movement, who would also take offense and certainly not want Trump as a member. But more to the point, yes, he behaves erratically. Is that our real complaint? Is that where our focus should really be? Some work has come out recently that seeks to delegitimize Trump by making an argument that he is "mentally unfit for office."

I don't support this work.

Why not call Trump mentally ill if he objectively is, you might say, and this is a reason he could be ejected from office? For one, it's not working. Two, to use language of ability with regard to employment and mental health is regressive to the work of the Americans with Disabilities Act and the millions of people like myself with mental health diagnoses who are more than capable of doing their jobs.

Finally, this is a naive project that stunts our political imagination and potential for social transformation and highlights the limitations of the biomedical understanding of human experience and suffering vis-à-vis the *DSM*.[2] We do need him out of power, but by using the rhetoric of "mental illness" and "unfit for office" we are aligning ourselves with the rhetoric of *individual* and *biological* illness, and sadly, his pattern of dominance and American fascism is a social and political one that comes out of many years of inequality and oppression in this country.

In short, Trump is not alone, nor is he an outlier or anomaly. And his followers are not duped. They know what they signed up for. Are we to say that "anyone who votes for Trump is crazy"? As tempting as this may sound to some, for those of us who have been slapped with the label "crazy," this is not acceptable discourse. Moreover, this is neither an idealistic nor pragmatic strategy for politics. To radically revise that narrative of Trump's "mental illness," we must hope that the traits of cruelty and hate are capable of being healed in every human. That is my hope as a spiritual idealist and teacher.

That's the long game.

But we've been too patient. For now, let's heal ourselves, and let's hope that the "us" we align ourselves with can be as expansive as possible. Then let's come up with a plan to fight what's coming next. Finding that plan is not easy, but this book is part of the progress toward its articulation. In the 1960s, James Baldwin wrote of "the fire next time"; perhaps that fire is already igniting. Or perhaps we are still gathering the kindling. We don't know yet how big the fire will be, or what will come of its burning.

But the cruel reality is that this metaphor has become literal and could be a trigger for many. Fires *are* burning and destroying lives and impacting the physical and mental health of millions due to climate change. Just accepting that we are decidedly moving into a period of history when these kinds of crises (powerful hurricanes, massive fires due to drought, intense winter storms) are becoming routine brings with it mental distress, and of course those most impacted by disaster suffer in all kinds of ways.

Is mass-scale upheaval, destruction, and loss due to human-induced climate change inevitable, or do we have a small window left to prevent future catastrophes in the coming decades? How can we convince government and industry to make the necessary changes? What will we live through if nothing, or too little, is done? These questions weigh on my psyche as I breathe in the Butte County Camp Fire smoke with poisonous microparticles small enough to bypass my lungs and directly enter my bloodstream.[3] Polluted smoke itself, not just the daunting questions it brings, can cause anxiety and depression among many other health problems. The World Health Organization cited climate change as the number one threat to health in the twenty-first century.

Fearing for our future not only in the current political climate, but in the earth's climate, is overwhelming and causes a great deal of depression and anxiety for many people. In this regard, the category of those who could be labeled with mental illness is growing in an age of perpetual political and environmental crisis, and those of us who have struggled and learned to manage can offer strategies and hope for those who may not have considered themselves in this kind of need before.[4] And hopefully, we can learn to come together in mutual aid communities sharing practical tips for emotional and physical survival in frightening times.

But, as is one strategy for emotional wellness, let's stay in the present and not "future-trip" our way into immobilizing despair. It may be helpful to return from the grim horizon back to this moment. Many young, progressive politicians—many of them women and people of color, and several of them in the LGBTQ+ community—have just been elected across the country. The midterm election had the highest voter turnout for a midterm election in history. People are taking to the streets more and more these days, and more than I've experienced in my lifetime—for Black Lives Matter, for the women's marches, for trans* rights, for immigrants' rights, for the climate. People are coming together in grief, in rage, and in the relentless pursuit of radical joy, and that energy has the power to change things. Are we on the cusp of something great? Or even hugely transformative? Do we have reason for hope, or is hope guided by faith, not reason?

To move forward with these inquiries, we can listen to another James Baldwin quote: "The purpose of art is to lay bare the questions that have been hidden by the answers." The writing in this book asks many things, and it would be to its disservice to name them all here. But at its core, we ask: what can individuals and communities do to heal themselves and others, and how can the process of that healing transform our broken systems?

NOTES

1. Claire Suddath, "Freaked-Out Americans Desperately Seek to Escape the News," *Bloomberg*, June 29, 2018, www.bloomberg.com/news/articles/2018-06-29 /freaked-out-americans-desperately-seek-to-escape-the-news.

2. Well, actually, I think the *DSM* has as much use as astrology, and I'm not opposed to astrology as an interesting, sometimes accurate, hazy reflection of *some* aspects of personality. But the *DSM* is regarded as a science, and yet it is very limited, and often oppressive. (For example, homosexuality was removed as a pathological diagnosis only in 1973).

3. The Butte County Camp Fire was the deadliest wildfire in California history; at the time of this writing, in late November 2018, it has killed dozens (hundreds are still missing at this point), left thousands homeless, destroyed an entire city, burned more than 130,000 acres, and polluted most of Northern California with toxic smoke from not just woods, but from the chemicals from a burned city, for weeks. To answer naysayers—this fire was sparked by PG&E, but its magnitude was definitely because of the dry forest, which is due to drought, which is due to climate change. Furthermore, the overall pattern of routine deadly fires all over the western United States is more than a clear indication of what's to come; it's already here.

4. In Leah Lakshmi Piepzna-Samarasinha's important 2018 book, *Care Work: Dreaming Disability Justice*, she has an essay with a sub-section entitled "Cripping the Apocalypse: We've Already Survived the End of the World." She describes how, in her experience after the 2017 fires, some folks with disabilities already had a handle on how to help their suffering communities with "masks, detox herbs, air purifiers, and somatic tricks for anxiety" (p. 134) among other things, including possessing the wherewithal to manage crisis. I cite her work here because it should be read and because what I express in this sentence is really her idea, including the concept that people can become disabled at any time; people can become mentally ill at any time.

AFTERWORD: DO YOUR PART

KELECHI UBOZOH

The world of mental health is gray, it is complicated and nuanced, and messy. When Liz and I embarked on this journey, I could not have imagined how our partnership would develop and the dynamic response from contributors would crystallize. Navigating painful and powerful stories is a gift, and I am grateful for those who taught me not to just listen, but to truly hear. Hear the pauses, the unsaid struggles, the aches, and the triumphs. Like an artist working on a large canvas, we put tenderness and care into our approach and our connection to these amazing individuals who are brave enough and have been patient for too long. And yet, the painting remains unfinished; the work is not done. For example, while my home state of California has a progressive approach to including peers in our mental health system through stakeholder planning processes and program design, we are *not* one of the thirty-plus states that have developed a peer specialist training and certification program ensuring that these services are codified, billable, and sustainable.*

When I first arrived in California and worked at a peer-run mental health organization, I thought I had found my tribe. Everyone in my organization had experienced either a mental health diagnosis, substance use, trauma, or an altered state. I was no longer alone. But integrating people with a diversity of experiences of mental health also requires simultaneously building a system that supports them. I wasn't equipped to hear the stories of trauma, or watch someone lose their home, friends, and job because of a psychiatric break caused by substances. Trauma-informed systems of

---

* While this book was going into production, California began the process of passing Peer Certification. (Hooray!)

care were missing and needed within the organization. Despite the good intentions of hiring peers in clinical settings, many have shared experiences of being tokenized or disregarded because their lived experiences weren't valued. Radical mental health suggests that it isn't merely enough to add mental health consumers to a system and hope they thrive; we must transform the system itself to validate and support those experiences and voices. Radical mental health involves our dignity, and the idea that we should have self-agency over our care, and not have our civil liberties taken away.

A system can be defined as a set of connected parts forming a complex whole. How many parts do we need to fix the whole? Aren't we all part of larger system? The thought of overhauling systematic oppression can be daunting. Instead, why not think of doing your part? If more people got involved, they could be part of the solution and slowly change outcomes. It might be advocating for policy change to improve mental health practices to be more inclusive, it could be ensuring that there is enough funding and implementation support to have real impact. It could be ensuring that peer voices are required to be in every conversation and implementation of mental health policy. There are quiet advocates working inside the system making changes and loud advocates protesting on the streets and in government lobbies. We need all of you. We hope these stories inspire you to take your own journey of self-discovery, not just for your own personal wellness, but because we need you. Many of us have moved from victim to survivor to advocate, and we need you to join us. Help us finish a complete picture that is inclusive of diverse views, voices, cultures, and experiences. Please, do your part, because everyone has a role to play.

EPILOGUE: THE POWER OF NARRATIVE THERAPY IN THE RECOVERY MODEL

JESSIE ROTH

Jessie Roth is a writer, artist, and activist interested in the ways in which storytelling can be used to spur social change. She has been working at the intersection of art, writing, and social justice for more than six years, with a particular focus on how narrative practices can be utilized to reform contemporary mental health care. She is a member of the Institute for the Development of Human Arts, a community initiative of providers, advocates, and survivors who support growth and change in the mental health system. Her writing has been published in *Intima: A Journal of Narrative Medicine* and the *Village Voice*. She received her BA from New York University's Gallatin School in 2015 with an individualized major in narrative psychology and a double minor in mental health studies and creative writing.

. . . .

We tell ourselves stories in order to live.

Joan Didion wrote these famous words in her essay collection *The White Album* in 1979. In the years since, countless people around the world have identified with the universal line. It speaks to both the human predilection for storytelling and to its necessity.

Every story blooms from the same place of self-preservation, but every story also has a place it wishes to go. The stories in this book are on a mission. They intend to heal the self, but they also intend to change a broken system—the mental health system.

Many people today agree that the predominantly biomedical mental health system is in need of reform. This book offers one way forward:

through uplifting and amplifying the voices of those who have survived the system. This book wonders: what could happen if we heard the voices of those directly affected by the mental health system?

Today, biochemical psychiatry dominates mental health practice, leaving little room for personal narrative, and little appreciation for lived experience.

The biomedical model of psychiatry can be traced all the way back to classical Greek civilization, when early physicians attributed severe sadness to a dysfunction of the humors. As the organized field of modern psychology developed and evolved from its Freudian roots, the biological method initially lost favor to alternative approaches. With the election of big business advocate Ronald Reagan and the publication of a new *DSM,* however, the year 1980 witnessed the rapid growth in the pharmaceutical industry and a corresponding resurgence of the biological model. According to psychiatrists who support this system, diseases of the mind are diseases of the brain. The paradigm shift from a Freudian psychoanalytic model to a disease model ushered in a new age of psychiatry that is very much in effect today.

In this book, Imogen Prism reflects on the myriad ways in which Western medicine generally failed to support her experience: "Western medicine's attempt to manage the trauma in my body when it was at its most acute expression was a massive fail for many reasons.... What I really feel like I need when I'm in those states is a place to rest and someone to listen to me until I run out of the story and land with necessarily rugged emotion."

Imogen explains the necessity of sharing her story as a way forward, and a way to heal. And yet: "For me, meds do the job. They do it quicker and dirtier, and with potentially devastating long-term results, but they do the job."

For Imogen and for so many, *medication is one piece of (her) wellness.*

This is important to acknowledge. This book is not categorically antipsychiatry. Taken as a whole, these stories merely intend to constructively critique the modern-day biomedical model of mental health care, and to offer a way forward through the lens of personal narrative that underscores the recovery model. If the biomedical model condemns "patients" to lifelong status as categorically "ill," narrative therapy poses an alternative method that can bring people out of suffering, toward healing, and into recovery.

Most modern medical decisions are made according to the biological model, which instantly grants tunnel vision to a treatment plan, and often forgoes the possibility of integrating alternative approaches. This book embraces the recovery model in contrast to mainstream psychiatry's allegiance to the medical model.

For some, an exclusively biological approach may be the most productive, whereas others may benefit from the addition of psychotherapy, or a combination of art, cognitive behavioral, and spiritual therapies. Rather than knock one approach in particular in favor of any other, this book supports attaining as much information as possible about all possible approaches in order to create the unique psychological framework that will ensure optimal functioning and well-being for each individual.

Recent studies estimate that approximately one in five adults in the United States—43.8 million, or 18.5 percent—experience mental health concerns in a given year.[1] Although numbers can tell us something about the pervasiveness of mental health challenges, they do not tell us anything about the intensity, quality, or variety of individual suffering. This is why narrative matters.

At the heart of this anthology is a simple idea: one of the ways we can implement the recovery model is through narrative. The narrative model supports participants to reclaim overwhelming and complex situations. It supports them to rewrite damaging stories, constructing better alternatives. This type of narrative inquiry lends a new model for navigating mental health. This mode of thinking and talking about mental health considers the unique stories of affected individuals and fosters a purpose for their participation in a system that historically has not supported them.

The act of translating a lived experience into a written one validates the fact that it happened. Textual evidence assigns meaning to an experience and makes it possible for a person to view a potentially painful experience from a distance. The discrepancy between the lived and textual selves provides strategies for future problem-solving and heightens the overall potential for self-understanding and growth. Writing is an empowering process that provides control and delivers a sense of satisfaction. At the end of the day, life is best understood when it is told as a story.

Historically, one of the best examples of a proactive campaign in favor of the recovery model is The Icarus Project. Started in 2002 by two activists diagnosed with bipolar disorder, Icarus encourages those with diagnoses to create a safe space and community where mental illness is celebrated instead of pathologized. The goal is not just to survive, but also to thrive. The mission statement of the organization is to acknowledge the creative, "dangerous" gifts possessed by those typically considered mad in a world that is arguably madder.

Icarus embraces narrative theory, and both of the organization's founders have published books of either poetry or memoir narrating their experiences with mental illness, proving that creativity can be a lasting salvation for anyone who has survived any number of damaging circumstances.

One of the founders of The Icarus Project, Sascha Altman DuBrul, writes: "I believe in the power of people's stories, and in the power of language, metaphor, and collective narratives. One of the keys to our larger political struggles lies in our ability to own and rewrite our personal stories."

Dismissing the power of personal narrative omits an essential voice in the conversation about mental health: the voice of those with lived experience. Mental health is too obscure and delicate, too intertwined with lived experience, to be assigned a single, medical story—or worse, to ignore the presence of story altogether.

The editors and contributors to this volume firmly believe that mental health research and practice can be improved by privileging the voices of those living with mental difference. Books such as this one illuminate the experience of mental health struggles for readers who would not understand otherwise. The reading experience allows an audience to bear witness to a story, which has the potential to foster empathy and reduce the stigma attached to mental health diagnoses.

How we heal is implicit within the unique story of our lives.

NOTE

1. "Mental Health by the Numbers," National Alliance on Mental Illness, www.nami.org/learn-more/mental-health-by-the-numbers.

GLOSSARY

ableism: Discrimination, prejudice, and oppression against people with disabilities; defining people by their disabilities, considering them inferior to the (temporarily) nondisabled.

biomedical model: The ideology and movement in mainstream psychiatry that defines mental distress as a physical, biological disease ("chemical imbalance"). These diagnoses of behavior are codified in the DSM, and the typical standard of treatment is lifelong pharmacology (psychiatric drugs).

consumer movement: Empowers mental health consumers to be advocates on their own behalf and change the mental health industry for the better.

consumer or mental health consumer: Someone with lived experience of mental health issues who is a consumer of the mental health system.

disability justice: An understanding of justice that centers people of color and LGBTQI+ people with disabilities and is intersectional and anti-capitalist. (sinsinvalid.org)

lived experience: A shorthand in the movement for saying "someone with lived experience of mental health issues/mental illness."

mad pride movement: Overlaps with the consumer movement, with more of a focus on the reclaiming of a socially maligned "mad" identity as something with positive features. Argues that mental illness should be understood as an issue of social justice and that a person's mental state can improve through greater social support and collective liberation. (Wikipedia's entry on The Icarus Project)

mentalism or sanism: Discrimination, prejudice, and oppression against a mental trait a person has or is perceived to have.

neuroatypical/neurodivergent: A broad umbrella term for anyone whose mental experience can be defined as "atypical" by the medical establishment. A reclamation and point of pride for many. Began with the autistic community and since expanded. See neurodiversity.

neurodiversity: The belief that the neuroatypical provide unique perspectives and make vital contributions to the world, and that this diversity should be celebrated.

neurotypical: A term for someone whose mental experience is deemed "normal" by the medical establishment.

recovery model: The idea that people with mental health concerns can get better and heal, and don't necessarily need lifelong "treatment" with psychiatry or even therapy.

trauma-informed care: An approach based on acknowledging the impact of trauma and aimed at ensuring that the environments where healing occurs are welcoming and safe for all—from policy and procedures to services. This includes therapeutic interventions that work to release trauma from the mind/body and speaks to the recovery model in that healing and resolving trauma to the best of one's ability goes a long way in resolving present-day mental distress. A large portion of trauma-informed care centers around resisting re-traumatization.

ABOUT THE EDITORS

L. D. Green

L. D. Green is a queer writer, performer, college educator, and mental health advocate living in Oakland, California. Her work has been published on *The Body Is Not an Apology*, *Truth-Out*, and in *Sinister Wisdom*, *Foglifter*, *sPARKLE + bLINK*, and elsewhere. She has been featured at dozens of reading series, slams, showcases, and workshops in schools, colleges, and open mics locally and across the country. She was on two national slam teams in 2004 and 2005. As a playwright and writer/performer, she has had her work performed at multiple local and national theater festivals including the National Queer Arts Festival three times as well as the San Francisco Fringe Festival. She received her BA from Vassar College and her MFA in creative writing from Mills College. She was a 2010 Lambda Literary Fellow in Fiction. She attended Tin House Writers' Workshop in 2012 and was a Catwalk Artist in Residence in 2013. She is assistant professor of English at Los Medanos College in Pittsburg, California, where she teaches composition, creative writing, and literature. She was an active member of the Bay Area chapter of The Icarus Project from 2009 to 2011. Green writes poetry, plays, fiction, and nonfiction. She has completed a novel and is working on a collection of short stories, all of which are speculative fiction. For more information, visit www.ldgreen.org.

Kelechi Ubozoh

Kelechi Ubozoh is a Nigerian American singer, writer, and mental health advocate. Originally from Brooklyn, New York, Ubozoh holds a BA in journalism from Purchase College and was the first undergraduate ever published in the *New York Times*.

Ubozoh was featured in *The S Word*, a documentary following the lives of suicide attempt survivors in an effort to end the stigma and silence around suicide, which won a Voice Award from the Substance Abuse and Mental Health Services Administration (SAMHSA). In 2018, Ubozoh appeared on *CBS This Morning* with Gayle King and *ABC Channel 7 News* to support a national conversation about suicide prevention. Her story of recovery is featured in the January 2019 edition of *O, The Oprah Magazine* and on the *Good Morning America* website.

Previously, Ubozoh supervised stigma discrimination reduction programs and led communications operations at a mental health nonprofit organization, PEERS, including a mental health stigma reduction research program for Chinese mental health consumers, where she partnered with Dr. Larry Yang and Columbia University. She also was the lead project coordinator in a statewide project funded by the California Mental Health Services Act, where she applied evidence-based research from working with Dr. Patrick Corrigan to train speakers' bureaus on how to share targeted mental health recovery stories across forty-one California counties.

Ubozoh currently works at California Mental Health Services Authority (CalMHSA) as the peer and community engagement manager. When she isn't working she runs a Bay Area quarterly submission-based reading series called MoonDrop Productions and performs at literary readings across the Bay Area. Her work was recently published in *Endangered Species, Enduring Values: An Anthology of San Francisco Area Writers and Artists of Color* from Pease Press. For more information, visit https://kelechiubozoh .wordpress.com.

About North Atlantic Books

North Atlantic Books (NAB) is an independent, nonprofit publisher committed to a bold exploration of the relationships between mind, body, spirit, and nature. Founded in 1974, NAB aims to nurture a holistic view of the arts, sciences, humanities, and healing. To make a donation or to learn more about our books, authors, events, and newsletter, please visit www.northatlanticbooks.com.

North Atlantic Books is the publishing arm of the Society for the Study of Native Arts and Sciences, a 501(c)(3) nonprofit educational organization that promotes cross-cultural perspectives linking scientific, social, and artistic fields. To learn how you can support us, please visit our website.